Dilemmas of Development

DILEMMAS OF DEVELOPMENT

Reflections on the Counter-Revolution
in Development Economics

John Toye

Second Edition

BLACKWELL
Oxford UK & Cambridge USA

First published 1987

Reprinted 1989

Second edition published in hardback and paperback 1993

Blackwell Publishers
108 Cowley Road
Oxford   OX4 1JF
UK

238 Main Street,
Cambridge, Massachusetts 02142
USA

British Library Cataloguing in Publication Data

A CIP catalogue record for this book is available from the British Library.

Library of Congress Cataloging-in-Publication Data

Toye, J. F. J.
Dilemmas of development : reflections on the counter-revolution in
  development economics / John Toye. – 2nd edn.
      p.   cm.
   Includes bibliographical references and index.
   ISBNs 0–631–18547–X (hbk.); 0–631–18548–8 (pbk.)
   1. Economic development.   2. Developing countries – Economic
policy.   I. Title.
HD82.T65   1993
338.9′009172′4–dc20   92–47385
                                                                  CIP

Typeset in 10 on 12 pt Plantin
by Graphicraft Typesetters Ltd., Hong Kong
Printed in Great Britain by T.J. Press (Padstow) Ltd., Padstow, Cornwall

This book is printed on acid-free paper

Contents

Tables

Preface to the First Edition

This book is about the ideas and opinions of a number of well-known professional economists who emerged in the 1970s and 1980s as the intellectual advance guard of what their friends and critics alike referred to as a 'counter-revolution' in development theory and practice. Among the major figures of this counter-revolution are the late Harry Johnson, Peter Bauer, Deepak Lal, Ian Little and Bela Balassa. They are united in opposition to Keynes and neo-Keynesianism, 'structuralist' theories of development and the use of economic planning for development purposes. On the positive side, they are united by the belief that the problems of economic development can only be solved by an economic system with freely operating markets and a government that undertakes a minimum of functions.

It seemed timely to address the doctrines of this group of economists because they have had, over the last ten years, a rising influence in the academic discourse about development policy. In turn, they have been taken up by the media and the policy-makers in governments of developed countries and in key international organizations. It therefore seemed important to try to provide an assessment of the development counter-revolution that is accessible in style and content to the undergraduate student of development studies and to the intelligent layperson who wants to know more about the strengths and weaknesses of its perspectives on the process of development.

There is a danger that, in trying to evaluate a group of like-minded writers, one exaggerates the similarities in their views and, if only for the sake of ease of comprehension, blurs some real differences. In the course of writing this book, I became aware of sharp differences on certain issues within the counter-revolutionary group. These issues are the usefulness of welfare economics for policy purposes, the effectiveness of foreign aid and the role of human capital formation in development. In the text, such differences are pointed out and an effort is made only to attribute views to particular named authors who have publicly expressed them. The effect of this may be to make the argument overloaded with references and over-personalized. This was unavoidable without falling into the opposite error of creating a composite straw person, with views that no one actually holds.

Another danger, when commenting on views which are controversial or polemical in nature, as those of the development counter-revolution often are, is to reply stridently to stridency, to cap slogan with anti-slogan and to caricature the propositions being criticized as the counter-revolution sometimes caricatures its opponents' views. Since some of what I have to say is critical of the counter-revolution, this particular danger has been ever-present. But I hope that I have succeeded in making the ground of each criticism sufficiently clear and avoided disparagement of anyone's motives or capacities. The validity of the concepts and arguments is all that matters. Everything else is irrelevant.

The reason for writing a book of this kind, so different from the narrowly focused, specialist studies undertaken before, is to alert its readers to both the theoretical problems and some of the practical mistakes which can arise from an over-simplified approach to development policy. When economic thinking is connected up with political movements of the right or the left, it seems almost impossible to avoid the ill consequences of over-simplification. As Albert Hirschman (1982b: 94–5) has said: 'The human capacity to imagine social change is notably limited . . . Attempts to imagine a better future have remained simplistic and schematic . . . We may simply be unable to conceive of the strictly limited advances, replete with compromises and concessions to opposing forces, that are the frequent outcomes of actions undertaken under the impulse of some magnificent vision'. The magnificent vision of the 1980s is of a world developing its resources and capacities in response only to the ups and downs of relative prices and the self-imposed stasis of limited government.

When magnificent visions dominate the political firmament, many people can find reasons for sharing, or claiming to share, the euphoria of total conviction. To such people, the exegesis of theoretical complexity and the demonstrations of flaws in the design of their policy experiments will appear as tiresome and unhelpful. Nevertheless, it is to them that the following pages are addressed, as well as to those who have remained sceptical of the manipulation of economic ideas by various kind of populists during the last decade.

The material in chapters 1, 2, 5 and 7 is entirely new. Chapters 3 and 4 draw to some extent on previously published articles (Toye 1983b and 1985), but with substantial revision and expansion. An earlier version of chapter 6 was presented at an ESRC Conference on South Asian Studies, held in Cambridge in July 1986, and has been published in *Modern Asian Studies*, Volume 22, Part 1, February 1988.

I am grateful to Sue Corbett, now Journals Publisher at Basil Blackwell, for suggesting that I should write this book and for her detailed comments on its first draft. Dr Chris Gerry, my colleague at Swansea, was very helpful and stimulating in his comments on the first version of what is now chapters 2–5, when we used it for our joint course on Development Theory for undergraduates in the Michaelmas Term, 1985. Chapter 6 benefited from comments by several participants in the ESRC South Asian Conference. I particularly wish to thank Robert Cassen, Meghnad Desai, John Harriss, Vijay Joshi, Michael Lipton and Douglas Rimmer in this connection. But none of them bears any responsibility for the form in which their comments have been used.

During the period of writing this book, Professor Hans Singer has been a delightful correspondent and an invaluable source of ideas and information. Again, he bears no responsibility for the text, some at least of which he would disagree with. But its writing has been made much easier and more pleasant by his generous interest and support. I feel deeply obliged to him.

Hazel Lewis has done a superb job of word-processing the entire text single-handed, apart from the bibliography on which she was assisted by Maureen Connew. Her endeavours, while coping with all her other tasks in the Centre for Development Studies, have been outstanding.

Lastly, I have had much sympathetic support during the period of writing from my wife, Janet. This has meant a great deal to me. It is to our children, Eleanor and Richard, that I dedicate this book.

John Toye

Introduction to the Second Edition

The Challenge of a New World Order

A gale of radical conservative rhetoric blew through the early 1980s. It took the frustrated and demoralized nations of the West by surprise and had consequences, both good and ill, that went far beyond the realm of rhetoric. An important part of this upheaval in the political world was concerned with economics and economic policy. Post-Keynesian economics, which had become almost a consensual foundation for Western macroeconomic policy, had its ascendency overturned by the advocates of monetarist policies. The developing countries of the world were then hit by the backwash of these doctrinal disputes. The economics of development, as it has evolved up to that time, suffered its own counter-revolution. It was aggressively disparaged as intellectually worthless and politically motivated. It was also convicted of guilt by association with the Keynesian economics which had 'failed'. In place of the old development economics, welfare economics was set up as the proper guide to development policy.

The first edition of this book had two aims. One was simply to draw attention to the development counter-revolution and to provide a brief sketch of the views of some of its leading proponents. The other was to try to assess a selection of its key propositions, separating what seemed important and valuable in its critique of the old development economics from the tendentious and over-blown claims which it also made. The development counter-revolution contained enough of the latter for the critical assessment to become – in the euphemism of the day – quite robust at times. The original book was essentially a response to a phenomenon of the early 1980s, rapidly written, quite selective in its choice of themes and exhibiting an air of unfinished business. It was a *livre de circonstance*, and showed both some of the defects of this kind of writing and some of its merits. It was described by one reviewer as 'passionate and hard-hitting' (Lundahl 1991: 155).

The publication of a second edition in the early 1990s demands some justification, particularly in the light of the recent rapid changes on the world scene, which have made the concerns of the early 1980s seem oddly remote. With hindsight, it is clear that by the time the first edition of was published in mid-1987, the populism of the right was already beginning to blow itself out. The Reagan presidency was drawing to an end, tarnished by the 'Irangate' affair. The Thatcher government, having won a third term, had already embarked on the economic and foreign policies which brought it down in 1990. The Kohl government in (then) West Germany was being drawn into the hasty *ostpolitik* which has brought it unprecedented triumph and unprecedented problems. The high tide of populist conservatism had already been reached.

If that is so, why bother to keep the book in print, let alone bring out a revised and expanded version? Authors of works which treat policy issues usually hope to have some influence on the trend of informed public opinion, however presumptuous that may seem. But that does not exhaust the reasons for producing them and wishing them to be read. One can influence the trend of public opinion, one can persuade one's readers, in all sorts of different ways. What is important is to do these things on the basis of sound principles and a well-grounded understanding of the underlying issues. Where there is a choice between the exercise of influence over public opinion and strict adherence to the logic of argument and to the empirical evidence, the academic's duty is to sacrifice the former. This is especially so today in the field of economics where some academic economists, when writing about development, have been tempted to make the opposite choice. So the fact that opinion has moved back towards the policy approach recommended in the book's first edition does not make it redundant. The key question is whether its arguments were and remain cogent, or 'not very cogent', as one of the leading counter-revolutionists of development has asserted (Lal 1992: ix).

This Introduction does three things in an attempt to look again at the cogency of the original ideas. It asks whether recent global events have undercut the original lines of argument. It examines the ideas which have become fashionable in the 1990s as a result of the post-1989 realignments. Fukuyama's *The End of History* is taken as the representative of these newly fashionable ideas, and its contents are contrasted with some of the main messages of the first edition. Finally, the revisions and expansions which this edition incorporates are detailed, so that the extent and nature of the changes which it now seems desirable to make are quite transparent.

The six years since the publication of the first edition have brought momentous changes in the international landscape. It is obligatory to consider what challenges recent world events have posed to our understanding of the development process. Have the pressures of these events brought not only fresher but also better responses from the intellectual world? Are more valid and valuable theories of development emerging? Just putting this last question forcefully reminds us that a truly original idea is a great rarity. Intellectual change comes much more from reappraising the significance of familiar ideas than from discovering ones without precedent or pedigree. Indeed, as this Introduction shows, the 'newest' ideas of all skip right back over the whole of the twentieth century. The freshly embroidered banners of the New World Order bear the strange devices 'Back to the Future' and 'Forward with G. W. F. Hegel, 1770–1823'.

The rise to power of Mikhail Gorbachev in the former Soviet Union in 1985 marked the real watershed of the 1980s, although the full extent of the changes which he was to usher in did not appear at first. Political liberalization at home was combined with renewed, but largely unsuccessful attempts to re-start economic reforms. The autumn of 1989, however, revealed Gorbachev's unwillingness to underwrite militarily those regimes in Eastern Europe which opposed this kind of reform programme. Without his support, they proceeded to collapse like dominoes in a veritable liberal revolution (Toye 1990). One immediate result was the rushed reunification of Germany. Even more dramatic was the result that Gorbachev had fought vainly to avoid – the break-up of the Soviet Union, as member republics began to seek the same degree of national, liberal independence as the states of Eastern Europe had achieved. A similar but much more violent process of disintegration has destroyed the former Yugoslavia. Political change has continued, in all the successor states, to be much easier to bring about than economic reform. China, North Korea and Cuba alone have managed to stay relatively aloof from the wave of political liberalization which Gorbachev initiated (Pérez-López 1992).

The collapse of the post-war regimes in the Soviet Union and Eastern Europe has been accompanied by a dramatic realignment in geopolitics. The cold war competition of two large blocs headed by superpowers (the United States and the Soviet Union) first eased and then was formally ended, and the consequences are still being untangled. In turn, the ending of the cold war led to the defusing of a whole range of conflicts around the world in which the US and the former Soviet Union had participated, directly or indirectly.[1] This has produced the most radical changes in the politics of developing countries in the past generation. Although conflict in some of these areas rumbles on,[2] its intensity and global significance have been drastically reduced.

The fading of war in Southern Africa has been accompanied by the dismantling of the apartheid regime in South Africa. The release of Nelson Mandela (February 1990) has been followed by President de Klerk's decision to scrap apartheid laws and an overwhelming victory in the white population's referendum on fundamental constitutional change. Although communal violence in the townships continues at a horrific level, the process of 'building a new South Africa' has not lost all of its momentum. The white population seems to have been convinced that the demise of the much-touted threat of communism has irretrievably undermined the conservative nationalist policies of the period 1948–88.

In Latin America, the end of the 1980s produced a return to democracy in a number of key countries. In Brazil, a civilian regime took over from the military, and in 1989, the first President since 1960 to be elected by popular suffrage came to power. In Chile, the dictatorship of General Pinochet which had lasted since 1973 gave way to the civilian rule of President Aylwin in 1990. Uruguay ended twelve years of military rule in 1985 and held its second free election of the decade in 1989. Argentina, which had returned to civilian rule in 1983, successfully conducted an electoral transfer of power to President Carlos Menem in 1989. All over Latin America, the military was returning to barracks in the late 1980s. More important, it was staying there, despite the economic failures of some of the early exponents of civilian rule like Sarney and Alfonsin, and the corruption of Collor. In Asia, too, the move to more democratic politics was evident, with the peaceful and democratic 1987 election of President Roh Tae Woo. Even in Africa, which has lagged behind in the 1980s, the first real sign of a return to more democratic politics arrived with the election of President Chiluba of Zambia, after 24 years of one-party rule, in 1991.

At the same time, the ending of the cold war has brought new dangers of its own. The outbreak of ethnic and national conflicts in Eastern Europe and the former Soviet Union have already been mentioned. In the Middle East, the un-freezing of the long moratorium on territorial changes led to the revival of dormant claims, as Iraq attempted to annex Kuwait. But this annexation was reversed by an American-dominated international force fighting under the flag and resolutions of the United Nations. This was the first time the UN had played such a major role in world affairs since the Korean War (1950–3). The new dangers were met with a new response, or rather with a reversion to more consensual style of international conflict management for which the mechanism had been established in the initial euphoria of the post-Second World War era.

This very brief glance at world events since 1987 makes it patently obvious that many of the assumptions about the world on which the first edition of *Dilemmas of Development* was based have changed beyond all recognition in a mere six years. The original book did not predict the end of US–USSR superpower confrontation; the outbreak of relative peace in many regional conflicts in LDCs; the strengthening of democratic politics in Latin America, Asia and Africa; the rapid moves towards a South Africa without apartheid; or the revival of the United Nations. On the economic reform front, it did not envisage the eager embrace of liberal market economics by Eastern Europe and Russia, or the rapidity of the spread of structural adjustment programmes in developing countries, including from 1991 onwards, in India, which was, however, extensively discussed. Like the dog which failed to bark in the night in *The Hound of the Baskervilles*, these silences raise questions. Was there enough of value in the original text to justify a second edition in such altered circumstances?

The Intellectual Response

Of all the so-called 'new theories' which have responded to the post-1989 geopolitical upheavals, Francis Fukuyama's *The End of History and the Last Man*, (1992), is the best known. Fukuyama is a former policy planner at the US State Department and a researcher at the Rand Corporation. He is very much at the heart of the Washington establishment. The thesis of Fukuyama's book is not the literal and absurd one that time has stopped, or historical events have ceased. Rather it is that recent events show that certain historical alternatives – socialist central planning and authoritarian government – have become irretrievably discredited. Liberal democracy (allied with free-market economics) is said to be left without any competition, as the only remaining ideology of potentially universal validity. The future can consist only of the continued spread of liberal democracy, albeit with the occasional temporary regression to one or other of the discarded and discredited alternatives.[3] But, in the (undefined) longer run, 'there is a fundamental process at work that dictates a common evolutionary pattern for *all* human societies, something like a Universal History of mankind in the direction of liberal democracy' (Fukuyama 1992: 48).

This new theory is, avowedly, a revival of an old theory. To be more precise, it is a revival, and combination, of two old theories. One of these is that most familiar and proto-typical development theory, the theory of economic modernisation. This starts from a positivist account of natural science as the accumulation of objective knowledge about nature. It then moves, through an engineering view of technology as the application of scientific knowledge, to the conclusion that the worldwide availability of advanced technical processes for economic production 'guarantees an increasing homogenisation of all human societies, regardless of their historical origins or cultural inheritances' (ibid.: xiv–xv). This will happen, according to the theory, even if its consequences for human happiness are ambivalent.

The other venerable theory which Fukuyama resurrects, in order to yoke it to economic modernization theory, is Hegel's account of history as the evolution of human nature. This addition is necessary because modernization (as explained above) is taken to be not sufficient to guarantee the spread of liberal democracy as well as of advanced industrialization. Something else is needed, and it is found in Hegel's account of human nature. Essentially, the human desire for recognition by other human beings sets up contradictions, which according to Hegel, can be resolved only by the mutual recognition of human rights in a framework of a liberal constitution. Only thus can the human spirit achieve its final fullness of freedom (see Hegel 1953 (1837)). And once this freedom has been achieved, no greater achievement is possible. This is the sense in which, once liberal democracy has been achieved, history as it has been experienced hitherto will be at an end. It will have nowhere else to go, so to speak, except for the occasional backward slide.

If this hybrid of economic modernization plus neo-Hegelianism is to be the theory of the New World Order, *Dilemmas of Development* has not lost its relevance. The first edition criticized economic modernization theory on a variety of different grounds, while at the same time distancing itself from theories of the development of under-development, which effectively provide a reverse image of modernization, or, in another metaphor, stand modernization theory on its head. This attempt to steer a middle course still seems, despite the upheavals of the last few years, both necessary and worthwhile. Leaving the flaws in the under-development account aside because of is current low profile, the modernization story as re-told by Fukuyama also glosses over most of the basic intellectual issues which animate development studies. Let us merely indicate a few of these issues.

Development studies takes it as axiomatic that modernization cannot be evolutionary and gradual, because it is human-directed historical process. It starts somewhere at some time because someone has so decided. Initial success confers not only increased prosperity, but also increased power on those who succeeded. It created the capability to colonize others. All subsequent modernization efforts are, on the one hand, defensive in character for the society attempting them, and, on the other hand, threatening to the societies which have previously succeeded. Global modernization is an inherently conflictual process. The circumstances in which the conflict is worked out is not the same in every case. But modernizing countries which do not enjoy the protection of a more powerful state during the process (as Korea and Taiwan have done) often adopt a strategy of militaristic modernization. Why, after all, has the USSR collapsed, if not because of the huge distortion of its economy to sustain a military-industrial complex? Did not a similar distortion also at one period afflict other, earlier modernizers, Germany and Japan? The logical point is that modernization can only become gradual, evolutionary and economically rational once a universal order of liberal democracies has already been established – but never before this has happened.[4]

Development studies has persistently questioned the proposition that technical progress 'guarantees' the increasing homogenization of all human societies. The implication of this must presumably be that homogeneity will occur at levels of consumption per head at least as high as those currently enjoyed by the most developed countries. (It is an unduly conservative assumption that the current living standards of the OECD countries will stand still while those in the rest of the world catch up. But ignore that, for the sake of simplicity.) How much extra production would be needed for all of the 5.2 billion in the world to be in a position to enjoy the same level of living as the 773 million who live inside the OECD? In 1989, the GNP per capita of the average OECD resident was 19,090 dollars (World Bank 1991: 182, Table A.2). That of the average non-OECD resident (in the low and middle income countries) was only 800 dollars (ibid.). For the whole world to enjoy current OECD levels of living would, on these figures, require world production to be almost five times as great as it was in 1989.

Could economic growth on that scale be sustainable? Surely it would become constrained by shortages of natural resources and the costs of avoiding environmental damage long before the required output target could be reached? Fukuyama recognizes people's desire for a safe environment, and, moreover, assumes that liberal democracy will somehow ensure that they get what they want.[5] But he does not convincingly confront the problem of reconciling the catching-up efforts of late modernizers with the availability of natural resources and the preservation of a clean and safe environment. Granted that it is a fallacy to claim that the quantity of natural resources is absolutely fixed. What counts as a natural resource depends on the composition of output, the technologies used to produce it and the possibilities of resource renewal and resource substitution. The early 1970s literature on the limits to growth was rightly criticized for neglecting these sources of flexibility (Nordhaus 1973). Nevertheless, it does require a truly cornucopian view of future technical progress to be confident that no resource and environmental constraints will bind on growth, and that the catching-up process will therefore be a positive-sum game.[6]

The first edition of *Dilemmas of Development* also pointed out that while the relative output growth rates between 1965 and 1980 showed some slight evidence that the low- and middle-income countries as a group were catching up with the OECD countries, this has not been the case since 1980 – rather the reverse. This has been the decade of free-market economic policies and, as have been seen, the beginning of a shift from authoritarian to democratic politics in many parts of the non-OECD world. In this decade of no general catching-up by the developing countries, economic performance has quite sharply polarized within the group. Excellent performance in East, and to a lesser extend, South Asia was in stark contrast to the economic retrogression in sub-Saharan Africa and Latin America. The correct interpretation of the East Asian experience is, therefore, crucial for understanding the real prospects for economic modernization. The analysis of the actual development process since 1980 suggests, in addition to the likelihood of future constraints on growth, the partial presence of a whole range of other short-term constraint: the debt squeeze, deteriorating terms of trade, the shortage of administrative capacity, and so on. These are the real and pressing daily problems of development policy. Whatever may be true of some unspecified 'longer run', without a solution to all of these and other urgent policy problems, the vision of universal modernization will be no more than a cruelly deceptive mirage.

The End of the Third World?

In its new version, the story of economic modernization is supplemented by the Hegelian interpretation of history as the progressive self-realization of the human spirit, culminating in the achievement of freedom. For Hegel, history was not merely the endless fluctuation, the rise and fall, of different political and social institutions. It had a pattern, a series of stages, each a more complete embodiment of freedom than the one before. The transition from stage to stage was driven by the psychological dissatisfaction experienced under each set of social arrangements with the recognition which people could achieve for their own sense of essential humanity. The end of history was the transcending of all the contradictions between social and political institutions and the striving for personal fulfilment.

Within this new Hegelian perspective, the collapse of central planning and authoritarian governments in East Europe and the former Soviet Union has been given a crucial significance as the final transcending of these contradictions. After slavery, feudalism and dynastic monarchy, the last plausible set of alternative institutions – state socialism or communism – has been consigned irretrievably to the past. Such a view certainly appeals to our sense of the suddenness and decisiveness of the events themselves. It also points up that they were not triggered exclusively by the failures and irrationalities of the chosen method of economic modernization. As many commentators noted, psychological alienation was just as potent a fuel for these liberal revolutions as the (often exaggerated) deprivations of consumption.

An obvious implication of the disappearance, once and for all, of authoritarian central planning as an historically viable system of political economy is that a 'Third World' must cease to exist. If the Second World of state socialism has indeed vanished into an historical limbo, what meaning or purpose can now be attributed to a Third World, defined in contrast to it? None, certainly, if the Third World had been nothing more than the creation of cold war politics, the group of neutrals who wished a plague on the houses of both capitalism and socialism. But, as the first edition argued, the Third World concept was always more complex than that. The political cement which held the Third World together was never merely a passive antipathy to the two competing cold war ideologies. It was the collective experience of colonization and a reasonable fear of neo-colonialism, which many, but not all, newly independent countries were determined to keep at bay.[7] The term 'Third World' must now vanish along with 'Second World'. But the persistence or otherwise of the key political attitudes which animated Third World politics will depend on many intangible and uncertain future developments, and how far these allow small or militarily weak nations to determine their own policies in their own interests. This, in turn, depends on how truly liberal the large and militarily strong nations turn out to be in their conduct of international relations.

Dilemmas also rejected the claim that the Third World was a creature conjured up by the guilt feelings of the West that was kept in being only by a common interest, in extracting foreign aid. This denial appears to be vindicated by recent events. The OECD countries seem keen to extend foreign aid to the former Second World, where no question of Western guilt arises, and to do so in a way which is additional to their aid commitments to the former Third World countries. They presumably believe that foreign aid is a rational policy instrument for achieving their foreign policy goals – including homogenizing the world to capitalist and liberal democratic practices. How far this belief is correct, and how far it is illusory is something that still remains to be seen.

Foreign aid, however, is but one of the instruments which will be used to shape 'the new world order' of the 1990s and beyond. World arrangements for trade are even more important. The outcome of the Uruguay Round of GATT negotiations is still awaited, keeping the issue of global free trade versus global protectionism hanging in the balance. The trade arrangements that will apply between the former Second and Third Worlds remain to be settled, and their consequences for the world's poorest remain in doubt (Stevens and Kennan 1992: 38–56). Apart from trade, the degree and nature of controls over labour migration from East to West and from South to North are climbing ever higher on the political agendas of the OECD countries. In this issue lurks at least one very pessimistic scenario, in which the old colonialist attitudes of racial superiority revive in potency to the point where they can enforce a much more ethnically divided world than has yet been seriously contemplated. Recent election results in France, Germany and Italy do not, unfortunately, allow this scenario to be rejected out of hand.

The End of Keynesianism in Development Economics?

The End of History regards 'capitalism' and 'economic liberalism' as the economic arrangement which, along with liberal democracy, constitutes the end-state for human development. The aspirations of political leaders in developing countries to work towards alternative ends by alternative means are regarded as illusory and misguided. The options for economic growth and social justice through mercantilism, socialism or a nationalist industrialization are dismissed after relatively brief discussion (Fukuyama 1992: 98–108). Such a brusque approach is inadequate. It glosses over too many critical distinctions. The disappearance of centrally planned socialism for all time (if that is indeed what recent events portend) leaves many possible policy choices. Capitalism and economic liberalism are terms which can be given a wide range of different definitions. Which one is adopted in practice is a matter of the greatest importance.

The central thrust of the first edition of *Dilemmas of Development* was to counter some of the more simplistic and eccentric claims made on behalf of free-market economics in the 1980s. It pointed out how poorly anchored such claims were to economic theory, particularly the theory of welfare economics to which some, at least, of their makers seemed to think that they were tightly linked. It counter-posed to such claims the essentially Keynesian idea that economic performance can be improved by intelligent state intervention. Its alternative to fundamentalist belief in the magic of the market was the older notion of managed capitalism which had prevailed in the golden age of global expansion between 1945 and 1973. According to this approach, government economic policy, both at the national and international levels, is in principle capable of achieving faster growth and a fairer distribution of income and wealth than would occur when market forces are allowed to operate completely unchecked. The caveat of 'in principle' is important. To hold that any or all forms of government intervention in economic affairs is beneficial would be absurd. A belief in managed capitalism does not require this. It merely asserts that, since some forms of government intervention occur in all complex economic systems, the question must be about how to improve the economic and social effectiveness of those interventions, rather than about whether they should be allowed to occur. In some cases, better management will require a reduction in the density of government activity – but not always, and not necessarily. For countries in pursuit of economic development, it may well be found that selective and analytically well-judged interventions will be highly beneficial.

The Keynesian approach to development policy is highly pragmatic. The pithiest statement of its style originates from Brian Reddaway, who worked in India, Bangladesh, the Middle East, Nigeria and Ghana on many practical problems of economic development. He sums up as follows:

> I class myself as a Keynesian, though I am willing to adopt what seem to be good ideas from any source . . . [In] my work in developing countries I found that common sense points on administration and the like have been more valuable than economic theory, even though the latter [on essentially Keynesian lines] doubtless provided an essential foundation.
>
> (Thirlwall 1987: 39)

The priority of political and administrative issues over economic theory in policy-making for developing countries is the critical insight here, and one that is pursued throughout the remainder of the text. Starting the other way round, by supposing that economic theory itself furnishes 'a body of settled conclusions immediately applicable to policy' is, as Keynes himself maintained in the original *Cambridge Economic Handbooks*, a serious mistake. Whether they are conclusions about the magic of the free market or the magic of central planning, Keynes's point remains valid, although it is on the former manifestation that the first edition of this book concentrated its fire.

The quotation from Reddaway captures the neo-Keynesian style, but does not say much about its content. As is well known. Keynes did not devote himself directly to the analytical treatment of the problems of economic development. Nor did he claim that his short-run analysis of money, interest and employment in developed economies was relevant to developing economies. Nevertheless, scattered through his writings are many insights which are relevant to development policy today. The original edition of *Dilemmas* highlighted the objections that had been raised in the 1970s and 1980s against Keynes's influence on development policy, and rejected them as ill-considered. It is now possible to go further and to show how carefully Keynes himself distinguished between the policies of limited protection and moderate state planning which he advocated in the British context, and strategies of wholesale forced industrialization at the expense of the rural sector which he vehemently rejected in his comments on Russian development. This part of Keynes's work has been largely neglected in the development debate. But Keynes did have clear views about Soviet economic policies in the 1920s and 1930s. It is manifest that he never believed that they provided a rational, or even tolerable, path to development (Toye 1993). Thus the recent collapse of the Soviet system in no way undermines the Keynesian approach to managing capitalism. Rather, it testifies to Keynes's insight into the defects of the Soviet strategy. To a Keynesian, it was always the ability of the Soviet economy to survive for as long as it did that created the puzzle.

The new discourse of *The End of History* makes the alternative of managed capitalism conspicuous by its absence. It thus simply bypasses the problem of what capitalism or the liberal economy is to be like, in detail and in practice. This rather extraordinary vagueness assists the general message of teleological thinking – that only *one* end is possible, and that only *one* real choice exists whether we reach that end directly or indirectly, now or a little later.

The supposition that 'capitalism' and 'economic liberalism' are unitary (and indeed interchangeable) concepts is bolstered by reliance on a particular misinterpretation of economic history that *Dilemmas of Development* was at pains to refute. It lumps together the Chicagoan free-market experiment in Pinochet's Chile with the economic strategies of the newly-industrializing economies of East Asia as indistinguishable examples of liberal economics. It pays no heed to the accumulating evidence of extensive intervention by the governments of South Korea and Taiwan in their economies in order to increase rapidly their exports of non-traditional manufactures. While noticing the extremely high growth rates of South Korea and Taiwan (much higher, incidentally, than for the genuinely free-market Chile[8]), no close enquiry is made into the means by which this economic performance was achieved. Rather, the role of the state is assumed to have been simply the control of struggles over income distribution, while 'truly liberal economic policies' were followed.

How far this assumption is from reality is shown by the most recent accounts of what the Taiwan and South Korean government actually did to promote their countries' economic development. Wade (1990: 297–8) has developed what he calls the governed market theory of East Asian economic success, and compared it with theories of the free market and the simulated free market using Taiwan as a case study. According to Wade, Taiwanese policies

> have aimed to channel resources into industry based within the national territory, and thereby raise the domestic demand for labour. By means of politically determined constraints and rigged prices, they have steered the competitive process into higher-wage, higher-technology alternatives and

away from short-term speculative and labour cost-reducing alternatives within or beyond the national territory.

Wade proceeds to detail the types of policies that have been used to steer resources in these ways. They include a ceiling on the ownership of agricultural land; control of domestic and cross-border sources of credit; macroeconomic stabilization; modulation of international competitive pressure in parts of the domestic economy; export promotion; investment in technological capacity and assistance to specific industries. He notes that 'under all these headings the governments have got well beyond the limits of what would be sanctioned' by either the free-market or the simulated free-market approaches. Having considered the arguments that such policies had a zero or negative effect, he concludes that 'governing the market is too important to ignore even in a parsimonious explanation of East Asian success'.

For South Korea, Chang (1991: 136–50) has examined the various arguments which admit the existence of considerable state intervention, but go on to deny that it affected the way in which the economy performed. Having been forced to abandon an empirically incorrect description of Korean economic policy, free-market theorists have fallen back on the claim that interventions have been self-cancelling, and so neutral in overall net effect, or that, being prescriptive only, have allowed the private sector to flourish outside the areas where the state has a directive policy. Chang finds both of these suggestions to be defective, the first because counter examples (such as the heavy and chemical industries started in the 1970s) were clearly a non-neutral intervention, and the second because it ignores the problem of opportunity cost of resources.

Both Taiwan and Korea remain, in the light of recent research, examples of countries where governments have improved economic performance by strong, but intelligent and selective, interventions in market behaviour. They show that managed capitalism remains not only a viable, but a potentially spectacular path of development. This is not to say that it is the only one, even in East Asia. The successes of the city-states of Singapore and Hong Kong have been much more the result of classic free market policies. The critical issues of the replicability of Taiwan and Korean successes outside East Asia, and their dependence for effective implementation on authoritarian rather than democratic regimes, are large ones which remain unresolved. To cite East Asian strategies under the label of Keynesianism is also liable to be confusing, given that they have resulted from long-term industrial policies, rather than the short-term demand management policies which are the hallmark of Keynesianism in its narrow (too narrow) sense. Nevertheless, Keynes was an advocate of reformed capitalism, in which the state plays a supplementary and co-ordinating role in a basically market economy. In this broader sense, Keynesianism is a national strategy which not only lives on in the developing world of the 1990s, but has some of the most dramatic development performances of recent times to its credit.

Global Keynesianism is also being revived in the light of recent events. The ending of the cold war has had economic consequences, in addition to the political ones already referred to. Heavy expenditures on armaments of ever-increasing sophistication and cost have been a major driving force of economic growth while the cold war lasted. This particular engine of growth has now lost most of its steam. Apart from military spending growth has depended on a cycle of monetary expansion and squeeze, boom and bust, which only at the top of the cycle has been able to maintain near-full employment in the developed countries. In the 1990s, the European Community will be struggling, via its exchange-rate mechanism, to pursue a steadier and more disciplined monetary regime, at a time when the long boom in Japan is flagging, as Japanese stock market values and property prices collapse. The US budget deficit also threatens to keep world interest rates high, and so impede a natural recovery. In these circumstances, some fresh impetus to the world economy seems to be called for. The case is being made again for global Keynesian policies, centred on substantial credits to the former Soviet Union to rehabilitate its infrastructure and re-equip its industries with more technologically advanced and environmentally appropriate capital goods (Skidelsky 1992). The need for a radical redesign of international economic coordinating institutions, such as was achieved at Bretton Woods in 1944, is also being strongly argued (UNDP 1992: 87–90). These plans should not attract automatic, or blanket, endoresement. But they can no longer be brushed off without serious examination, as they could in the early 1980s.

What Does Teleology Tell Us?

The sudden death of one of the competitors in the peaceful competition between alternative social systems, as Nikita Khrushchev described the cold war in 1956, has been accepted as an epochal event, and a cause for general rejoicing. No sociological conservationists have yet bemoaned the extinction of the state socialist species of society as an irreparable loss of the richness of sociological diversity. Rather, it is seen as a necessary step towards a better life for all, an extension of prosperity, security and freedom. In this public mood, the theorizing of development as teleology, as the gradual movement to a single desired social state has a strong intuitive appeal.

This new teleology is not an entirely deterministic approach to social analysis. It leaves people free to explore as they will, to construct and reconstruct their social relations as they see fit – but with the major proviso that most experiments will fail so badly, so many times, that in the end they will no longer be repeated. People will learn from their experience of history that, as Mrs Thatcher used to proclaim, 'there is no alternative' to one way of arranging social, economic and political affairs. So ultimately choice is transformed into the redundancy of choice; freedom into acceptance of constraint; and human variety into human homogeneity.

At one level, therefore, the recent revival of teleological explanations in development is no more than another kind of triumphalism, a celebration of victory over threatening political forces and unpleasant social regimes. It is also an attempt to fill an ideological vacuum, which the discrediting of Marxism-Leninism has created, with some equivalent certainties about the future of capitalism and liberal democracy. The reassuring message is that history is on *our* side, that there is a deep resonance between *our* economic and political arrangements and the fundamentals of human nature – just, indeed, as Marxism-Leninism taught about the Soviet state and socialist man.

How does one take this kind of cosmic comfort? Is it really reassuring? One alternative reaction is to exclaim: the fulfilment of human freedom – us? Do we really represent the apotheosis of human nature so much better than did the Prussian citizenry of Hegel's day? Are we self-satisfied enough to believe that no more can be done to solve the problems of our environment, our economic antagonisms, our ethnic and nationalistic egotisms, the deep poverty of our global neighbours than what our present-day liberal capitalism has already achieved? Surely any conception of human nature must leave room for the spirit of unsatisfied striving for self-improvement, for self-transformation without knowing in advance how, or even whether, it can be achieved? Is the Promethean element in human nature now also extinct?

Another reaction of a less Romantic kind is to raise the question of morality. Kant's teleology looked forward to the emergence of a universal moral order. The lessons of history led humanity to understand a moral imperative which could ultimately be universally agreed to be such. Kant's vision was of a set of moral values in which all humanity – irrespective of culture, colour or creed – not only could participate, but would voluntarily participate. This moral code would doubtless contain important implications for social arrangements. But it did not necessarily imply social homogenization, and certainly did not look forward to it regardless of a moral convergence. That, however, is what the modern teleologists do.

A third reaction is to question the prospect of social homogenization outright. Even if one grants that human societies undergo evolutionary processes, it does not follow that homogeneity rather than variety will be the inevitable consequence. If the theory of biological evolution is relevant for understanding the long vista of history, it is important to remind ourselves that biological evolution does not appear to have any predetermined end-state. It explicitly allows 'niching', the preservation of earlier products of the evolutionary process undisturbed in an appropriate environment (Runciman 1989: 25–37). Although the nineteenth-century social Darwinists may have thought otherwise, biological evolution is a theory whose validity is independent of the worth of particular social and political ideals, and which does not indeed underwrite any of them.

Finally, do we really believe in the law of diminishing marginal surprises? In 1987, the first edition of *Dilemmas* failed to predict so much. Of course it did. Who had predicted the campus rebellions of the 1960s, the economic shocks of the 1970s, the plunge into populist conservatism in the early 1980s? The world is suffused with much greater uncertainty than we ordinarily like to contemplate, as we decide on our purposes and plans and try to do what we think best for the future. It seems deeply counter-intuitive to suppose that, increasingly, we need no longer bother to expect the unexpected. As for Hegel himself, he 'seems to have drastically under-estimated the essential openness and unpredictability of experience' (Smith 1989: 225). Keynes, by contrast, makes the uncertainty of life the fundamental premise of his economic vision.

Hegel's Political Philosophy

The teleologists of the 1990s draw much more from Hegel's philosophy of history than they do from his account of civil society and politics. In rejecting the revival of historical teleology of a Hegelian kind, it should be emphasised that one is not thereby rejecting the whole of Hegelian thought. Although Hegel saw no radical separation of his philosophies of history and of society and politics – very much the opposite – it is possible for the modern reader to find more that is illuminating in the latter than in the former. While resisting the temptation to enter into a deep discussion of Hegelian political philosophy, it may be useful to point to some of his beliefs which have been neglected in the rush to rediscover his relevance to the circumstances of today.

He was fundamentally opposed on methodological grounds to the analysis of society and politics exclusively in terms of the behaviour of individuals. The actions of individuals could only be understood, he thought, when they were seen as situated within their particular historical social context. Apart from opposing methodological individualism, so favoured by the orthodox economists and rational choice theorists of today, he also regarded individual self-seeking as unethical and socially undesirable. The idea of freedom, for Hegel, did not mean the freedom of each person to maximize his or her own utility with the minimum of interference by the state. In common with other major thinkers of his time, such as John Stuart Mill, atomistic 'mere self-seeking' was seen by Hegel as the problem, not as the solution, in the quest for the realization of human freedom.

Hegelian freedom requires the achievement of an 'ethical social life'. This in turn, outside the family, was found in civil society and in the state. Civil society is the realm of free, voluntary association, but not only in the impersonal transactions of buying and selling in the market-place. Apart from markets, the crucial constituents of Hegelian civil society were 'corporations' – professional associations, social and sporting clubs, charities, churches and what today would be called non-governmental organizations (NGOs). These all provided fora for the development of ethical social life to counter the alienation that inevitably arises from isolated self-seeking activity. They would also serve as interest groups which could be a source of group representation in political life. Hegel believed that universal suffrage would generate political apathy rather than political participation – so great was his distance from modern liberal democracy.

As for the state, it had to be based on the rule of law, embodied in a constitution that was generally accepted as legitimate. State officials were drawn from a civil service recruited by education and merit, who constituted a 'universal class' capable of acting impartially in the public interest. Hegel's view was thus at dramatic variance with modern critiques of the state which deny the very possibility of benevolent government and demand its confinement to an absolute minimum of functions.

A New Political Economy of Development?

The first version of *Dilemmas of Development* commented critically on the work of analysts of India who based themselves on 'the new political economy' of development (NPE). The NPE grew out of work by Krueger on 'rent-seeking', which showed how foreign trade controls (but not only such controls) created windfall gains, and thereby stimulated both corruption and directly unproductive activities in developing countries. The NPE has meanwhile continued to flourish, and has stimulated new and more comprehensive accounts of politics, based on the underlying assumption that, because rulers pursue their own self-interest rationally, they cannot constitute themselves as a benevolent state. But any advocacy of intelligent government intervention in the economy for the purpose of managing capitalism pre-supposes some degree of benevolence in the state. It therefore implies the need to revise the propositions of the NPE in a way that admits this possibility.

The basic problem of the NPE is the disjunction between its strong anti-state rhetoric and the different and partial analytical apparatuses which are used to illustrate the rhetoric. The rhetoric is cynical in the extreme about the intentions and behaviour of leaders and politicians and deeply pessimistic about the prospects for sound public policies. This is justified on the basis of a variety of highly simplified models of rent-seeking and fiscal exploitation. The models themselves are often incoherent. The rent-seeking model, for example, is incompatible with patronage politics, as it is usually understood. Fiscal exploitation turns out to mean a number of quite different things, and the choice between them, using only the simple assumption of rulers' self-interest, is left undetermined. The underlying analyses are quite primitive. They would justify a sweepingly negative view of political performance only to those who were already convinced of its validity. Thus the new political economy seems to be deeply founded on prior belief – perhaps as much so as the old political economy of Marxism, which it resembles in so many other ways (Meier 1991: 111–19).

Its chief value is that a critique of it forces us to look again at the familiar dichotomy of individualism versus structuralism. The NPE's flaw is that it tries to account for political behaviour entirely on the basis of individual motivation, disregarding the structural features of political life which act as constraints on what is politically possible. This is as limiting as the opposite approach, which reads off political outcomes only from structures – the existence of a state dedicated to the public welfare, or (from the Marxian perspective) of a state dedicated to the interests of a given dominant class. There is no point in rejecting the NPE only to embrace again the old structuralist approach. A synthesis of both is required, which admits both the freely self-determining political actor and the variegated structures – social, economic and political – within which action takes place, and which are modified by the action itself. Agent and structure must be seen realistically as mutually interdependent.

In the post-cold war world, one of the great resurgent forces has been nationalism. Already it has reintroduced into Europe violent conflict on a scale not experienced for forty years. This phenomenon defies analysis by means of methodological individualism. But equally clearly it is not just an historical given, which individuals' choices are powerless to intensify or abate. A fruitful analysis of nationalism has to integrate both dimensions and explain how they act and re-act on each other. Understanding nationalism is just one example of the many intellectual tasks that remain undone in the political economy of development, and on which a more sophisticated methodology than either individualism or structuralism needs to be employed.

Revisions to the Original Text

The major revisions to the original text, apart from the inclusion of this new Introduction, are as follows. Chapter 2 has been re-written with two objectives in mind. The first was to remove the sections on the structuralists' critique of Keynes which some reviewers thought were a distraction from the main line of argument. The second was to incorporate a discussion of Keynes's views on the economic policies of the Soviet Union, whose development experience was an influential model for some developing countries after decolonization.

The changes to chapters 4 have been made to accommodate some of the post-1987 work that has appeared on the East Asian development model, along with recent discussions of the role of the state and the policy of privatization. Following on from this, a substantial addition has been made to chapter 5, to explore the ways in which the neo-Marxian political economy of the left was followed, and countered by the 'new political economy of development'. This addition to chapter 5 provides a bridge to chapter 6, which explores the application of this 'new political economy' to the explanation of India's development.

In chapter 7, the original section on 'Exchanging Aid for Policy Reforms' has been re-written to incorporate some up-to-date evaluations of the World Bank's structural adjustment lending and the new policy emphases that have been placed on the international agencies' agendas for the 1990s.

A new final chapter has been added in this edition. Chapter 8 describes the origins of the world debt crisis and the various attempts to resolve it, focusing on the policy stances of the US and UK governments during the decade of the counter-revolution. This is intended as a case study of the economic damage which was done to many developing countries by the economic policies in two leading industrialized countries, arising both from the ideological spirit in which they were conceived and the incompetence with which they were realized.

Notes

1 A partial list would include the Iran – Iraq war, the Soviet withdrawal from Afghanistan, the Ethiopian and Angolan civil wars, the conflict in El Salvador, the insurgency in Mozambique and the independence of Namibia. The hostages held in Lebanon since 1985 have all been released and the preliminaries of peace talks on the Israel–Palestinian question have begun.

2 The disintegration of civil and military authority in Somalia in 1992 exposed between four and six million people to the risk of starvation. Hundreds of thousands actually died before US forces intervened under a UN humanitarian mandate in late 1992.

3   To underline this point, Fukuyama actually predicted that Peru might lapse into dictatorship, a shrewd guess which President Fujimori's subsequent coup from above vindicated.
4   The history of the United States shows that, even when a liberal democratic order already exists, economic modernization can lead to acute military conflict – between the industrializing northern states and the traditional agrarian southern states in the American Civil War (1861–5).
5   At the same time, incidentally, portraying environmentalists as reactionaries opposed to scientific progress or as exponents of morally confused claims about animal rights.
6   Five-fold growth of output assumes not only no further rise of living standards within the OECD, but also no further growth in world population – an assumption which is certainly false. The environmental problem will in fact be much more problematic than the estimate in the text suggests. I make these points in expiation for the relative neglect of environmental issues in the first edition of *Dilemmas* – see criticism by Brookfield (1988: 126).
7   The best presentation of the credo of non-alignment that I know is President Nyerere of Tanzania's address to the Non-aligned Movement's conference in Lusaka in 1970 (as quoted by Williams 1987: 60–1):

> [It] is a policy of involvement in world affairs . . . Our role arises from the fact that we have very definite international policies of our own, but ones which are separate from the independent of those of either of the power blocs. By non-alignment we are saying to the Big Powers that we also belong to this planet. We are asserting the right of small, or militarily weaker, nations to determine their own policies in their own interests, and to have an influence on world affairs . . . Non-alignment does not imply agreement (among the non-aligned) on major issues, it is simply a statement by a particular country that it will determine its policies for itself according to its own judgements about its needs and the merits of the case. It is thus a refusal to be party to any permanent diplomatic or military identification with the Great Powers

Not all 'Third World' countries participated in the Non-aligned Movement. A majority did, but some others were members of military alliances with First World countries, e.g. CENTO and SEATO.
8   The growth records of South Korea, Taiwan, Chile and three comparator countries were:

Some comparative growth performances, 1950–87 (average annual growth rates)

	1950–64	1964–87	1950–87
Korea	6.1	8.5	7.6
Taiwan	8.3	9.1	8.8
Chile	4.2	2.2	3.0
India	4.3	3.6	3.8
China	5.2	7.2	6.5
Japan	9.5	5.7	7.1

Source: Chang (1991: 125)

CHAPTER ONE

Is the Third World Still There?

Diverse Reports from Distant Places

One summer when there was nothing more amusing for them to do, the subeditors working on *The Times* held a competition to see which of them could insert the most boring headline into their famous newspaper. The most boring headline to appear in print was unanimously agreed to be: 'Small Earthquake in Chile: Not Many Hurt'. A routine disaster a long way away – is there anything with less power to attract our attention than that? But sometimes the scale of the disaster is so great that the news of it manages to sneak behind our mental defences. When hundreds of thousands, or even millions of people are involved, curiosity may get the better of long-established habit. When there are also colour photographs of the suffering, or television footage, curiosity may turn briefly to sympathy, or even indignation that too little is being done to help. Indignation may then be followed by a definite resolve to do something helpful for the distant victims, or at least to try and find out more about the causes of their plight.

The most dramatic recent distant disaster has been the terrible famine in Somalia, which occurred almost unnoticed, obscured by the civil wars in the Balkans. Terrible though the loss of human life has been, not to mention the suffering and the disruption experienced by those who have survived, these events will not have been entirely without mitigation if, as seems likely, they have created greater concern for the human misery endured by many in remote regions of the world.

The first lesson which great disasters like the Somalian famine should have taught is that, although disaster relief is the top priority in the short term, the long-term avoidance of vulnerability to disaster requires a successful development policy. Those who would transform their concern into more permanently constructive action will thus necessarily have to try to come to grips with development issues and the many debates which surround the question of devising a successful development policy. For a start, they will have to go back to their newspapers, weekly magazines and television programmes and discipline themselves to read and watch those boring bits. These should indeed become very much less boring, if one wrestles to make sense of them and fit them into an overall pattern. Not everything is going to fit in at the first, or even the second or third attempt. But many things do become clearer as one struggles to put different pieces of the development jigsaw together.

Widespread famine represents the most visible and most shocking distant disaster. But it is also a complex event, for which simple and obvious explanations will not always suffice. Famines can occur in the midst of plenty, when particular groups of people lose their accustomed means of access to the available food supply. Famine among pastoralists often occurs in a deteriorating natural environment. But it is difficult to sort out whether the deterioration has autonomous physical causes, or whether it results from population growth, or simple abuse of the habitat based on ignorance. And what role does politics play in causing famine? Cultivators who are moved on to new land for military reasons may be being put at risk, and governments may give or withhold relief supplies as a weapon in a political game.

A country will not suffer from famine just because its inhabitants are poor. India's per capita income lies in between those of Ethiopia and Sudan, but India has managed to avoid famines for all of the forty-odd years since she became independent.[1] There are many other poor countries which can make the same claim. Although at present famine and the threat of famine seem to haunt Africa, particularly sub-Saharan Africa, the contrast between Africa and Asia is not absolute. China experienced severe famine in the early 1960s, as did Bangladesh in the early 1970s. Clearly, the cause and the incidence of famine are not easy to unravel.

The reports from faraway places do not tell only of famine. Finance as well as food is currently a major issue of development policy. When the oil price rose by leaps and bounds in 1973 and again in 1979, its effect was to withdraw substantial amounts of purchasing power from oil-consuming economies, and to transfer these amounts in the first instance to oil producers who were unable all at once to spend their great increases in income. This was evidently a depressing influence on world economic activity and, in an attempt to lessen the impact of the depression, oil revenues (or petro-dollars) were 'recycled' by the private banking system. A large part of this recycling was done by lending petro-dollars to governments of poor countries, in the belief that this kind of lending ('sovereign debt') carried minimal risks of default. From 1973 to 1982, the governments of many countries took on more loans than they could possibly repay, given their ability to generate foreign exchange earnings. Their poor foreign exchange earning ability at the end of the borrowing spree indicated that many had borrowed more than they could invest in hard-currency-earning enterprises.

In the last few years, the media have carried many reports on this debt crisis, which was allowed to reach the point where the stability of some large private US banks began to be questioned, as well as where numerous governments of poor countries were pleading to have their debts re-scheduled. Bail-out plan has followed bail-out plan, bankers' revolts and debtors' revolts have come and gone, austerity packages have been devised, imposed, evaded and re-imposed. The crisis is far from over and its management shifts from tactic to tactic, trying to learn something along the way.[2]

Just as famine is said to be Africa's problem, so the debt crisis is said to be Latin America's. This is because it was Mexico and Brazil in 1982 who first indicated that their debt burden had become unsustainable. But no continent has exclusive proprietorship of particular development problems. Although ten of the fifteen countries which the IMF defines as heavily indebted are Latin American, three are African (Nigeria, Morocco and the Ivory Coast), one is Asian (Philippines) and one is European (the former Yugoslavia).

The examples of Mexico and Nigeria indicate that having indigenous supplies of oil was no guarantee of being able to avoid the debt crisis. Borrowing undertaken when the oil price was high quickly became unsustainable when the oil price softened and collapsed. The crux of the matter was never just the possession or non-possession of domestic oil supplies. It was the ability to manage resources well in the face of great turbulence in a key commodity price. India, though on balance hurt economically by the oil price rise, did wot begin heavy commercial borrowing until the mid-1980s. The debt crisis did not reach India until the early 1990s.

In oil-exporting countries, the rapid growth of the 1970s has been followed by stagnation in the 1980s as the oil price has fallen. In addition to Mexico and Nigeria, it is the countries of the Middle East which have been the most seriously affected. In the 1980s, countries that relied on primary product exports had somewhat faster growth than the Middle East, benefiting from the slight acceleration in economic activity in industrialized countries after the trough of the recession in 1982. But the only group of poor countries to have grown consistently fast in the 1970s and 1980s are those that export manufactures. These include the newly industrializing countries (NICs) whose growth performance has been held up as a model for the development of countries still caught up in the toils of famine or debt.

It is important not to confuse economic growth, the expansion of the measured output of goods and services, with development. One can imagine some forms of economic growth that would not seem much like development. For example, output can be produced by the severe exploitation of labour – the payment of mere subsistence wages, bad health and safety conditions and the unfair treatment of workers – with the resulting profits being channelled to private bank accounts in foreign tax havens. This would be the kind of development that few people would vote for, if they were allowed to vote. So would growth that was accompanied by environmental pollution and gross overcrowding. The process of very rapid industrialization, new or old, can create widespread social distress and conflict, as well as previously undreamt-of levels of material wealth and technical advance.

These ambivalences of rapid industrialization are characteristic of what have become known to journalists as 'the four Asian tigers' – the two city-states of Hong Kong and Singapore, and the two larger political entities of South Korea and Taiwan. But these are not the only NICs. There is another important group in Eastern Europe (Romania, Hungary and Yugoslavia before its break-up), plus the big, heavily populated, countries which have pursued industrialization by import-substitution, India and Brazil.

Trying to make sense of the information which reaches us about poor countries a long way away seems, then, to lead to the identification of a set of contemporary problems – famine and the related problems of the production and distribution of food; the financing of development through the private banking system and the related problems of debt, the oil price, inflation and the choice of productive investments; and the social costs of rapid industrialization.

Although at first glance, it might appear that these problems were to be found in different continents – famine in Africa, the debt crisis in Latin America and the agony and the ecstasy of rapid industrialization in Asia – a closer look showed that this was not entirely so. Although each problem was concentrated to a noticeable degree in one continent more than the others, a sharp geographical demarcation of problem locations was not warranted. Similar phenomena appeared to a lesser degree elsewhere.

The continents of Africa, Asia and Latin America are diverse, both geographically and historically. This diversity accounts for the tendency of particular development problems to concentrate in particular continents. Asia has much greater pressure of population on cultivable land than Latin America or Africa, but Africa has a much more unfavourable ratio of food availability from domestic supply and imports to its food requirements than does Latin America, or (to a lesser extent) Asia. Land is but one term in the agricultural equation and other historical and geographical factors have put Africa at a special disadvantage.[3]

Latin America (apart from Colombia and Venezuela) is much more diversified economically than Africa, where even the discovery of oil has hardly altered the pattern of relying on one or two sectors to generate most export revenue. But Latin America has also drawn much more heavily than either Africa or Asia on foreign sources for its direct investment. So its economies are much more influenced by decisions taken by multinational corporations (particularly US multinationals) than are those of Asia or Africa (notably excepting Liberia). Politically, Latin America and Africa have been more prone to military *coups d'état*, while Asia has found greater political stability, although often by authoritarian means. Given these contrasts, it is explicable why Latin America has had less sustained rapid industrialization than parts of Asia and greater entanglement in the problems of international debt.

The Basis of the Third World: Politics and Psychology

These continental contrasts, combined with the evident differences between the most pressing problems of development in different places, naturally lead people to ask whether there really is 'a Third World'. Does it make sense to lump the problems and circumstances of Latin America, Africa and Asia together as those of 'the Third World', and talk of that world in a way which inevitably emphasizes similarities rather than differences? Might it not be better to confine discussion of development policy to a regional rather than a global perspective?

In the flood of comment on the dilemmas of development policy, an abrasive new approach came strongly to the fore in the 1980s. This new approach has been called a counter-revolution in the theory and practice of development. The later chapters of this book look quite closely at the teaching of the apostles of this counter-revolution, to examine what they have to say and the evidence they produce for their views. But before going on to do that in a systematic way, it may be instructive to pick out first one particular opinion which is highly relevant to the question posed in the previous paragraph – does the Third World really exist?

The answer of the development counter-revolution is that the Third World exists only because it has been created. Further, the creative force was not history or geography, or economics. It was psychology and politics, namely 'Western guilt' and the politics of foreign aid, which between them conjured up 'the Third World'.

The Third World and its antecedents and synonyms, such as the underdeveloped world, the less developed world and the developing world (all still used) and now also the South, are for all practical purposes the collection of countries whose governments, with the odd exception, demand and receive cffcial aid from the West . . . The Third World is the creation of foreign aid: without foreign aid there is no Third World.

(Bauer 1981: 87)

In turn, 'insistence on foreign aid is a major theme of the recent literature of Western guilt', which holds that the West is responsible for the poverty of most of Asia, Africa and Latin America. If there is no truth in this suggestion of 'responsibility' and no virtue in the policy of aid, as some development counter-revolutionaries believe, the Third World itself exists only as a kind of collective psychological delusion.

In responding to assertions of the kind just quoted, it is necessary to begin by examining the psychological and political aspects of the concept of a Third World. What truth is there in the suggestion that it denotes an association of countries dedicated to the moral blackmail of a guilt-afflicted West? Once the psychological and political influences on the identity of the Third World have been clarified, the further question of whether they share a common type of economy will be addressed.

In would be misleading to argue that being a Third World country is simply a matter of experiencing certain economic conditions and problems. There are also, and possibly even predominantly, psychological and political elements in 'Third Worldliness'. But they are of a distinctly different character than that alleged by the development counter-revolutionaries.

What then is the political significance of a Third World? The term has been traced to several different origins. In Europe in the 1920s, there was some talk in political circles of finding a 'third way', meaning a political programme that was neither explicitly capitalist nor explicitly socialist in orientation. The details of the programmes, clerical, fascist and business variants of social corporatism, are less important than the enduring idea that some third alternative was possible, and that the struggle between capitalism and socialism did not have to be all-engulfing. An alternative origin with a related connotation lies in the French term 'the third estate'. Just as, in the approach to the French Revolution, the third estate found its political opportunity in the quarrel between nobility and clergy, so at the end of the Second World War, the US–USSR conflict provided the political opportunity for independence in the less developed countries. The analogy here is with benefiting from the struggle between two superior forces, not merely surviving it.

This is not the political interpretation which the development counter-revolutionaries gave to the idea of the Third World. They ignored the struggle between two superpowers with opposing ideologies and, therefore, Third Worldism was seen by them as form of hostility to the West which was inspired by a positive (if covert) preference for socialism. Hence their constant criticism of developing countries for socialistic behaviour, or what is read as such. Third World countries as a group were blamed for over-extended public sectors – which are actually smaller proportionally than that of the US is to the size of its total economy – and excessive reliance on government controls, even when those controls are known to be easily circumvented by private enterprise firms, which are nowhere near to being centrally planned in Soviet style.

If the political thrust of Third Worldism were merely anti-Western, it should have found some favour with those committed to socialism. But this presumption is wrong. On the contrary, 'radicals . . . are usually reluctant to posit a third world, for they see most, perhaps all, of these countries as under-developed capitalist ones, tied in subordinately to the first world. Thus, the main radical view is that there are only two worlds, one of capitalism and one on Marxian socialism' (Griffin and Gurley 1985: 1090). The orthodox socialist position is thus that the Third World does not exist, because it is really subordinated to the first, capitalist world. This is uncannily similar to the position of the counter-revolution itself, that the Third World only exists to the extent that it is able, by exploiting Western guilt feelings, to be insubordinate and anti-Western. The second world (socialism) did not recognize the third, on the pretext that it was really part of the first. But the first did not do so either, on the pretext that the third was indistinguishable from the second.

The political interpretation which the development counter-revolution gives to the concept of the Third World is one which derives from its continuing political engagement with the struggle against socialism. By the same token, the orthodox socialist position on the Third World derives, although much more self-consciously and with much more open public acknowledgement, from the struggle against capitalism. Both are declaring, in effect, that there cannot be independents or non-combatants in their ideological confrontations. It is precisely this kind of doctrinaire exclusiveness which fuelled, until the collapse of the USSR, the search for a 'third way'.

Moving on from political ideas to political practice, the origin of the Third World as an active group of cooperating countries was a desire to establish a strong group of neutrals during the US–USSR 'cold war'. Their aims were to avoid any entanglement with superpower rivalries and to safeguard their national sovereignty as (mainly) countries which had recently become independent of European colonial powers. In fact, the actual political coherence of the Third World nations as a group has been greater in relation to the politics of decolonization than in relation to the politics of US-USSR superpower rivalry. Ironically, the posture of non-alignment adopted by many Third World countries since 1961 was adhered to less strictly than the posture of opposition to colonialism and imperialism (Willetts 1978). It is the latter, rather than the now-defunct competition between capitalism and socialism as social systems and as power blocs, which holds the key to the politics of the Third World.

The advocates of a counter-revolution in development thinking place the emphasis the other way round from this. They stress the anti-West attitudes of Third Worldism, the West's irrational guilt that supposedly encourages these attitudes and the alleged crypto-socialist policies of Third World governments. For them, Third World politics is nothing if not a by-product of the cold war. That Third World politics is centrally about decolonization and the future security and prosperity of former colonial countries is thus denied and treated as an irrelevant distraction.

The basis for dismissing decolonization as the central Third World issue is the fact that some countries which are now generally recognized to be part of the Third World have been continuously independent of formal control by a foreign power at least since 1815. Paraguay, Saudi Arabia, Turkey and Nepal fall into this category (Crow and Thomas 1983: 11). There are a few other countries where either the period of colonization was relatively brief or relatively informal, such as Thailand, Iran and Ethiopia. The fact that colonial expansion was to this degree less than worldwide in its reach is taken as an argument against the political definition of the Third World in terms of the politics of decolonization. It is difficult to follow the logic of this. Some very inhospitable parts of the world are both relatively unattractive to foreign imperialists and relatively inaccessible for military conquest. But countries located there still share with their neighbours who have experienced colonization a common interest in avoiding it. There is no country so remote, so inaccessible and so well entrenched in its history of independence that it cannot become a battleground for foreign troops. The history of Afghanistan in the 1980s should illustrate that proposition vividly. And the real experience of colonization has been overwhelmingly more commonplace than the untutored fear of it.

Decolonization

'Decolonization', like 'Third World' itself, is a modern term of mid-twentieth-century vintage. The modern politics of decolonization have not directly affected Latin America very much, with the exception of Guyana and Surinam and the 1982 conflict over the Falklands/Malvinas. Most Central and South American countries had freed themselves from Spanish and Portuguese colonialism in the nineteenth century, only to find themselves, from the Monroe Doctrine of 1842 onwards, coming under the growing hemispheric overlordship of a rapidly industrializing United States. Thus by the end of the Second World War, and the arrival of the modern episode of decolonization, any declaration of non-alignment by the Latin American states would have been construed by the United States as a hostile act. Latin America, therefore, occupied a special position within the Third World. It was the first continent to liberate itself from colonialism and, yet, it was not able to participate fully in the political construction of the Third World.

The psychology of Third Worldism is the psychology of decolonization. If decolonization wrongly implies that the initiative for independence was always taken by the colonial powers, the psychology of Third Worldism can also be described as the psychology of national liberation (Chamberlain 1985: 1). The classic account of the psychology of national liberation was that of Fanon. According to Fanon, the social relationships of colonial societies denied the native populations a true human identity. True identity could only be achieved by a violent struggle against the colonialists who created and imposed a sub-human personality on the native. In turn, this historical necessity for redeeming violence created a dilemma for the supporters of decolonization in the colonial countries. Their support derived from a Western cultural humanism. But Western culture has to be rejected because it condemns violence and also because it is shot through with a racially biased hypocrisy. Its claim to universal values is said to be contradicted by the racism practised in the colonial situation.

Sartre paraphrased Fanon's essential message as follows: 'The rival blocks take opposite sides and hold each other in check; let us [i.e. the Third World] take advantage of this paralysis, let us burst into history, forcing it by our invasion into universality for the first time. Let us start fighting; and if we have no other arms, the waiting knife's enough' (Fanon 1967: 11). It was this message that led Sartre to conclude that 'the Third World finds itself and speaks to *itself* through [Fanon's] voice' (p. 9).

There is much to quarrel with in *The Wretched of the Earth*. The notion of redeeming violence is inexcusably romantic; the understanding of Western humanism is superficial; the politics of a national peasant revolution are wildly utopian. So one could go on. What it provides is neither an accurate description of colonialism, nor a useful prescription for how to overcome it. What it provides instead is an excellent intuitive account of the psycho-pathology caused by colonial wars and the deformations of values and vision caused by the acutely stressful conflicts of decolonization. How else than like Fanon could people feel, at the end of a long war of atrocity and counter-atrocity, such as that of Algerian liberation between 1954 and 1962?

Fanon usefully reminds Anglo-Saxon readers that decolonization has not just been a matter of the peaceful transfer of power by metropolitan countries benignly seeking the future welfare of colonial populations. Although in India the worst bloodshed was caused by communal violence within the newly independent country, Britain itself has conducted fierce military campaigns against 'terrorists' in countries soon to become independent, for example, in Palestine (1946–8), Kenya (1952–5), Malaya (1957–63), Cyprus (1956–60) and Aden in the 1960s. The war in Algeria, however, dwarfed all of these, with France committing an army of half a million men there by 1962. When decolonization intersected with superpower rivalry, as it did in Vietnam between 1965 and 1973, the scale of conflict was even larger. There the US committed over two million ground troops, of whom 55,000 were killed, while half a million Vietnamese were slaughtered in both ground and aerial bombing attacks.

The voices of the development counter-revolution speak of 'Western guilt' as the psychological force which gives coherence to the Third World. Western guilt is presented as an abstract neurosis, a subjective feeling detached from the objective circumstances of contemporary history. But objectively, colonial conflicts create intense brutalization and trauma on both sides. The effects do not cease when the conflict ceases. The intensification of racism and drug abuse in ex-colonial countries is directly connected to the brutalization of some participants and the trauma of others in the course of recent colonial wars. Anxiety about these self-inflicted social evils combines with the self-doubt of Western humanism described by Fanon to create a psychological unease which is well grounded in fact and history.

The ex-colonies themselves do not escape unscarred. The counter-revolution in development thinking is quick to condemn the many instances of illiberalism to be found in countries of the Third World. But it does not pause to consider the social forces which make oppression and persecution so relatively simple to organize. One important force is the great power of the army, often with foreign training and technology, when political independence comes at the end of a long armed struggle, as in Mozambique and Zimbabwe. It takes immense political skill to keep the armed forces under civilian control in such circumstances. Too often that political skill is lacking.

The full trauma of the process of decolonization is not yet over. South Africa still has to find its way out from white settler colonialism, despite the fact that, since 1991, the apartheid legislation has begun to be dismantled. The pressure towards violence; the unwillingness of liberals to support wholeheartedly the national liberation struggle; the dragon's teeth, to use the phrase of Kiernan (1982: 227) about armies, sown in the course of conflict and bringing forth their harvest once the political victory has been won – all of these could be replayed one more time and perhaps more fiercely than ever before, in the years ahead.

The Third World is not, despite all that the development counter-revolution says, yet able to be dismissed from our minds. It is not a figment of our imagination ready to vanish when we blink. It is a result of our collective lack of imagination, our inability in our present difficult circumstances yet to see ourselves as belonging to one world, and not several.

The Basis of the Third World: Economics

The term 'Third World' when applied to a country is often taken to be synonomous with descriptions like underdeveloped, less developed and developing. But these latter terms have a different point of reference, the degree of economic and social backwardness. 'Underdeveloped' and 'less developed' imply relative backwardness, while 'developing' implies movement away from backwardness. That is, perhaps, clear enough. But what is 'backwardness'? Evidently, being at some remove from 'forwardness'. So what is 'forwardness'? Well, there can be more than one opinion about that, surely?

It is important to realize that an apparently neutral and scientific word like 'development' is no such thing. Definitions of the goals of development and of the process by which these goals should be striven for, unavoidably depend on the values of the person doing the defining, as well as on facts that are in principle falsifiable. Further, people's values are not identical, nor are they completely at variance, fortunately. Although all theories are to some extent contestable because of differences in values rather than problems of logic or observation, theories of development are particularly subject to disagreements arising out of value differences.

Modernization Theory

The original theory of socioeconomic development that accompanied the post-1945 decolonization of Asia and Africa rested on the idea of modern society as the goal of development. Modern society supposedly had typical social patterns of demography, urbanization and literacy; typical economic patterns of production and consumption, investment, trade and government finance; and typical psychological attributes of rationality, ascriptive identity and achievement motivation. The process of development consisted, on this theory, of moving from traditional society, which was taken as the polar opposite of the modern type, through a series of stages of development – derived essentially from the history of Europe, North America and Japan – to modernity, that is, approximately the United States of the 1950s.

It was the idea of countries that were less developed (LDCs) according to the above modernization paradigm of development which was most closely linked in practice to the giving of foreign aid. Within this paradigm, Western experts have an extremely prominent and powerful position as guides and advisers in poor countries. Not only are their values being imported wholesale, usually without much awareness on anyone's part that this is what is happening, but Western technology is assumed to be appropriate and the embodied technology of Western machines and equipment is assumed to be transferrable with only modest difficulty. All of these assumptions are convenient to support large-scale capital aid programmes.

This theory and practice of development was bound to come into question before long. Leaving aside the social and psychological side of modernization theory and concentrating on the economic side, it had a conception of a typical less developed economy. This was predominantly agricultural, with small cultivators growing crops primarily for household subsistence needs. It had low rates of investment, low stocks of capital employed per worker and low rates of economic growth. The foreign trade sector was small, and so was the share of national resources passing through the government budget. Infrastructure was poor as a result of low government investment. The typical less developed economy admittedly showed some variation from place to place, but the variations were essentially natural. Some were islands, some were landlocked; some were big and some were small; some were arid, some were flood-prone; some were mountainous and some were on the plain. But all were typical less developed economies.[4]

Criticism gradually focused on the part of this story that concerned trade. Two main reasons for this focus stand out. The idea of development as the passage through a series of predetermined stages assumes that *timing* of the development process, in relation to the development of other countries, is of no major consequence. Countries can embark on their journey and reach their desired destination without regard for the timetables that others have followed, or are about to follow. In other words, development is independent, national development and there are no 'late developers' whose prospects are damaged by their very lateness. Trade forms part of the network of international interdependence. It is, therefore, one of the key linkages that binds the national development processes together – for better or worse.

The second reason why criticism of the idea of the typical LDC focused on trade was that the link did not appear, on inspection, to be of the negligible kind posited by modernization theory. Most LDCs seemed to have developed one or more major export sectors: specialized

agricultural commodities like cocoa, bananas, sugar or tea; raw materials like rubber or jute; or minerals, particularly copper, tin or bauxite.
Moreover, 'underdeveloped countries generally trade with advanced
countries and not with each other. This pattern is clearly quite unlike
that of an "untouched" pre-capitalist economy . . .' (Brewer 1980: 9).
This raised the possibility not allowed for in modernization accounts of
development that the typical LDC economy had already been shaped
by its trade contacts with other countries into a distorted form, from
which a 'normal' development process, through the usual stages of
modernization, would not be possible.

This possibility was seized on as a certainty by some writers in the
1960s who believed that modernization theory was a way of denying
the adverse economic effects of colonial rule and legitimizing foreign
aid as an instrument to maintain former, colonial patterns of international relations. The nexus of international exchange, often referred to
loosely as 'the capitalist system', was credited with the major role in
creating the specific form of backwardness found in the Third World.
This specific form was called 'underdevelopment': it was not a pristine
condition of low productivity and poverty but an historical condition of
blocked, distorted and dependent development.

It is this conception of underdevelopment created by the capitalist
system which the counter-revolution in development rejects most vehemently. Rightly so, because it is an extreme position, the logical and
empirical supports for which were never properly worked out by its
own advocates. In adopting this position for the decade between 1965
and 1975, its partisans were allowing values, in this case strident anti-
imperialism, to dominate almost completely their choice of theory.

The theory of underdevelopment implied a continuous polarization
in income and welfare between developed and underdeveloped countries. However, the normal indicators of income and welfare did not
show that such a polarization was taking place. The average rate of
growth of income per head in both groups of countries was, between
1950 and 1975, just over 3 per cent a year. If anything (though recalling that these kinds of statistics are subject to large margins of error),
the under-developed group grew more quickly, indicating a slight
movement towards closing the relative income gap (Morawetz 1977:
26). A rate of growth of just over 3 per cent a year was also faster
than that of today's developed countries during the second half of the
nineteenth century.

Physical indicators told a story that was consistent with that of the
group growth rates. Between 1950 and 1979, life expectancy rose on
average in all developing countries from 43 to 58 years, while literacy
rose from 33 to 56 persons in every hundred and the mortality rate in
children between 1 and 4 years old fell from 28 to 12 per thousand.

Again, these rates of improvement are faster than those experienced by today's developed countries during their period of fastest development. At the same time, there is still massive scope for further improvement before developing countries reach the levels of health and education currently enjoyed by today's developed countries (Killick 1986).

If the facts rule against the idea of a long-period process of polarization between rich countries and poor, there is no need to spend time discussing the causes of such a process. However, that does not mean that one must deny that colonialism produced negative economic effects. Certain pre-colonial forms of economic activity were destroyed, certain colonial investments were inappropriate except within the context of colonialism itself and liberation conflicts have often burdened countries after independence with costly and turbulent military establishments. Economies have been distorted by colonialism in a way which hampers their future action for development. But these negative effects are not insuperable; they can be struggled against successfully. In the end, whatever the extent of the economic damage of colonialism, countries which do nothing but persuade themselves that they are the victims of history will let slip such opportunities for development as they do have now.

The evident absence of a long-period process of polarization should lead us neither to deny the negative economic impacts of colonialism nor to deny short-period setbacks which developing countries have experienced as a group. Certainly, since about 1980, economic recession has badly affected all countries, developed and developing, by greatly slowing their growth of income per head. It has also affected the developing countries as a group more seriously than the developed countries. Any past tendency for the relative income gap to narrow has thus, since 1980, been put into reverse. The main causes of the present severe slackening in developing countries' growth have been falling commodity prices, rising real interest rates and the reduction in concessional and other financial flows (Singh 1986).

What at present appears to be a short-period interruption to a long period of buoyant growth may, unless wise policy action is taken, stretch out some considerable way into the future. The prospects for quick remedies to the specific problems of debt, food availability and falling export prices do not at present (early 1993) seem bright, although one always hopes that such statements will be disproved.

Growing Diversity in the Third World

But looking at the economic performance of developing countries only as a group would conceal something that is highly relevant to the question of whether, from an economic perspective, the Third World is still with us. For within the average results for the whole Third World group, an increasing differentiation between regions and types of countries has been taking place. The growth that has been achieved has not been uniform and across the board. It has affected some countries and some regions very much more than others. As a result, the Third World in the last twenty years has increasingly departed from economic homogeneity.

The relative position of Africa has worsened steadily during the last twenty years, with the continent as a whole seeing little growth in the 1970s and falls in output in the 1980s. Some African countries were not affected by stagnation (for example, Cameroon and Tunisia), but the general picture has been very bleak. More recently, economic retrogression has extended itself, via the debt crisis and falling oil prices, to Central and Latin America and the OPEC countries. Economies least affected by the recession of the 1980s were those already growing very fast. Important in this group were the East Asian economies achieving their growth through investment in industries that could produce manufactured exports, plus India and China, who were following an inward-looking strategy of industrialization.

The differentiation within the Third World economies has resulted in two very different responses, one at each end of the economic spectrum. At the top, a debate has been begun on the issue of 'graduation', that is, the formal recognition that a developing country has developed sufficiently for it no longer to be regarded as a developing country. Rather little has been achieved except verbal sparring on the graduation issue. Whatever its degree of economic progress, a developing country is reluctant to graduate, because it thereby loses its access to certain privileged financial facilities, like concessional World Bank loans. There is also reluctance on the part of international organizations concerned with developing country interests to lose the participation of their more successful and powerful members. These institutional pressures obscure the degree of differentiation that has taken place at the top of the group.

At the bottom of the group, however, the inhibitions to recognition have been less powerful. Although UNCTAD was initially unhappy about doing so, a separate lower-end sub-group has been identified since 1979 among the members of the 'Group of 77' (which confusingly contains over 100 Third World countries). This sub-group is composed of 31 'least developed countries', also known as LLDCs. The LLDCs are defined as countries with an average income of less than $100 per head, an adult literacy rate of less than 20 per cent and a manufacturing sector which provides less than 10 per cent of gross domestic product. The Third World average for literacy was 56 per cent and for share of industry in output was about 20 per cent in 1980.

The emergence of the LLDCs is a reflection of the particular development problem faced by small, underpopulated and often landlocked

African states like Chad, Mali, Niger, Burkina Faso, Uganda, Malawi, Rwanda and Burundi. In all, Africa has two-thirds of all LLDCs. With a few exceptions like Nepal, Ethiopia and Afghanistan, the great majority of LLDCs are former European colonies.

What has happened then over the last forty years has been neither the uncomplicated succession of economic take-offs which modernization theory predicted, nor the continuously growing gap in income and welfare between the rich countries and the poor countries prophesied by underdevelopment theorists. Instead, there has been a combination of some take-offs, mainly in East Asia, and some severe cases of economic retrogression, mainly in Africa. Thus the polarization that has taken place has done so *within* the Third World, but not between the Third World taken as a group and the developed economies of the non-socialist world.

Does this intra-Third World economic differentiation matter? The answer to this depends on one's values and viewpoint. Politically, it makes the cohesion of the Third World more difficult, as conflicts between different sub-groups increase. In the 1970s, such a conflict was always threatening between the oil exporters and the oil importers in the Third World. In the 1980s, with new commercial lending almost non-existent, the main conflict was over the division of the remaining concessional finance between the least developed countries – whose need is greater – and the rest – whose ability to use the finance productively is probably greater. So to all who see the building up of the political unity of the Third World as the major task, economic differentiation does matter because it makes that task more difficult.

Economically, what most people would say mattered ultimately is the ending of large-scale poverty. It is the sickness, ignorance and premature death, not to mention the violence, ugliness and despair of daily life, which accompany poverty and underemployment, that revolt most people. Those things can be found in any Third World country on a scale that would never be tolerated elsewhere and they must be eliminated as quickly as humanly possible. Thus increasing inequality between countries is, in itself, a matter of indifference. What matters is whether mass poverty is expanding or contracting and whether the means are at hand for doing something effective to reduce it. Economic development should have as its fundamental objective the reduction of poverty (cf. World Bank 1990: 24).

If that is how one sees things, then it could be argued further that inequality within Third World countries is of concern to the extent that it prevents the reduction of mass poverty. How much scope does the existing degree of inequality provide for redistributing resources towards the desperately poor? What incentives are necessary to encourage and sustain economic growth and increase the resources available for

redistribution? How much of the existing inequalities arise from oppression and exploitation which cause and perpetuate poverty, as well
as being intrinsically unjust? Although judgements are hard to make in
particular cases, these at least are the relevant questions about inequality. They suggest that the reduction of inequality should be seen as a
secondary rather than a primary goal of development policy. Inequality
appears to have no systematic link with poverty in the Third World, or
indeed with the type of economic system – capitalist or socialist – which
is in operation. Income distribution is only slightly less unequal in
Nepal than in Brazil, and among the more equal distributions, there
is nothing to choose between that of Tanzania and that of Thailand.
Simple guidelines are not forthcoming from the bald statistics.

Backwardness, and specifically the interaction between poverty and
inequality, can thus take many varied forms. As Griffin and Gurley
remarked 'heterogeneity is the name of the game in the Third World'
(1985: 1090). The development counter-revolutionaries are right
when they criticize envisaging 'the Third World as an undifferentiated,
passive entity, helplessly at the mercy of its environment and of the
powerful West' (Bauer 1981: 84). Economically, it is certainly not
undifferentiated, one of the differences being precisely in the extent to
which particular countries are exposed to hazards either of their natural
environment, or of their international economic environment.[5]

Politically, too, the Third World is not passive, although it certainly
is relatively weak. This weakness has always been recognized as stem-
ming in part from lack of unity and the absence of solidarity. As long
ago as 1961, Sartre wrote of the Third World:

> We know that it is not a homogeneous world; we know too that enslaved
> peoples are still to be found there; together with some who have achieved
> a simulacrum of phoney independence, others who are still fighting to
> attain sovereignty and others again who have obtained complete freedom,
> but who live under the constant menace of imperialist aggression . . . Thus
> the unity of the Third World is not yet achieved. It is a work in progress . . .
> (Fanon 1967: 9–10)

From the 1950s onwards, much has been done to strengthen the collective organization of Third World states, both as a global grouping
and at the level of regional co-operation. Most recently, as the recession
has undermined their economic prospects, certain developed countries
have come out in open opposition to the Third World's political pre-
tensions, particularly in the United Nations organizations where the
one vote per country system of decision-making operates. However one
cares to evaluate these trends, the Third World cannot correctly be described as either passive or homogeneous. It has been actively seeking
a political unity it does not yet fully possess.

The Consequences of Third World Complexity

The two previous sections of this chapter have raised and then tried to give some general answers to the question of the definition of the Third World. They started from the assertion made by Bauer that the Third World owes its existence to the weakness of the West, its feelings of guilt about episodes of colonialism and imperialism and a willingness to provide foreign aid to assuage this neurotic guilt.

While acknowledging that the constitution of the Third World is based in an important way on both politics and psychology, so that it is not merely (or even, at all) a congeries of similarly structured economies, there is clearly a misunderstanding involved in examining the politics of the Third World in relation to the West alone. Historically, the Third World originates in the period of the first US-USSR cold war. It is difficult to see why groups of states referred to themselves as a 'world', or why one such 'world' called itself the 'third world', if with Bauer we ignore the 'second world' of the socialist states which were engaged in tense superpower rivalry with the West. This rivalry makes explicable the West's willingness to provide foreign aid to a group of states which, if one believed Bauer, had no more substance than ectoplasm.

But the political practice of the Third World gradually shifted from non-alignment in the competition between superpowers, to a common front on issues of decolonization. A few remote and inaccessible states which had escaped colonization joined in this common front, while others in Latin America did not do so, despite their former status as European colonies. None of these historical and geographical oddities detract, however, from the fact that the political coherence of the Third World, such as it is, is greatest in relation to the problems of decolonization. The psychology of Third Worldism, as stated classically by Fanon, revolves around the attitudes of both colonized and colonizer during the struggle for independence and not just an abstract 'guilt' experienced in former colonial countries, as Bauer would have it.

It was tempting, in the interests of strengthening the common front on colonial issues, to insist that the economic structure and performance of Third World countries was shaped decisively by their colonial experience, and that currently their development was being retarded by the effects of neo-colonial influences, such as aid, multinational corporations and Western-style advertising. This myth, just like the myth it overthrew of national modernization, rested on the notion of a typical Third World economy. All that changed – and changed radically – were the features that were said to be typical.

Whatever validity this notion may originally have had, it has been progressively weakened by changes within the Third World over the last forty years. The initial differences of location, climate and size have been added to as a result of international price movements, financial flows, differential population pressures, political choices, management performance and so on. Today, the economic position of Third World countries is more variegated than ever, with some having reached the point of being indistinguishable from developed economies, while others are retrogressing despite a succession of schemes and strategies of development. Nor are there simple correlations to be found between this range of economic performance and the incidence of poverty and oppressive forms of inequality in the Third World.

To say this may seem to be singularly unhelpful. To present poverty and exploitation as a massive human challenge that exists in the Third World, but to refuse to give any guidance as to its incidence, causes and cures must seem highly perverse. The reason for doing so at this point is to emphasize as strongly as possible that standard-formula approaches to development policy are a handicap rather than a help. People are thereby induced to analyse the particular situation in which they are working according to a set of rigid preconceptions. As often as not, such preconceptions turn out to be entirely irrelevant.

There is no simple or special way to analyse the realities of the Third World and therefore there is no simple or special set of instructions that can be given to change those realities successfully. In one sense, this is good news. It means that there is no arcane form of social science that has to be mastered before one can begin to think about development policy. For example, there are no pre-packaged intellectual tool-kits labelled 'Third World Economics' or 'Third World Sociology' which can be directly applied to Third World situations whatever they are.

It is worth pausing to emphasize this point, because one of the assumptions of the counter-revolution in development is the existence of a Third World economics which has to be swept aside. In fact, development economics as a sub-discipline of economics has not been engaged on the construction of a Third World economics. The reason for this has always been clear to development economists. 'Developing countries themselves are not homogeneous: ideas that are appropriate to India, for example, are often inappropriate to Africa . . . Equally, there are important differences between countries within Africa . . . Equally, there are important differences between countries within Africa, because of differences in customs, colonial experience, geography and culture. No single development economics is likely to be appropriate to all' (Stewart 1971: 324). Development economics is rather the practice of applying relevant concepts and theories of economic analysis to the study of the process of development. That process does not occur exclusively inside the Third World. Wherever it occurs, to analyse it requires a thorough knowledge of the particular circumstances of the time and place where it is occurring. The particular difficulty of the Third World is that full knowledge of relevant circumstances is very hard to achieve.

The analysis of development sequences is only one part of a development economist's activities. Mass poverty can be caused by the dynamics of social change, as when cultivators or forest-dwellers are turned off the land in great numbers. But it can also be caused by stable structures of oppression, the continuous extraction of all surplus beyond subsistence through tenure systems and money-lending. Having understood something about how favourable development sequences have worked, that is, dynamic social change without poverty-inducing effects, that knowledge has to be transferred to different situations of stagnant oppression and deployed pragmatically to stimulate favourable change. In making the transfer, allowance must be made for all relevant differences of circumstances.

This is a task which self-evidently requires great intellectual sophistication, imagination and practical skills. Given the complexity of the Third World, as it confronts any outsiders, the only valuable advice is not just to begin by shedding preconceptions, but actively to learn how to become more open-minded. There are a number of subtle biases which distort outside perceptions of problems of poverty. The best general advice to those approaching Third World problems for the first time is to get to grips with these endemic perception difficulties, along the lines mapped out by Chambers (1983).[6]

The unhelpfulness of the counter-revolution in development derives from its particularly powerful preconception of the actions that need to be taken to promote development. That preconception is that development problems are problems of resource allocation; that the price mechanism should be relied on to allocate resources optimally; and that government intervention in markets should be minimal. It may be seen as more than a little ironic that, having dismissed a non-existent Third World economics on the grounds of the heterogeneity of the Third World, its proposed replacement is a 'First and Third World economics' which makes even fewer concessions to heterogeneity.

Before delving deeper into the analytical basis of these policy preconceptions, a final example may serve to illustrate their practical unhelpfulness in the context of poverty alleviation. This particular example comes from Sri Lanka and its context is the conservation of fuelwood. When people have become so poor that they can no longer afford to buy commercial fuels in the market place, they scavenge for wood to use for cooking their food. Provided that the off-take from the forest is only of dead wood, no harm is done to the renewal of future wood supplies. When so many poor people are scavenging that the live wood begins to be cut down, it becomes only a matter of time before the supply is exhausted and the users become progressively more impoverished. So what should be done?

Should we raise the price of fuelwood, to discourage the marginal users with the least intense preference for it? One might start to debate the familiar question of whether demand for fuelwood is highly price inelastic, or whether quantities demanded would respond to a price rise rather flexibly. But that is hardly relevant, because there is no fuelwood price. There is no fuelwood price because there is no fuelwood market.

So should we create a market for fuelwood, so that we can have a price to raise? This is not possible for economic reasons. The costs of creating such a market would be too great in relation to the revenue that could be raised from the indigent potential customers. It would involve establishing undisputed legal rights to the product of all the trees and policing and enforcing this right against non-paying scavengers who might come by night, perhaps, in their desperation, armed.

Should we at any rate avoid all government intervention, in the belief that governments only make already difficult situations worse? Not necessarily. Robert Wade (1988) has shown that in some circumstances, this problem of 'the tragedy of the commons' can be handled by communities coming together to regulate demands on the commons. But when neither market-based nor community-based solution are feasible, intelligent governments can intervene helpfully. The government in this case, decided to design a new type of cooking stove which used fuelwood twice as efficiently as the existing design and to sell the new stoves at a subsidized price in the areas where destructive scavenging was most prevalent. The effect of this move was to slow down the rate of forest destruction and create a breathing space in which a long-term conservation policy could be devised and implemented.

This was not an 'ideal' solution, because the improvement in forest conservation and the economic security of the scavengers was not achieved without making anyone else worse off. The vendors of the old-style, fuel-inefficient stoves were made worse off so were the Sri Lankan taxpayers who paid for the new design and the subsidy on its sales. But development policy is all about the dilemmas of balancing the gains of one group against the losses of others. In this case, the balance that was in fact struck would probably be widely agreed to be the correct one, in that it simultaneously improved the efficiency and the equity of the economy.

The rejection of preconceptions in favour of a free-market solution does not rest on any ideological antipathy to solutions of that kind. It is simply that, in the circumstances of Third World (or other) poverty, such solutions are often not solutions, because they fail to address the problem. Rejection also has nothing to do with any tendency, often detected by the counter-revolution in old-style development economists 'to ignore microeconomic problems altogether in the design of public policies' (Lal 1983: 9). Although forest conservation is a sector-level problem, the strategy of government intervention was adopted because it was the one that made the best microeconomic sense.[7]

Notes

1   See the discussion of India's experience with famine, in contrast with that of China, in Sen (1983: 757–60).

2   The origins and current state of the debt crisis are discussed in more detail in chapter 8.

3   The varying characteristics of soils in tropical areas can be found in brief in Kamarck (1976: 22–9).

4   The failure of development economists to take some of these natural variations more seriously as discriminators of radically different modes of rural economy has been attacked by economic anthropologists, notably Polly Hill (see Grillo and Rew 1985: 117–30).

5   Mention of the hazards of developing countries' natural environments serves to remind us of one unifying characteristic of the Third World which has been insufficiently stressed in the foregoing discussion. Many Third World countries share, by virtue of their geographical location, a special set of hazards which the now developed countries did not have to negotiate successfully – namely poor soils for agriculture, abundant pests and plagues of predators and the tropical diseases of trypanosomiasis, bilharzia, malaria, river blindness and hookworm disease (Kamarck 1976: passim). The degree of exposure to these tropical hazards does differ between individual Third World countries, however, as does the ability to adopt policies that will reduce the degree of exposure. In the context of the development counter-revolution's account of the Third World, it is interesting to note that the references to climatic influences on development prospects which are to be found in Bauer (1972) disappear in his subsequent books (1981, 1984).

6   See particularly Chambers's account of the biases in perception which inhibit an understanding of rural poverty in the Third World. These arise from such things as the habit of viewing rural areas from vehicles, looking at projects, meeting mainly male elite persons, avoiding the wet season and trying to be polite. From the view point of the would-be development economist, perhaps it is professional bias which is most relevant:

> Knowing what they want to know and short of time to find out, professionals in rural areas become even more narrowly single-minded. They do their own thing and only their own thing. *They look for and find what fits their ideas.* There is neither inclination nor time for the open-ended question or for other ways of perceiving people, events and things.
>
> (Chambers 1983: 23, with emphasis added)

7   The source of this illustration is Munasinghe (1985). This case study vividly demonstrates the futility of what Albert Hirschman has called 'the visiting-economist syndrome, that is, . . . the habit of issuing peremptory advice and prescription by calling on universally valid economic principles and remedies – be they old or brand new – after a strictly minimal acquaintance with the "patient" ' (Meier and Seers 1984: 93).

CHAPTER TWO

Development Policy in the Shadow of Keynes

Reaction against the Keynesian Revolution

The counter-revolution in development theory and policy which has characterized the 1980s can be understood, in part, by examining what it was reacting against. The present counter-revolution is dedicated to countering a previous revolution. That previous revolution was the work of John Maynard Keynes and its impact on the economic thought and policy-making of the 1930s and 1940s. It is no exaggeration to say that Keynes transformed economics and the practice of economists. On the theoretical plane, he showed the way out of the beautiful, self-balancing clockwork economics to which so many of his contemporaries had subordinated their minds. On the practical plane, he inspired whole new sub-disciplines of economics – macro economics, national accounting, econometrics – which had to be created before economists could make a continuous, operational contribution to national policy-making.

No revolution carries all before it. Notwithstanding the unprecedented post-war rates of economic growth, the virtual elimination of involuntary unemployment in developed economies and the very rapid expansion of world trade, all of which came about when economists of Keynesian outlook were more actively involved with economic policy-making than any previous generation of economists had been, criticism of this outlook persisted, although in a minor key. One theme of criticism – represented in the UK by economists belonging to the Institute of Economic Affairs – was that Keynesian economists engaged in economic policy-making tended to favour government intervention to achieve aggregate-level policy objectives where microeconomic theory suggested that a freely working market would produce a superior outcome.

Another theme of criticism, which was stronger in the US, was that the Keynesian analysis of the interaction of the monetary variables in the economy was incorrect. Contrary to Keynes's view, monetary expansion to increase national income could not be practical for long without causing accelerating rates of inflation. These two themes, the overriding of market forces and the alleged failure to analyse inflation correctly, converged in the early 1970s in the great debate over incomes policy. The spectacle of otherwise conservative administrations, led by Nixon and Heath, both attempting to enforce wage and price 'guidelines' in 1971–2 as a crucial part of their macroeconomic strategies, was the event which, more than any other, converted grumbling dissent among right-wing economists into an outright anti-Keynesian counter-revolution.

Thus it was that the doctrines of free-market forces and monetarism were, in the 1970s, rapidly absorbed by conservative political parties in Europe and the US (Keegan 1984: 33–104). Their return to government in 1979–80 in the UK, the US and West Germany was partly on the strength of their adoption of a strident anti-Keynesian in domestic economic policy. Their broad political success in turn increased the confidence of the academic anti-Keynesian counter-revolutionaries. It also expanded their access to public platforms and their prospects of honour and reward. This has had profound implications for development policy. The late Professor Harry Johnson is a central figure in the story of the development counter-revolution. He was a technically proficient economist who specialized in monetary theory. He held chairs at both Chicago and the London School of Economics. As well as developing the free-market ideas of Chicago with formal elegance, he conducted a personal crusade against the influence of Fabianism (said to be entrenched in LSE in the 1930s despite Hayek, Robbins and Paish) on post-war British economics.

One of the lessons which Johnson drew from the history of the Keynesian revolution was that intellectual movements in economics take place in response to perceived social needs. They do not, in other words, arise from an autonomous dynamic of scientific progress within the discipline itself. As he put it in his Richard T. Ely Lecture on revolutions and counter-revolutions in economics: 'New ideas win a public and professional hearing, not on their scientific merits, but on whether or not they promise a solution to important problems that the established orthodoxy has proved itself incapable of solving' (Johnson 1971a: 12). Keynes had promised to cure mass unemployment in the 1930s when no one else seemed able to: that, for Johnson, was the secret of the Keynesian revolution's success, not its scientific merit.

This may seem like a useful argument for dismissing an earlier theory, while at the same time explaining its triumph, and so it is. But its corollary is that any counter-revolution must also be of the same non-scientific kind. The public and professional acclaim for the economics of free-market forces and monetarism must then also derive from its promise to solve an apparently insoluble problem – the problem of accelerating inflation. Johnson does not appear to see anything paradoxical in accepting this corollary. On the contrary, he speaks with disarming frankness of the 'invention' by the anti-Keynesian counter-revolution of important parts of its own intellectual history and the 'scholarly chicanery' used in presenting its case (1971a: 10–11). The intellectual pragmatism of Keynes had become, in the hands of the counter-revolution, a much more manipulative approach to the intellectual standards of economics.

A second major lesson which Johnson drew – among many others on the right – was that the Keynesian revolution's central message was unjustifiably critical of capitalism. Just as those on the left condemned Keynes for having found a way to stave off the inevitable collapse of capitalism, so those on the right condemned him for daring to suggest that capitalism left to itself tends to produce mass unemployment and economic stagnation. Johnson could not agree with that, arguing instead that the Depression of the 1930s was simply a couple of quite different national problems which happened unfortunately to coincide: 'We now know . . . that the British problem of the inter-war period was a *special* problem compounded of industrial senility and an overvalued exchange rate, while the Great Crash was a matter of national and international monetary mismanagement by central bankers . . .' (Johnson 1971b: 4). None of this was any reflection on the efficacy of the capitalist system as a mode of economic organization.

In the light of these two conclusions, Johnson considered the state of development policy, as he perceived it at the end of the 1960s. He found much to deplore. In particular, he deduced from their actions that policy-makers in developing countries had been affected by the same lack of confidence in the efficacy of capitalism which he thought that Keynes had created in the developed countries. Coupled with this, they had adopted industrialization and national self-sufficiency as prime objectives of development policy, an error which he attributed largely to 'the flight of well-trained Central European scholars to the West during the 1930s' (1971b). Finally, they accepted economic planning as the major instrument of development policy, because the past economic successes of the Soviet Union's and National Socialist Germany's planners were taken at their face value, instead of as outcomes only possible in highly authoritarian societies.

From these three central policy attitudes – doubts about the capitalist system's ability to deliver 'development', a desire for industrial self-sufficiency and an admiration for authoritarian economic planning – Johnson traced out the causes of many policy problems which developing countries faced. For example, to this trinity of beliefs was attributed the rash of unproductive industrial investments which appeared in many developing countries – but particularly Africa – in the wake of independence. It was said also to encourage the corruption which often surrounded the administration of economic controls. It was blamed for policies of import-substituting industrialization which produced chronic balance of payments problems and for misguided interventions in economic life, made in a futile attempt to achieve social justice and fairness. Johnson effectively built up by a hypothesized link between selected features of Third World countries – their propensity to corruption, their chronic shortage of foreign exchange, their unproductive industry – and certain policy decisions – to protect domestic industry, to make extensive use of controls on trade, wages and prices and to try to compress income differentials. Having connected outcomes with policies, a second link was then projected between these policies and selected social attitudes. In Johnson's analysis, the social attitudes that generate wrong policies in developing countries are the social attitudes propagated by Keynes.

As far as the Third World is concerned, therefore, the Keynesian revolution had, on this interpretation, created a blight on its hopes for development. The problems of the Third World were not a legacy of colonial history or the reflection of global structural inequalities: they were the result of current policies erroneously undertaken in the deluded belief that they would foster development. Moreover, the policies themselves would not be altered as long as policy-makers in developing countries continued to stand in the shadow of Keynes.

Johnson's 1971 account of how the shadow of Keynes clouded development policy can now be seen as rather unsatisfactory, even in its own terms. As a challenge to Keynesian thinking, it suffered from various weaknesses and contradictions. How sensible was it, for example, to appear to be challenging the objectives which developing countries set themselves, such as rapid industrialization? How libertarian could one realistically be, in opposing economic planning? How rigorously could the social attitudes which Johnson criticized be identified, with chapter and verse, in Keynes's own work?

Neo-classical versus Economic Nationalism

Denouncing the quest for industrial self-sufficiency in developing countries seemed to question their right of political self-determination, the chief fruit of the long anti-colonial struggle. It could well be asked, by what authority do neo-classical economists, who pose as value-free social scientists, presume to specify what objectives a developing country should have? Neo-classical economists make a virtue of taking preferences as given, and showing how they interact to generate an equilibrium of prices. As policy advisers, they claim to be technicians who can appropriately prescribe the efficient means to achieve given ends. None of this provides an intellectual basis from which to challenge particular preferred ends of policy, such as rapid industrialization or industrial self-sufficiency.

The argument from history on this point looks no stronger than the argument from neo-classical economics. Today's developing countries are the latest on a long list of 'late developers'. Every late developer faces the problem of establishing itself in a world dominated by countries with greater economic strength. Because economic resources are a necessary condition of military strength, economic strength usually implies that the already established countries are militarily superior was well. (This is certainly true of today's late developers, most of which have had to compete with a former colonial or imperial power). The already developed countries do not welcome the development of late developers. Why should they? Success achieved by a late developer country will cause economic disruption (through lost industrial markets and lost access to cheap food and raw materials) and it may also pose a military threat from a new direction. It is hardly surprising that, in the hostile world environment in which they must succeed, successful late developers – from the US, Germany, the USSR and Japan, down to contemporary South Korea – have given a very high priority to industrialization and have not allowed this to be shaped simply by the pressure of world market forces on their individual private firms. History does not forecast the future, but some good reasons would be needed to believe that the next successful late developers will use a radically different approach from all previous ones.

India may serve as a specific example, because it has been the *bête noire* of the development counter-revolution. It was labelled as the slow-growth country which listened to the wrong set of economists, that is, not the neo-classical ones. The fact is that India has successfully defended itself in three conflicts with Pakistan since gaining political independence and achieved its geopolitical objective of being the dominant power in the south Asian region. Its industrialization strategy has contributed materially to its ability to defend itself. The USA, as the global hegemonic power, has never shared India's aspirations to regional dominance. It was, until the USSR's demise in 1991, much more interested in building up the military strength of Pakistan as a counter to a perceived threat of Soviet expansionism. India's independent military strength, based on its capability to manufacture its own weapons, munitions and now aircraft, has rarely been an object of US policy. It was concerned in 1962, during the brief conflict with China, but in 1965, and again in 1971, the US expressed its active displeasure when India was in conflict with Pakistan.

The Indian case illustrates the kind of geopolitical circumstances in which developing countries often decide on policies of rapid industrialization. To preach directly against such policies, and the accompanying policies of economic nationalism – particularly in a totally economistic discourse which blandly ignores the geopolitical dimension of decision-making – is to court irrelevance, or even charges of bad faith, if the preacher is a North American academic.

The same could be said about denouncing economic planning on the grounds that it could only work in authoritarian societies, like Germany and the Soviet Union in the 1930s. Supposing one takes this equation of planning and authoritarianism at its face value, its force is again mediated by its geopolitical context. While the US, as the hegemonic power, was seen to be actively supporting authoritarian regimes in the Third World, for its own strategic reasons, the claim that economic planning only works within such regimes was not a very strong indictment of economic planning in the Third World. The geopolitical strategy of 'freedom' often gave rise to local manifestations of illiberalism. Taiwan and South Korea developed very fast using a form of economic planning implemented by authoritarian governments supported by the United States.

Again, the south Asian example is helpful here. When democracy collapsed in Pakistan in the mid-1950s, the US government tried to help the new authoritarian regime of Ayub Khan (1958–69). It did so by building up Pakistan's economic planning skills. Planned development was supposed to make the absence of democracy (and of 'political instability') acceptable to the population.[1] It failed precisely because it studiously ignored all questions of equity and social fairness, particularly as between the west and east wings of the country. These were the political realities of the developing world at the time when Johnson was writing. They made much of what he was saying seem rather controversial.

Finally, anyone who is at all familiar with Keynes's views would be highly sceptical that he did actually share the social attitudes which are said to lie at the root of developing countries' policy mistakes. It is one thing to thunder against a non-economic approach to industrial development, an illiberal endorsement of economic planning and a radical anti-capitalism. It is task of much greater difficulty to demonstrate that these attitudes can be logically deduced from any of the writings of Keynes, as will be shown in a later section of this chapter.

The Shadow of Keynes Redefined

Towards the end of the 1970s, Johnson tried again to define the undesirable influence which be believed that Keynes had exerted on policies of economic development. While admitting that Keynes himself had, for a variety of reasons, written little about economic development, Johnson highlighted some alleged characteristics of Keynes's approach to economics which had lingered harmfully in the minds of those making policy in the post-war Third World. The characteristics complained of were an over-emphasis on the importance of physical capital formation in economic processes; a neglect of the possibilities of technical change; and a contempt for entrepreneurship.

The channel by which Keynes's economic concepts were transmitted to post-war development economists was the Harrod–Domar model. This model provided the elementary framework for considering the relationship between the growth rate of output, the growth rate of population and the growth rate of savings. The Harrod–Domar construction was interpreted to suggest that a key problem of development might be a too high or too low rate of growth of savings and, therefore, that knife-edge instability characterized any steady-state growth path (Hahn and Matthews 1965: 5–8).

Johnson claimed that a misleading obsession with fixed investment connects the Harrod–Domar model with Keynes' *General Theory*. In his own words: 'The Harrod–Domar equation – while not of Keynes' own coining [is] essentially Keynesian both by direct discipleship and by intellectual affinity with the concentration on fixed capital investment as the prime economic mover in *The General Theory*' (Johnson and Johnson 1978: 232). Johnson attributes to Keynes the view that 'policy directed at fixed capital investment was the key to full employment and social bliss' and speaks of 'the crucial importance of the level of fixed capital investment' in the Keynesian system (1978: 228, 233). While agreeing that no economist can be held responsible for the intellectual production of his disciples, does Keynes's fascination with fixed capital formation mean that the defects of the Harrod–Domar model are rightly seen as part of the Keynesian inheritance?

Keynes's supposed fascination with fixed capital formation is something of a canard. Keynes does describe the level of investment as the *causa causans*, but only because 'it is usual in a complex system to regard as the *causa causans* that factor which is most prone to sudden and wide fluctuation' (Keynes CW XIV: 121). Only in this special sense does fixed capital formation play a particularly 'prime' or 'crucial' role in Keynes's macroeconomics. What, after all, was the essential analytical novelty of the *General Theory*? In Patinkin's words, it was 'the argument that an excess aggregate supply exerts a direct depressing effect on the level of output, and that the decline in output itself ultimately eliminates the excess supply and thus brings the economy to a position of unemployment equilibrium' (Patinkin 1982: 80). Fixed capital formation is exogenous to this process of equilibration. It enters the picture only because failure to invest reduces aggregate supply which starts the move to an unemployment equilibrium. Keynes in fact does not have one theory of fixed capital formation, he has two: 'animal spirits' of entrepreneurs, which self-evidently cannot be modelled, and the marginal efficiency of capital schedule, which may however shift about for all sorts of unpredictable reasons. Fixed capital formation plays approximately the same role in Keynesian macroeconomics as the weather plays in agricultural economics. It is indeed recognized as important. But it is hard to forecast, and there is nothing much one can do about it. Compared with the forces affecting the production of wealth, according to Keynes, 'even the weather is only moderately uncertain' (CW XIV: 113).

Nor is the role of fixed capital formation, *pace* Johnson, central in Keynesian economic policy. A fiscal policy for increasing aggregate demand is indifferent between capital formation and consumption expenditures. Keynes was prepared to have the government pay people to dig holes in the ground and fill them up again, as a means of reducing unemployment. He also hoped that the government would then see that it would be even better if they were building houses, roads or sewers. This indifference between investment or consumption expenditure in Keynesian fiscal policy is reflected in the absence of classification of government expenditure into these two categories during Keynes's lifetime.

The Harrod–Domar model was not the only growth model constructed by economists in the 1940s and 1950s. There was a whole family of growth models that were analytically very similar, both in terms of the general level of aggregation at which they operated (they were highly aggregative) and in the definition of the component variables. One of this family of models was the neo-classical growth model. This variant produced different analytical results from Harrod–Domar, because it made different assumptions about which of its variables were fixed and which were flexible. By permitting the capital/output ratio of the economy to vary, it was possible to imagine an adujstment mechanism which solved the Harrod–Domar problem of knife-edge instability on the steady-state growth path (Solow 1970: 8–38).

This neo-classical model of growth shared exactly the same conception of fixed capital as that of the Harrod–Domar model. Since both models were of economies which produced only one commodity, that commodity had a dual role; it could either be consumed or be invested. Although dual purpose in this way, it was clearly physical in nature. The labour inputs into its production were assumed to be homogeneous. So in both models, 'human capital formation' was ruled out by assumption, and all capital formation was fixed and physical. Far form exemplifying a Keynesian fetish with fixed capital formation, as Johnson contended, the Harrod–Domar model rather shared a general tendency of all early growth model theorists, including neo-classical, to use highly simplified, but analytically tractable, conceptions of capital and labour.

Such models, whether Keynesian or not, tend to be short on policy implications that can be applied to the real world. Both Harrod–Domar and the neo-classical model contribute little to the discussion of economic policy. Harrod–Domar presents a policy problem, but a problem with no suggested solution. The neo-classical model denies that failure to control the saving rate does constitute a policy problem, but contributes neither problems nor solutions of its own.

The neo-classical model can be read as pointing to other factors outside itself as influences on the growth rate of real output per person. One such outside influence is technical progress. Johnson's next line of attack on the shadow of Keynes is to suggest that Keynes encouraged policy-makers to neglect the possibilities of technical progress. He suggests that the concept of disguised unemployment, which is Keynesian in lineage, has mesmerized policy-makers in developing countries to the exclusion of problems of technical change. 'The notion that there exist masses of "disguised unemployed" people leads easily into the idea that "development" involves merely the mobilisation and transfer of these presumable costless productive resources into economic activities, primarily investment or industrial production, at an obvious and virtually costless social economic gain' (Johnson and Johnson 1978: 229). This kind of policy is contrasted unfavourably with the Chicago view of the rural sector of developing countries. This regards farmers as efficient profit-maximizers, only poor, so that the phenomena of disguised un-employment are really just the symptoms of a low productivity technology – the view of T. W. Schultz (1964).

It is true that a famous early model of economic development, that of Lewis (1954), focused on the transfer of surplus labour from the sub-sistence to the capitalist sector of the economy as part of the process of output and income growth and capital accumulation. The Lewis model also contributed substantially to debates on development policy in the 1950s and 1960s. This was particularly so in relation to debates on rural–urban migration and the correct methods of investment appraisal (or cost–benefit analysis).

The Lewis model, which in lineage was explicitly classical rather than Keynesian, has been extensively discussed. Any simple model has to ignore important aspects of reality, and it is quite plausible to say that the Lewis model misled practical policy-makers in developing countries. In particular, the view of the subsistence sector in this model was misleading and may well have held back a proper understanding of the role of small-scale agriculture in assisting development. Lewis saw the rural subsistence sector almost exclusively as a sector to be milked of labour that it could not use, so that the capitalist labour force could swell.

For practical development policy, this vision was in several ways quite unhelpful (Thirlwall 1984: 102–4). Capitalists did not want raw country labour, because of population growth in urban areas. Or they wanted it, but only on a temporary and rotating basis. The process of capitalist expansion went on unevenly and slowly. This was because many investments chosen were not productive and surplus-generating; industrial growth could also be demand-constrained, and not just supply-constrained; and food and raw materials were subject to shortages and price inflation. The rural subsistence sector turned out to have a complementary role to play in national economic growth and raising its productivity soon became identified as a goal rather than an obstacle in development policy.

Even so, Johnson's dichotomy of either capital accumulation or technical change is much too sharply drawn. By developing a model without technical change, Lewis was not *ipso facto* denying the desirability of technical change. His choice of focus was undoubtedly influenced by what seemed to be the most practical option for policy in 1954. The possibility of rapid technical progress in agriculture had become much more visible only ten years later, when Schultz wrote. It was, after all, during the period 1954–64 that the scientific basis of a green revolution in agriculture was laid.[2]

Moreover, even if technical change is the better policy option, in some sense, how much of it can a country undergo without accompanying capital accumulation? The case of the 'miracle seeds' of the green revolution is the one usually discussed is this context, since it comes nearer than most others to the idea of pure technical change (Singer 1975: 41; Johnson and Johnson 1978: 230). It is clear from this that miracle seeds need complementary inputs, some of which are fixed capital – the dams and canals for large-scale irrigation, the electric pump sets for minor irrigation, the fertilizer factories to produce domestic fertilizer or the handling and transport infrastructure if it is to be imported. In countries other than India, tractors or combine-harvesters might also be useful complementary inputs to miracle seeds. Less obviously, the use of miracle seeds in India required their adaptation to the local Indian agro-climatic environments. This presupposes a network of agricultural research institutes capable of undertaking the necessary adaptation. Even the education of the farmer, the human capital approach so strongly urged by Johnson, requires the creation of agricultural colleges for extension workers and the vehicles to take them from farm to farm. Capital formation and technical change are not alternatives, they are complementary.

It is, therefore, no real surprise to discover that countries with a high share of output going to gross domestic investment (excluding human capital formation) have also enjoyed high growth rates of output (Sen 1983: 749); or that countries like Uganda, Sudan and Mozambique, which devote very little of their output to investment, are economically stagnant or contracting; or that this relationship holds up for countries at a range of different income levels. These results themselves tell us nothing about the direction of causation, let alone whether the achieved growth has increased welfare. But they do serve the minimal purpose of suggesting that a strong contrast between sound Chicago theories basing growth on technical change and unsound, Keynesian theories basing growth on fixed capital formation was a false antithesis.

Uncertainty, Entrepreneurship and Incentives

As well as neglecting technical change, Keynes was said to have neglected the problem of entrepreneurial incentives. The reason given was that he shared 'the mixture of attribution of entrepreneurial decisions to unexplained but vaguely contemptible "animal spirits" and denial of any economic justification of profits' (Johnson and Johnson 1978: 232). This criticism reverses the truth. Keynesian economics is able to explain why entrepreneurship is so important, in a way that neo-classical general equilibrium theory cannot, because of its own assumptions. The explanation is a structuralist one. It is simply that intertemporal markets for goods over the lifetime of capital assets do not exist (Hahn 1981: 132). In the absence of such future markets for goods, rational calculation as the basis for investment decisions is simply impossible. Thus entrepreneurship is defined as 'our rational selves choosing between the alternatives as best we are able, calculating where we can, but often falling back for our motive on whim or sentiment or chance' (Keynes CW VII: 163). In other words, entrepreneurs are not accountants, they are people who hire accountants and make difficult decisions on the basis of the limited help which accountants can give them.[3]

There is nothing contemptible in this for Keynes. Entrepreneurship was valuable for him precisely because, as he explained it, 'if the animal spirits are dimmed and the spontaneous optimism falters, leaving us to depend on nothing but a mathematical expectation, enterprise will fade and die' (CW VII: 162).

Because of uncertainty about the long-term future, the fading of enterprise may be based on low expectations that are no more reasonable than the high expectations which buoy up entrepreneurship. It would, however, produce an involuntary unemployment equilibrium in the short term. The cure for unemployment depends on the creation of a more solid framework for business expectation. A larger role for the state in the direct organization of investment was one way to provide such a framework.

The reward for entrepreneurship is explicitly linked by Keynes to the priority to be given to capital accumulation. If his critics are to be believed, Keynes both had an accumulation fetish and recommended confining entrepreneurs to relatively small rewards. Keynes may have made mistakes, but was he really too foolish to see this contradiction? Obviously it is only once capital accumulation has diminished in social importance that dividends and interest payments can be relatively reduced. That day seemed only a generation away to Keynes because a stationary or declining population for Britain was forecast when he was writing – a fact which ironically reinforces his own account of the impossibility of forecasting the future with any tolerable accuracy. There is the further point that Keynes was also assuming 'the separation between ownership and management . . . and . . . the development of organised investment market's (CW VII: 150). Once this separation has occurred, the rewards of entrepreneurship become a cost of production, determined in the markets for enterprise managers and not an element in gross profit. Keynes very exactly distinguishes speculation in securities prices from enterprise, 'the activity of forecasting the prospective yield of assets over their whole life' (CW VII: 158). The latter activity becomes 'professionalized' in mature capitalism and its performance does not rely, in any essential manner, on the existence of high average rates of return on investment.

Johnson rests his case against Keynes on three counts: his investment fetish, his distraction of policy-makers' attention from technical change and his contempt for entrepreneurship. No significance is attached to Keynes's work on international finance. Johnson mentions that Keynes supported international commodity agreements, but refers to this fact as 'a culturally insignificant part of his literary legacy to modern economic culture' (Johnson and Johnson 1978: 227).

At the end of the 1970s the counter-revolution had still produced only a limited indictment of Keynesian thinking. The differences between Keynes's way of conceptualizing capital formation, of modelling growth and of noticing the importance of technical change, and the ways of other economists seem, overall, to have been relatively minor. The biggest difference is Keynes's explicit acknowledgement of the role of uncertainty in economic behaviour and decision-making, his recognition of the non-existence of crucial markets and his consequent ability to explain what entrepreneurship is, and just why it is important.

Keynes on Soviet Development Strategy

Having examined Johnson's critiques, it is time now to focus attention on what Keynes really *did* say about policies for economic development. To do so, we must look at his writings about Russia and the economic experiment of the Bolsheviks in the Soviet Union. This material has been unduly neglected in the debate about the relevance of Keynes's thinking to the problems of today's poor countries. It turns out to be very pertinent, allowing two important conclusions to be reached. The first of these is that Keynes anticipated many of the development counter – revolution's theoretical criticisms of the economic distortions generated by interventionist governments. In their attacks on the shadow of Keynes, critics like Harry Johnson failed to see that Keynes himself had, in his commentaries on Soviet economic policy, made most of their own points first. The second key conclusion is that when later, in the 1930s, Keynes advocated a form of state planning and limited protection, he expressly did so for the developed, industrial countries alone, and of them only for those that had maintained a liberal political system. His unwavering opposition to Stalinist planning is beyond doubt.

The urban bias of the early Soviet economy was maintained by government interventions which Keynes called 'the official method of exploiting the peasants'. This method he described as follows in *A Short View of Russia* (1925):

> [It] is not so much by taxation . . . as by price policy. The monopoly of import and export trade and the virtual control of industrial output enable the authorities to maintain relative prices at levels highly disadvantageous to the peasant. They buy his wheat from him at much below the world price, and they sell to him textile and other manufactured goods appreciably above the world price, the difference providing a fund out of which can be financed their high overhead costs and the general inefficiency of manufacture and distribution. The monopoly of import and export trade, by permitting a divorce between the internal and external price levels, can be operated in such a way as to maintain the parity of foreign exchange in spite of a depreciation in the purchasing power of money. The real value of the rouble inside Russia is, admittedly, much depreciated compared with its external value as measured by the current exchange.
>
> (CW, IX: 264)

Keynes had identified, before his 1925 visit to Russia, three interrelated components of the Soviet regime's management of its economy, namely:

1   state monopoly of the import and export trade;
2   deliberate government inflation of the domestic currency as a means of taxation;
3   a foreign exchange currency rate which had become greatly overvalued in terms of the domestic currency.[4]

The *Short View* adds two new features to Keynes's understanding of the Soviet system, namely:

4   the distortion of relative prices, in a way that turns the internal terms of trade against the agricultural sector; and
5   state subsidies for a government-controlled industry that is inefficient.

These five features taken together form the core of the counter-revolutionary critique of economic policy in developing countries, as embodied in, for example, Little, Scitovsky and Scott (1970) *Industry and Trade in Developing Countries*. To see this, one has only to compare Keynes's account with the theses of Little, Scitovsky and Scott (1970) as summarized on their opening page:

> The main theses in this book are that industry has been over-encouraged in relation to agriculture and that, although there are arguments for giving special encouragement to industry, this encouragement could be provided in forms which would not, as present policies do, discourage exports, including agricultural exports; which would promote greater efficiency in the use of resources; and which would create a less unequal distribution of income and higher levels of employment in both industry and agriculture.

Given his diagnosis, Keynes's prescription was that Soviet Russia's economy required 'structural adjustment'. In an analysis which must have a familiar ring to readers of World Bank publications in the 1980s, he declared:

> The low value of agricultural products in terms of industrial products is a serious deterrent to the output of the former, which is the real wealth of the country. The fundamental problem of the Soviet government is to get itself into a sufficiently strong financial position to be able to pay the peasant more nearly the real value of his produce – which would surely have the effect of giving him both the means and the incentive to a far higher output.
>
> (CW IX: 264)

In the absence of this adjustment, one major inefficiency of the Soviet system would be the under-production of agricultural goods.

The other drawback would be excessive stimulus to rural–urban migration. Keynes argues that the artificially high urban wages will draw too many people from the rural areas, because they will fail to calculate correctly the probability of their finding employment in the towns. Hence the flow of rural migrants will only be checked 'after the towns have become over-crowded and unemployment has reached unheard-of proportions'. Because they are paid a dole 'from their trade', 'this vast army of unemployed is a heavy burden on the financial resources of the state establishments'. This outcome is a very far cry from Arthur Lewis's vision of industrialization via the employment of surplus rural labour at a constant real wage. Instead, it prefigures the rural urban migration theory of Harris and Todaro (1970).

Keynes had already criticized the Bolsheviks for their inability to understand what institutions had to operate in any society and economy, whatever its politics and ideology. Post-1925, he made this criticism focus specifically on the role of relative prices:

> This state of affairs serves but to enforce a lesson of bourgeois economics as being equally applicable in a Communist state, namely that it impairs wealth to interfere with the normal levels of relative prices or with the normal levels of relative wages.
>
> (CW IX: 265)

The major economic difference between the theses of the development counter-revolution and Keynes's on Soviet Russia's economy is that Little, Scitovsky and Scott concede that *some* state promotion of industry is desirable. Keynes in 1925 did not make the same concession to the interventionist viewpoint. This unwillingness to countenance a state-engineered industrialization drive was not limited to the Russian context, but applied equally to India, whose: 'future prosperity is to be sought almost entirely in the application of more skill and knowledge, and especially of more capital, to the methods of agriculture' (Chandavarkar, 1989: 135–6).

Keynes was, at the political level, unsympathetic to the then swelling Indian economic nationalism, and, at the economic level, ready to base himself on the static version of the principle of comparative advantage. Thus, in both India and Russia, he was *even less* interventionist than the neo-classical critics of 'premature industrialization' in the 1970s. Indeed, his dictum that agriculture constituted 'the real wealth' of Russia has an almost physiocratic flavour which lays him open to the accusation of 'rural bias'.

Let us turn now from economics to political economy. It is natural to ask now whether, if Keynes anticipated much of the counter-revolution's critique of the development policies of today's less developed countries, he also anticipated its 'new political economy', with its emphasis on corruption, rent-seeking and the predatory state. It is usual to think that he did not, and to attribute to him a Platonist view of the state, essentially guided by benevolent and intelligent intellectuals, like himself. Keynes's true position was stated succinctly in the early 1930s. 'My own aim', he declared, 'is economic reform by the methods of political liberalism' (CW XVIII: 29). In a liberal democracy, the methods of influence and persuasion are manifold, and Keynes made use of most of them, although he never ran for elective office. Apart from publishing books and academic articles, he wrote for newspapers and journals, gave radio talks, sat on and gave evidence to committees of enquiry and held positions of high responsibility in the government administration, private firms, national boards and the House of Lords. The ideal state, for Keynes, was the one which kept open all these channels of influence on a government that was itself democratically elected. His view of actual states differed profoundly depending on whether or not they were embedded in an institutional context of political liberalism. Keynes had plenty of criticisms of individual politicians and statesmen and of the cumbersomeness of the working of the democratic political process itself. But he never tried to subvert or circumvent it.

A Platonic state is one *not* necessarily committed to liberal institutions. It is ruled by an elite, guided by intellectuals with their own idea of the good. Russia in the early 1920s could be dubbed a Platonic state, and was by Popper in *The Open Society and its Enemies*. But Keynes certainly did not regard the Bolsheviks as providing much other than a new tyranny for an old one. He saw them as deliberate exploiters of the peasantry, whose methods had achieved some elements of permanence. He also saw Leninism as 'a missionary religion', because of which he allowed the possibility that 'beneath the cruelty and stupidity of New Russia some speck of the ideal may lie hid' (CW IX: 271).[5] But that minuscule caveat itself had evaporated in his mind by 1928.

But to this interpretation of Keynes's views, there is one very obvious objection. All of the evidence cited above relates to the 1920s, which is the period (it will be objected) *before* Keynes abandoned conventional economics and developed distinctively 'Keynesian' economic ideas. It is hardly a surprise, therefore, that he analysed the Russian economy conventionally and came up with a critical verdict on unorthodox economic policies employed by the post-revolutionary regime. Further, (to continue the objection) Keynes's own views then changed dramatically. He responded to the crisis of the post-1929 Depression by embracing both protectionism and a form of state planning. This brought him much closer to the interventionist, closed-economy policies which Russia had adopted. It is precisely whether these novel and dissenting policies of the 1930s promote development, which is the heart of the question of Keynes's relevance to developing countries today. This objection assumes a strong discontinuity between Keynes's views of the 1920s and those of the post-1929 period with respect to the economic policies of Russia. It is undoubtedly true that Keynes changed from a defender of free trade to an advocate of tariffs and expanded those functions of the state (in addition to protection) which he claimed to be legitimate and socially beneficial. The central issue, however, is whether these changes in Keynes's beliefs caused him to soften, either expressly or by implication, his critique of the economic policies of Soviet Russia and his prescription for the removal of economic distortions and adjustment through increased agricultural exports. The evidence shows that:

1   Keynes never recanted the substance of his critique of Soviet economic policy under the NEP;
2   the normative basis of his critique was, however, shifted from the

principles of 'bourgeois economics', to the prudence and intelligence of the practice of intervention;
3   as the NEP gave way after 1929 to the economics of Stalinism, his critique of Soviet policy became more extensive and condemnatory than it had been in the 1920s.

The potential for securing benefits from trade protection large enough to outweigh the costs did not lead Keynes to endorse all the actions taken by countries in the name of national self-sufficiency. One the contrary, he candidly declares that 'in those countries where the advocates of national self-sufficiency have attained power, it appears to my judgement that, without exception, many foolish things are being done'. Russia, significantly, is singled out for special criticism in this regard: 'Russia exhibits the worst example which the world, perhaps, has ever seen of administrative incompetence and of the sacrifice of almost everything that makes life worth living to wooden heads' (CW XXI: 243–4).

Keynes is adamant that he 'must not be supposed to be endorsing all those things which are being done in the political world today in the name of economic nationalism' (ibid.). But having dropped his previous absolute rejection of the principle of protection, he has to criticize what he believes to be wrong in schemes of economic nationalism on a different set of criteria from the simple 'lessons of bourgeois economics' on which he relied in 1925. These new criteria concern the prudence and intelligence of the practice of protection.

The kind of planning which Keynes was prepared to advocate was, therefore, quite different in kind from 'the official method of exploitation' which he had analysed in 1925, let alone Stalinist planning. For him, the essence of state planning was, by contrast, 'to do those things which in the nature of the case lie outside the scope of the individual'.[6] State planning 'differs from Socialism and from Communism in that it does not seek to aggrandize the province of the state for its own sake'. Its purpose is supplementary and additional to private enterprise purposes, modifying through the use of deliberate central foresight the environment in which the private economy operates. (CW XXI: 86). Taxation, tariffs, exchange control, regulation of transport and town and country physical planning were the examples cited of existing forms of planning. But Keynes also explored problems of externality to speculate about other forms of state planning that might be needed in the near future. He contemplated controls on the location of industry, given the social costs of wasted infrastructure in areas which industry deserts. He also contemplated controls on emigration and immigration, given the need to regulate the growth of the population. He advocated state support for the arts and a state lottery. Most famously, he advocated state action to mitigate economic slumps.

The *General Theory* itself proposed that 'a somewhat comprehensive socialization of investment will prove to be the only means of securing an approximation to full employment'. It acknowledged also that 'the central controls necessary to ensure full employment will, of course, involve a large extension of the traditional functions of government' (CW VII: 378–7). To these rather sweeping, and imprecise, statements, two riders are added. All manner of compromises and devices could be used by the public sector to cooperate with the private to achieve the required levels and directions of investment. Additionally, the reasoning behind the proposal for the socialization of investment gave no warrant for 'a system of State Socialism which would embrace most of the economic life of the community'.

In his treatment both of protection and planning, Keynes explicitly separated what he was advocating in the context of the developed capitalist economies of the West – an experimental 'middle course' involving selective protection and 'moderate' planning of the framework of private enterprise – from communism, state socialism and the actual management of the Soviet economy. In his writings, this separation could hardly be clearer. He also denied that 'moderate' planning would lead on to either Bolshevism or fascism. Although in an obvious sense state planning is politically easier for an autocratic government, Keynes saw with great clarity that, in the medium term, autocratic planning suffers two fatal flaws. Its lack of legitimacy leads to popular apathy, and an inability to recruit 'the best available and most disinterested talent'. Democratic planning would be able to retain and attract such talent into its administration, which could thereby be modernized and improved.

But was a 'middle course' feasible? The response of the political right was to a argue that the attempt to advance beyond the existing achievements of capitalism would jeopardize what Keynes also evidently held dear: 'the old nineteenth century ideals' of liberty. This jeopardy thesis is one of the three classical arguments used to undermine proposals for political and social progress (Hirschman 1991: 110–15). The thesis is that the next step forward (reformed capitalism) would inevitably be at the cost of losing a previous valued reform (liberal institutions). This would happen irrespective of the intentions of the actual reformers (i.e. people like Keynes). The attempt to steer a middle course which avoided the excesses of economic nationalism and autocratic planning would be bound to fail. The extremism of the jeopardy thesis is evident. Keynes late in his life debated this point with Hayek after reading his recently published diatribe against planning, *The Road to Serfdom*. He reiterated his view that, in evaluating the practice of planning, the moral and political climate in which the planning is done is all-important in determining its social consequences. He believed that moderate planning, where the state supplements but does not substitute for individual enterprise, would be much less socially threatening than Hayek prophesied, provided that a liberal moral and political culture could be sustained and strengthened (CW XXVII: 385–8).

This close look at Keynes's writings shows that, although he did in the 1930s expand his vision of the appropriate role of the state – both with regard to selective protection and moderate planning – these changes do not provide a warrant for the view that his analysis of, and prescription for, the Soviet economy also changed in material respects. After 1929, his criticisms of Soviet methods of economic management could no longer be rested on an appeal to the general principle of free trade, because Keynes had argued that the cost of retreat from free trade might be outweighed by various non-economic national advantages. Government intervention could also no longer be opposed as a matter of principle, once Keynes began to contemplate various fiscal and monetary manipulations to reduce unemployment in the developed economies of the West. But there is no reason to suppose that Keynes took a more lenient or sanguine view of Soviet economic management as a result of these changes in his basic approach to economic policy. His new principles did not, and do not, validate 'the official method of exploitation' as he described it in 1925. Moreover, after the rise of Stalin, his remarks on Russian performance and policies become much sharper and more critical. The enormity of the mistakes which planning regimes can make if they are too ambitious, too weak in administration and too unfettered by liberal and democratic institutions impressed him ever more strongly as the era of Stalin unfolded. Joan Robinson had it right when she said of Keynes: 'Capitalism was in some ways repugnant to him but Stalinism was much worse' (Robinson 1975: 128).

Keynes and the Development Counter-revolution

The counter-revolution in development economics, as in macroeconomics, was a deliberate and self-conscious revolution against Keynes and 'Keynesianism'. The generation of economists which came to maturity in the 1950s and 1960s, when Keynes's influence was paramount, came to feel the need – professionally, politically and in some cases intellectually, too – for some collective iconoclasm. For many of that generation, their claim to the grand career prizes, their desire to promote new and different policy ideas and their doubts about unresolved issues in the Keynesian legacy came together to motivate a well-publicized and well-contrived overthrow of Keynes in the course of the 1970s.

As far as the counter-revolution in development economics was concerned, the link between the theories and policies of the 1950s and 1960s and Keynes was extremely tenuous. It proved quite difficult to show that their overthrow was logically or historically related to *his* overthrow

– which was the grand banner for a general move to the political right. Nevertheless, some economists – most notably, Harry G. Johnson – took it upon themselves to provide various equally implausible versions of this link. (Chandavarkar (1989: 138, 180, and 185) provides appropriate rebuttals.) As has been argued here, the attack by the development counter-revolutionaries on Keynes completely overlooked what he had written in the 1920s about the Soviet economy. The fact that at this time Keynes had anticipated the key points of their own critique of development policies in poor countries was therefore not noticed. It was the mild radicalism of Keynes's conversion to protection and state planning after the Great Crash which monopolized the attention of his modern neo-liberal critics. But in order to claim a link between Keynes's post-1929 radicalism and various mistaken development policies of the 1970s, his writings had again to be misrepresented, this time by ignoring the tight limitations which surrounded his recommendations for protection and planning, and his explicit separation between policies appropriate to the developed economies of Western capitalism and other cases.[7]

It may be objected that by focusing on what Keynes actually said on these issues, one loses sight of 'Keynesianism' – what others preached and practised in his name – and that 'Keynesianism' was the real target of counter-revolutionaries like Johnson. Apart from noting that this was not what they said, there is a straightforward answer to this objection. It is that, before attacking Keynes, the development counter-revolutionaries should have undertaken to discriminate precisely and in detail between the doctrine of Keynes and the propagators of 'Keynesianism'. The precedent for just such an exercise had already been set by the superbly scholarly work of Leijonhufvud (1968: 315–85). This revealed with great clarity for macroeconomists the differences between Keynes's and post-Keynesian monetary theory, permitting an informed reappraisal of Keynes's own position, including what are now regarded as analytical errors or inadequacies. Keynes's reputation emerged from this examination relatively unscathed; that of his followers less so. The same probably would have applied in the development field if such an exercise had been done.

It certainly seems to do so in one area – the importance of 'good governance', to use a currently fashionable term. On 'good governance', Keynes now has a very modern air. His prescriptions for structural adjustment–reformed public finances, extra investment in agriculture for export proceeds, the removal of wage and price distortions – were blocked, as he gradually came to realize, by the basic nature of the Bolshevik regime, particularly its increasing inability to learn from its past mistakes. As a result, the same problems which afflicted the Russian economy in the 1920s are still with it in the 1990s, after the Soviet regime has finally come to its end (Dyker 1992: 102–70). At the same time, the mid-century experiments with state planning in the Western economies did not prove to harbour the social and political disasters which Hayek prophesied and Keynes gently doubted. Political liberalism remained robust under state planning – at least as robust (if not more so) as it was after the counter-revolution received its electoral opportunities in the 1980s. Keynes's relevance to developing countries today rests not least on his sensitivity to these political factors, not only in promoting economic success, but also in sustaining national well-being in its broadest sense. His programme of 'economic reform by the methods of political liberalism' still confronts both the countries of the former Soviet Union and other developing countries with an awesome challenge.

In addition, as Hans Singer has argued recently, for the study of development, 'the relevance of Keynes is particularly strong in the international field (the Keynes of Bretton Woods . . .) as distinct from the domestic Keynes of the "General Theory" (1985: 3). In the 1970s and early 1980s, the counter-revolution concentrated its fire on the Keynes of the 'General Theory'. In this too-narrow focus they were aided and abetted by structuralist anti-Keynesians, like Dudley Seers (1983). The criticisms may have been different (neglect of human capital, technical change and entrepreneurship versus neglect of development sequences, distributional questions and national security). But the exclusive focus on Keynesian and neo-Keynesian macroeconomics was shared by counter-revolutionary and structuralist critics alike.

A focus on the Keynes of Bretton Woods, and particularly the 'Keynes Plan' for a post-Second World War international monetary order might have been more illuminating. Keynes had proposed a new International Clearing Union (ICU). The key differences between the ICU of Keynes and the IMF (as it existed before 1971) were:

1   The ICU's quotas were to be provided by international credit creation (not a general subscription of capita, as with the IMF).
2   All foreign exchange transactions would be subject to national controls, before being cleared by the International Clearing Bank (rather than the continuation of free individual dealings in foreign exchange on current account, as with the IMF).
3   Control of capital movements required national scrutiny, inviting preventive action if excessive (compared with *ex post facto* correction with IMF).
4   Pressures for correction of disequilibrium exchange rates to be applied to both surplus and deficit countries (not just deficit countries, as with the IMF).

The interesting question is what difference the ICU would have made to world development, compared with the actual trajectory of the last forty years. Any answer is necessarily highly speculative, but some informed guesses have been forthcoming (Williamson 1985). The ICU's capital movement controls should have prevented the collapse of fixed exchange rates in 1971, or permitted a transition to a crawling peg system. This would have benefited developing countries who suffer from the present fluctuating rate system.

Further, a system of universal capital controls would effectively have prevented the huge borrowings of the 1970s by developing countries through the commercial banking system. Their growth through the 1970s may well have been slower as a result, but it would have been much more solidly based. They would not have faced the 1980s caught in the tight grip of a debt crisis. The rates of growth that would have been enjoyed would have depended on how far the figures in the Keynes Plan proved sustainable in practice. The plan was designed to be expansionist. Perhaps such generous quotas as it embodied would have had to be scaled down in the face of inflationary pressures and global economic overheating. But even with such a scaling down, the ICU may well have commanded more resources than the present IMF. That is important because lack of resources was at the root of the IMFs difficulties in managing the developing countries' payment deficits in the post-oil-shock era (Killick 1984: 271).[8]

One must beware of pursuing historical will-o'-the-wisps too far. What actually happened was quite different. The burden of adjusting the world's real and financial systems was placed on the private banks of the developed world. This has allowed many, but not all, developing countries to try to solve their problems of economic stability by going deeper into debt, until many cannot keep up their interest payments, let alone repay the huge outstanding sums of principal. As the developed countries themselves moved, after 1979, more heavily into a recession, the developing countries felt through their trade sectors the backwash effects. The intelligent joint management of the international financial system by the world's central banks, so necessary in Keynes's eyes, then reached its lowest post-war ebb. But by this point, Keynes's views had been effectively deleted from the political agenda.

Notes

1   As one chronicler of this series of events records:

> The rationale for the military takeover by Ayub Khan was the threat of 'national disintegration' of Pakistan. His government's instrument to defuse that threat was to be economic development . . . Planning was now a major political instrument to achieve the goal of national integration through economic development . . . The Harvard group [of US economists], by advising on the

preparation of those plans and then on economic policy to implement them, inevitably became a significant supporter of the new government. Thus the [Harvard Advisory Group] moved from the periphery of politics to its centre.

(Rosen 1985: 164–5)

2   T. W. Schultz himself was co-author in 1951 of a UN study entitled *Measures for the Economic Development of Under-Developed Countries*. This report stated that 'it is a commonplace that economic progress is a function, among other things, of the rate of new capital formation . . . How to increase the rate of capital formation is therefore a question of great urgency' (p. 35). It continued: 'In many under-developed areas, the population on the land is so great that large numbers could be withdrawn from agriculture without any fall in agricultural output and with very little change of capital techniques. If this labour were employed on public works, capital would be created without any fall in other output, or in total consumption' (p. 41). It thus appears that Schultz fully shared the general belief in the Lewis doctrine of surplus labour in the early 1950s, before agronomic advances opened up the technical progress option. Johnson's contrast between Lewis (supposedly a representative of Keynesian thinking) and Schultz is thus thoroughly misleading.

3   The same point is made by asking: what function could entrepreneurs conceivably perform in a Walrasian market system? The answer is simple: 'In an ideal-type market system, without uncertainty, factor-market imperfections and externalities, entrepreneurship would not be necessary. These conditions are clearly not satisfied in the LDCs' (Leff 1979: 60).

4   Evidence that Keynes saw these connections clearly is also to be found in the notes he made for his reply to Professor Mansiloff after giving his paper on 'The Economic Transition in England' to the Soviet Academy of Sciences on 15 September 1925. His noted include the following:

> Russian currency – a new experiment altogether, because the State monopolisation of import and export allows the maintenance of an internal level of prices which is *not* in equilibrium with prices at the stabilized rate of exchange.
> (King's College Library, Cambridge (KCLC), Keynes Archive folio A25.2.)

5   In his paper on 'The Economic Transition in England' given in Moscow in September 1925, Keynes characterized Leninism as 'at the same time a *persecuting* religion and an experimental technique' (emphasis added) (KCLC, Keynes Archive, folio A25.2).

6   In fact, Keynes had already formulated this distinction on his first visit to Moscow in 1925. His notes for a reply to Professor Mansiloff say: 'England not moving in the direction of Communism . . . The important changes in my opinion will consist of the State undertaking, not matters which are now undertaken by particular individuals, but matters which are not now undertaken by anyone but are left to chance and to the resultant of the free play of economic force' (KCLC, Keynes Archive, A25.2).

7   A recent example of such misrepresentation is provided by Mulji. He discussed Keynes's preference for socialisation of investment along with Nehru's admiration of Stalinist planning as if both were essentially similar examples of a general trend towards 'collectivism' (Mulji 1990: 126–9).

8   The relevance of the Keynes Plan for an International Clearing Union to the current debt crisis had been pointed out as follows:

> the growth of commercial bank leading during the 1970s was a response – however ill thought out – to the lack of any mechanism in the international monetary system akin to Lord Keynes' proposal for an International Clearing Union which would be able to provide extended credit to ensure that balance-of-payments difficulties never caused world instability or deflation.
>
> (Lever and Huhne 1985: 129)

CHAPTER THREE

Bauer's Dissent and the New Vision of Growth

The New Vision of Growth

In a remarkably short period, hardly more than five years, the counter-revolution in development policy made a dramatic leap. In the late 1970s, its status is best represented by Professor H. G. Johnson's attempts to exorcize the shadow of Keynes. By the mid-1980s, the counter-revolution had triumphantly proclaimed itself. Key sections of the Western media and government aid agencies, not to mention very influential international organizations like the World Bank, had by this time publicly announced their conversion to the development policy of the counter-revolution. They had done so jubilantly. The mood in many important centres of power was of a euphoric acknowledgement of fundamental truths about development which had been long suppressed.

This mood was nicely caught in the summer of 1985 by the headline in the World Bank's publication *Research News*. The headline read:

NEW RESEARCH PRIORITIES
THE WORLD HAS CHANGED – SO HAS THE BANK

The accompanying article did not give any attention to one major way in which the Bank's world had changed in the recent past. It did not refer to the coming to power of conservative administrations in the United States, West Germany and the United Kingdom at the start of the decade, or their opinions of the Bank's strategy, under its former President Robert McNamara, of concentrating Bank resources on programmes targeted at the poorest of the world's poor. Instead it talked about shifts in perceptions about the development process, without being specific about whose perception had shifted, and why.

Nevertheless, the vague generalities of this particular article are important because they set out, in a kind of passive impersonal code, the three crucial doctrines of the counter-revolutionary view of development. To help to gain some insight into this view, it is worth looking at an extended quotation:

> First, the record of development and the growing store of empirical research have heightened recognition of the importance of markets and incentives – and of the limits of government intervention and central planning. The new vision of growth is that markets and incentives can work in developing countries. But they are filtered through government policies and agencies, which, if inappropriate, can reduce or even negate the possible benefits. Second, physical investment is only one determinant of the spread of development. Human development is at least as important and sound government action remains at its core. Third, the economic policies of governments, and the distortions they induce, are now a major focus of the analysis of development policy.
>
> (World Bank 1985a: 1)

The clear emphases here are on the benefits of markets and the danger that government action will negate these benefits; the relative unimportance of physical capital compared with human development policies; and the distorting effect of government economic policies. These are the main components of the counter-revolution's new vision of growth.[1]

Given the miserable material conditions in many countries of the world today, it is not surprising that most people who are aware of these conditions are dissatisfied with the pace and character of development in the Third World. The need for improved living standards for the mass of the people is obvious enough and expectations of improvement are continually being created. Whatever the empirical record of development performance in the last thirty years had been, it would be easy to find a consensus that it was 'not enough'. But this perfectly genuine and well-founded consensus can lead to all points of the compass of policy. A more precisely defined problem is necessary for the link with a specific set of policies to be plausible. The inadequacy of development has always to be related to some particular causes, and given a particular interpretation. In the late 1960s and 1970s, it had been urged that these causes were structural inequalities in international economic relations, the lack of internal political will or ability to redistribute assets and income, and the neglect of popular participation in development. A novel set of policies would have to lay its stress elsewhere. The particular causes which the counter-revolution advanced for inadequate development in the Third World are indeed quite different from these.

The promise of the counter-revolution in development policy was to solve the problem of inadequate development by neutralizing three particular causes. They were:

1   *The over-extended public sector.* It is claimed that the developing country governments have damaged national economic performance by taking on functions which are beyond the proper, appropriate or normal functions of government, especially in the sphere of production.
2   *The over-emphasis on physical capital formation.* It was suggested that governments have been irrationally concerned with accumulating physical assets for production, while neglecting the improvement of human abilities and skills.
3   *The proliferation of distorting economic controls.* In addition to the two previously mentioned policy errors, governments of developing countries were charged with multiplying needlessly and damagingly controls over aspects of economic life. This is often attributed to egalitarian intentions which are pursued without regard to calculations of efficiency losses.

In sum, these three insights propose that poor development performance is due primarily, if not exclusively, to incorrect policies of developing country governments. This interpretation of the problem of inadequate development clearly carries with it a strong promise, implicit but often explicit as well, that the problem can be solved. The solution simply involves finding ways of getting the governments of developing countries to modify their current set of policies.

The proposal to view the problem of development like this could never have achieved its current state of enthusiastic acceptance unless there had been widespread doubt and anxiety about the wisdom of government activity in many developing countries. New interpretations and new programmes of action cannot support themselves entirely on their own hyperbole. These doubts and anxieties must be addressed, and understood, by those whom the counter-revolution still has to convince. There is some truth in them, albeit now presented by the counter-revolution in an ideological disguise.

Few people could disagree that public enterprises can be inefficient in the performance of their productive tasks. If, for example, the government of a developing country is prepared to make up the losses of a public electricity corporation, year after year, by giving it subsidies from general tax revenue, the corporation's management will have little incentive to minimize their costs of production. It may even be tempted to embark on expensive and ill-conceived experiments with nuclear technology, as happened in the 1970s in Brazil. The constant search for lower unit costs of production, which is a tiresome, vexing and tricky business, is unlikely to take place without some equally constant pressure, or incentive, to make it happen. If a government removes that pressure from a public enterprise (or, indeed from a private enterprise), the enterprise will tend to become complacent and high cost.

Public enterprises are also said to fail to respond adequately to consumers' preferences. This claim is not quite so straightforward. To the extent that a public enterprise is a monopoly, it is in the same position to insulate itself from the pressure of consumer demand as is any private monopoly. The question then becomes whether it is justifiable to have a monopoly in this area of production. Some public monopolies have been created thoughtlessly and, in other cases, the circumstances that originally justified them (for example, exploitative behaviour of the former private owners) may have long passed into history. The maintenance of monopolies, public or private, needs constant monitoring and evaluation. Apart from this, high-cost public enterprises will provide the consumer with poor value for money and an insufficiently diversified range of products. There may, however, be some justifiable reasons for its not meeting all expressed consumers' preferences – for example, safety reasons and the prevention of the exploitation of the industry's workforce.

These general concerns about the economic weaknesses which public enterprises can exhibit were reinforced when, in the late 1960s especially, a number of developing countries embarked on some dramatic nationalization projects. In 1969, for example, India nationalized all domestically-owned private banks. At about the same time, Chile and Zambia both nationalized foreign mining interests operating in their borders. The reasons for these moves were generally, in different ways, political rather than economic. The reasonable anxiety here was that Third World political leaders, like Kenneth Kaunda or Indira Gandhi, felt that they had to bolster their popular support by actions that undermined economic performance, and, therefore their country's development prospects.

Nor is this just a matter of individual dramatic cases. One sees that entire sectors of economic activity in the Third World show a tendency for Third World countries to rely more heavily on public enterprises than non-Third-World countries do. Table 3.1 shows the position in the mining and processing of non-ferrous metals in 1975 and 1982. In all of the industries in the table, a smaller share is publicly owned in North America, Western Europe and Japan than in other non-socialist countries, that is, the Third World.

If all the public sector enterprises in the Third World in these industries had been thriving, it would have been hard to pinpoint them as a major

TABLE 3.1   EXTENT OF PUBLIC OWNERSHIP OF BASE METALS
CAPACITY, 1975 AND 1982 (PERCENTAGE SHARE)

		N. America, Western Europe and Japan	Other non-socialist countries
Lead mining	1975	9.7	17.5
	1982	14.4	16.2
Lead smelting	1975	9.2	16.6
	1982	8.6	16.9
Zinc mining	1975	7.1	29.3
	1982	19.3	27.9
Zinc smelting	1975	10.5	27.2
	1982	11.9	37.3
Copper mining	1975	5.2	67.9
	1982	8.2	65.1
Copper smelting	1975	3.9	76.8
	1982	5.4	69.9
Nickel mining	1975	2.0	19.2
	1982	7.0	15.2
Nickel production	1975	1.8	17.1
	1982	4.3	21.9
Bauxite mining	1975	21.2	45.3
	1982	39.4	50.3
Aluminium smelting	1975	17.6	52.9
	1982	24.3	64.9

Source: Toye (1984: 930)

issue for development. But many – especially in Africa – were performing indifferently. This provided prima facie evidence that nationalization had been a mistake and that, therefore, the public sector was 'over-extended'.

Evidence of the wasteful use of physical capital in developing countries was not hard to come by either. It can be categorized under various headings. Spending on lavish prestige projects, such as sports facilities and conference centres for international events, or building a brand new capital city (for example, in Brazil, Tanzania, Malawi and now Argentina) is one category. Infrastructure projects that suffered from major design faults is another: roads that lead to nowhere, irrigation schemes that damage the soil or lower the water table, electricity grids with grossly inadequate generating capacity, major rail links built on sand, and so on. More important in the eyes of the counter-revolution was a third category – manufacturing capacity protected by tariffs, but with low, or sometimes even negative, economic returns.[2]

The importance of this third category lay in the fact that it can be seen as part of a pathological syndrome which includes the over-extended public sector and inappropriate government economic controls. In a number of countries, Ghana and Nigeria being favourite examples, protected, low-return industrial projects had been undertaken by public sector industrial development corporations. Their continued existence was made possible not only by government subsidies, but also by government restrictions on the inflow of competitive imports. From the early 1970s onwards this entire syndrome came to be seen as the malaise of Third World development.

The call for more attention to human development and less for physical capital formation is derived from the analysis of wasteful capital use. At the simplest level, if an aircraft fleet is under-utilized for lack of trained pilots or maintenance engineers, or if hospitals and clinics are half-empty through a shortage of trained doctors and nurses, the remedy is to change the balance of expenditure in the programme away from plant and towards education and training. At the next level, if projects are being badly planned and designed, more expenditure is needed on project evaluation, the training of project planners and of those who appraise the viability of the projects.

In the case of protected industry, the relevance of the call for greater emphasis on human development is not so clear. It is commonplace to prescribe more management training for industrial managers in developing countries. It is hard to demur. But if the industry is part of a wider structure of heavily protected and subsidized public corporations, even managers who are quite capable of managing well without any training may be prevented from doing so by the institutional structure. Once this has happened, no remedy will suffice short of radical political and social change.

The other great anxiety which fuelled the counter-revolutionary view was the ease with which developing country governments resorted to physical controls over foreign trade and industry. Part of the reason why capital was being used wastefully was that government controls distorted key prices in the economy (especially the price of foreign exchange) and the distorted prices were then used in the calculations appraising the worthwhileness of new investment. In other words, in a heavily controlled economy it becomes very difficult for anyone to know which resources are really scarce and to make sensible decisions to economize on their use.

People tend to respond to the prices which they actually face. If, because of controls, they face prices which understate the value of imports and exports, they will try to use more imports than is economically desirable and produce less exports than is economically desirable. The balance of payments problem which many Third World countries face could therefore be attributable to the policy of maintaining, with the help of controls, an overvalued foreign exchange rate.

Apart from this basic point that controls are an impediment to rational economic calculation, some important ancillary criticisms were made. The operation of controls is itself a use of resources which has an opportunity cost. If a massive bureaucracy of controllers emerges, the cost will be accordingly high. More significantly, the existence of controls creates opportunities for bureaucratic corruption. This may then insert another set of uncertainties and costs into the conduct of economic life. Specifically, politicians and officials will gain power over the business of economic activity: this became known as 'the politicization of economic life'.

The New Vision's Common Sense

A discussion of the new vision of growth must, if it is to be useful, start by recognizing those elements of it which constitute genuine advances in understanding the dilemmas of development policy. Development policy is a very large and complex subject, and it is certainly possible for important issues to be neglected for a while, when other issues – perhaps equally or more important – are being pursued too single-mindedly. The history of any area of study is the story of the way in which neglected issues are taken up, force themselves on the collective awareness and then are analytically integrated.

That public enterprise, physical investment and government economic controls have characteristic defects which make them fallible instruments of development policy is not perhaps very surprising news and need not be disputed. If development economists have in the past regarded them as infallible, or simply forgotten their frailties, they have been remiss. One cannot simply close one's eyes to all the awkward facts that spoil the neat, new development plan, and hope serenely for the best. Sooner or later, and usually sooner, the facts rebel.

If this were all that the counter-revolution in development were saying, it would be uncontroversial. But in fact it is making much stronger claims. Going beyond the raising of neglected issues, it treats these issues in a reductionist manner which brushes aside complex analytical issues and then, having over-simplified the problem, matches it up with a correspondingly over-simplified 'solution'. As a result, the new vision of growth is made both blinkered and myopic.

To examine some of the stronger claims that have been made on behalf of the development counter-revolution, it is proposed to look closely at the work of Lord Bauer.[3] Since it is not possible to comment on every aspect of Bauer's approach to development policy except at great length, those aspects have been selected for discussion which are most germane to the new vision of growth. They are his views on the public ownership of industry, on physical capital and development and on the use of government economic controls.

Bauer's Dissent on Development

P. T. Bauer engaged in research on smallholder agriculture and on trade in primary products in West Africa and Malaya in the 1940s and 1950s. According to a recent re-evaluation of his own work, what he found in the course of that research was 'starkly at variance with the components of the emerging consensus of mainstream development economics' (Bauer 1984: 2). Such a stark variance in turn seemed to warrant further conclusions about the status of the mainstream development economics of the day, although Bauer's researches were 'altogether unconnected' with that economic specialization (1984: 1).

Bauer came to the view that development economics was not merely irrelevant and not even merely wrong; far worse, it was intellectually corrupt. This charge begins to be developed as a favourite theme from the early 1970s (Bauer 1972). Although critical of aspects of modern economics (the habit of taking economic statistics at face value; an excessive concern with quantification; the use of models which omit crucial variables), he argues that development economics is in a much worse state than other branches of economics. Its errors are said to be 'simple and readily demonstrable', but it is claimed that their exposure as errors has been frustrated by an effective phalanx of professional colleagues who stand 'ready to shield the perpetration of even the crudest lapses' (Bauer 1981: 259–61). Further, this obstinate propagation of error was either politically motivated or induced by economic self-interest, or preferably both.

Apart from this general qualification as a pioneer of the counter-revolution, Bauer had other specific qualifications. Since his encounter with Indian planning in the late 1950s, he had preached against the evil of the over-extended public sector as an impediment to economic development. At a time when it was still unfashionable and unpopular to say such things (except to the American Enterprise Association, whom Bauer chose to address), he advised that 'what is required in India is essentially a redirection of the activities of Government, away from policies restricting the energies and opportunities of its subjects and away from acts of emulation of the pattern of the Soviet world, into directions aimed at releasing the energies of millions of people' (1959: 115). Although it was not very clear what policies would be likely to achieve this desirable release of energy, other than those already being undertaken by the Indian government, Bauer was specific about what the government should turn away from. It was 'the socialisation of the economy by the extension of government ownership and operation of industry and commerce', or the over-extended public sector. It was also 'extensive and specific control over what is left of the private sector outside subsistence agriculture', or distorting economic controls (1959: 106–7). Thus, Bauer's negative proposals on India did anticipate two of the three key policies of the current development counter-revolution.

On the third issue, the role of physical capital in development, Bauer apparently started with the conventional view that the accumulation of physical capital was necessary for the steady growth of output and incomes. Such a view was implied by his criticisms of colonial policy towards rubber smallholders in Malaya, for example. If physical capital (that is, rubber trees) is not normally productive, how was the colonial prohibition on new planting of trees in any way harmful to the interests of the smallholder, as Bauer maintained that it was (1947: 84–100)? He naturally, and rightly, took it for granted that because capital formation in the form of trees would be productive of higher output and incomes, prohibiting such capital formation would therefore be economically injurious to the smallholders. More recently, however, he has argued that the concern with physical forms of investment is merely a fetish. Now it is denied that 'investment spending is . . . the primary, much less the decisive, determinant of economic performance' (1981: 241). It is claimed that 'emergence from poverty [in the Third World] does not require large-scale capital formation' (1981: 248).

Bauer's doctrine that large-scale capital formation is unnecessary for the Third World's emergence from poverty is much more extreme and much more misleading than anything in the 'new vision of growth'. That vision includes the useful reminder that a balance needs constantly to be maintained between the provision of new physical capital and the development of the human resources needed for its optimal use. Bauer seems to believe that the alleviation of mass poverty hardly requires the provision of new physical capital at all. But that is not all. He not only seems to believe that physical capital formation is not needed for output and income growth, but is also sceptical of the importance of human capital formation. His Malayan research had convinced him that observed differences in the economic performance of rubber-tappers 'could not be explained in terms of differences in human capital formation' (1984: 7). Instead, economic performance was conditioned by 'personal preferences, motivations and social arrangements', not only in Malaya, but also in West Africa, the Levant and India (1984). Giving pride of place to intractable psychological and social forces, as Bauer does, is not at all the same as calling for a re-balancing of investment away from physical to human forms.

The discounting of investment as a cause of economic growth has a corollary in Bauer's thinking which is also relevant to the question of his relationship with the 'new vision of growth'. If investment plays at best a minor role in growth, then foreign capital aid and technical assistance can do very little good and may do great harm. That proposition had indeed become a major ingredient in Bauer's recent writing. Endless lists of pro-aid arguments are drawn up only to be comprehensively contradicted. The conclusion is categorical that 'foreign aid cannot achieve its declared objectives and has far-reaching damaging political and economic results' (1984: 60).

Bauer's rejection of aid as a policy instrument sets him at variance, in a significant way, with the development counter-revolution of the 1980s. Underpinning the new vision of growth is a political assumption – that the means can be found to change the 'wrong' internal policies which are singled out as the particular cause of the Third World's failure to develop. The counter-revolutionaries' own analysis of the Keynesian revolution tells them that it is useless to pontificate about 'wrong policies' adopted by developing country governments, unless some method of changing such policies can credibly be promised. Foreign aid, and its conditioning on internal policy changes, is the principal instrument for redeeming the promise of the developmental counter-revolution and the hidden political assumption of the new vision of growth.

The central tension in Bauer's thinking, between the conflicting imperatives to denounce policies of socialization and politicization of economic life and foreign aid itself as a distorting government intervention, was decisively resolved by the development counter-revolution in favour of the former thrust. Bauer himself, by contrast, remains perpetually torn. He is too much the relentless economist to countenance easily setting a thief to catch a thief, or perhaps too close an observer of administrative systems to believe that such a stratagem has much chance of success. Either way, on the several occasions in the last thirty years when this situation presented itself to him, he has never been able to give an outright endorsement to the use of foreign aid to secure changes in the domestic economic policies of developing countries.

At the time of preparing the Indian Third Five Year Plan, Bauer had to decide whether to join Milton Friedman in seeking to persuade the US Congress to cut off foreign aid, on the ground that Indian planning was too socialistic. In fact, the decision was sidestepped, on the ground that political forces would ensure the continuation of aid in any case. In a curious combination of recommendations, Bauer advocated both drastically reducing the size of the aid flow and making the level of aid depend on 'the performance of the Government [of India] in pursuing a policy designed to raise living standards and to promote an anti-totalitarian society, insofar as these aims can be promoted by government policy' (1959: 105–6). That position has been maintained ever since. Aid ought to be abolished; but since it will not be abolished, it ought to be reduced and used as a reward for changing to non-socialistic policies (1984: 60–1). This is much too contorted to find favour with the more pragmatic advocates of the development counter-revolution. In their view aid is good, provided its policy conditions are accepted and acted on: it does not have nasty side-effects on the economy or on political life.[4]

The Privatization of Industry

That public enterprises can be allowed, by weak or careless governments, to become inefficient would be very generally agreed. That governments in the Third World (with some notable exceptions such as post-Allende Chile) increasingly resorted to public enterprise as a mode of industrial organization in the 1970s is not in dispute. That problems of public sector inefficiency in the Third World call for increased attention should be a broadly acceptable conclusion. But, as one might expect, the common-sense element in the new vision of growth tends to get quickly superseded by more dramatic and more contentious policy proposals. In the context of public enterprise, the proposal is to 'roll back' the over-expanded public sectors in developing countries.

The proposal is based on the assumption that some norm exists which defines the proper functions of governments in developing countries. In chapter 2, H. G. Johnson was seen to appeal to such a norm: he suggested that there were certain kinds of policy-making 'that historical and contemporary experience have shown to be vital to economic success', and that governments should concentrate their energies on them. He actually named three areas of policy-making – public expenditure, taxation and the foreign exchange rate – but did not imply that these were exhaustive of the proper functions of government (Johnson 1971b: 10).

Bauer, like Johnson, implies that some norm exists, and gives a few examples of proper government activities without ever committing himself to an exhaustive list. He tells us that his personal list includes the maintenance of law and order, the control of the money supply, the provision of basic health and education services, the establishment of basic communications and 'often' agricultural extension work (1959: 96). The basis of selection is not discussed. Many advocates of privatization would find it much too long – why should telecommunications and air transport, for example, not be privatized? Others would find it much too short and would ask what other functions of government are also included, but not mentioned: environmental conservation? employment creation? export promotion? support for arts and culture? regional policies? The plain fact of the matter is that no one has yet succeeded in devising a division of functions between the public and private sectors which is both universally applicable and defensible on economic, rather than political grounds. The notion of 'over-expansion' is thus an arbitrary and subjective one.

Indeed, it is precisely on political grounds that Bauer proscribes certain kinds of activity by the government. As he puts it, 'a society resistant to totalitarian appeal implies that the government refrains from substantial government participation in industry and trade' (1959: 97). The oxymoron 'totalitarian appeal' exactly captures the emotional loading of the anti-communist crusades of the 1950s.[5] The extent of the government sector in India was to be determined, according to Bauer, by the requirements of developing 'a society resistant to the appeal of a totalitarian regime', which was 'the essential American interest in India' (1959: 95). If that is not a political criterion for deciding whether or not the public sector is over-extended, it is difficult to imagine one. Yet Bauer himself complains bitterly that development economists subordinate knowledge to political purpose (Senses 1984: 130, n. 41).

The purely economic considerations which bear on the size and composition of the public sector concern the current and future supply of entrepreneurship, the possible sub-optimality of savings and the absence of conventional policy instruments for the redistribution of income and assets. On the first point, Bauer (1984: 6) has argued that the requirement for entrepreneurship cannot justify state ownership. The reason for this is that if a society lacks entrepreneurship, there is no source from which the public sector will be able to draw it.[6] Now it is certainly true that many a development economist has put forward an essentially *faute de mieux* defence of government investment in industry and services: the state must do it because the private sector either cannot or will not. This is unsatisfactory and incomplete because it does not establish the competence of the state relative to the competence of the private sector (Toye 1981: 14–20). As a general defence, then, it will not do.

But correctly pointing this out by no means creates a presumption of the opposite kind, that the state can never be relatively more competent to perform entrepreneurial functions than the private sector. It may be, or it may not, depending on time, place and the circumstances of a particular sector or industry within an economy. There is no case for adopting a simple rule of thumb one way or another. Public enterprise performance varies greatly between industries at any one time in India, for example. Japan launched its development by setting up a series of government-owned industries but, as economic growth speeded up, it gradually sold them to the private sector. For many years, the Dutch government operated publicly owned coal mines more profitably than the private mines, but this was not the case with other industries (Tinbergen 1984: 12). Indeed, one could propose, as a major task for the development economist, that of identifying those areas of activity which only the government can undertake successfully beyond the minimalist tasks of Adam Smith's 'justice, police, revenue and arms'.

Bauer condemns all forms of government investment for necessarily overriding the preferences of ordinary people. In fact, the argument for government intervention to raise the rate of investment in no way rests on the overriding of people's preferences. Exactly the opposite. It rests on the notion of fulfilling preferences which are frustrated when people act individualistically, but which are capable of fulfilment when they act collectively. The claim is that people actually want to save and invest significantly more than they do under the constraint of atomistic decision-making, because in that situation they have no assurance that others will take complementary action (Sen 1984: 113–34). It is this version of what game theorists call 'the prisoner's dilemma' that underpins the case for government action to overcome the sub-optimality of saving and investment. Whether this argument is right or wrong, it is the one that needs to be addressed. Bauer never does this, except by stating axiomatically that people's preferences should never be interfered with by direct compulsion, a position which rules out government action by definition. By contrast, indirect or social compulsion is always acceptable to him.

The third reason for expanding the public sector in developing countries is that public enterprise pricing can be a more powerful method of redistributing income than more conventional methods of taxation and government expenditure. A government facing intractable obstacles, such as illiteracy, to a direct tax system, can levy an implicit tax on luxury items – like residential telephones – and grant an implicit subsidy to essentials for the poor – like bus fares. This device admittedly assumes that a government which cannot run an effective tax and social security system can organize the relevant public enterprises and cope with the necessary pricing calculations. For some developing countries, at least, such an assumption is realistic.

The distributive justification of an expanded public sector is attacked by the development counter-revolution in two related ways. It is contended that income redistribution is morally illegitimate and that it is practically counter-productive. But the moral illegitimacy argument cannot be sustained. It runs into the objection that in a society, as opposed to a desert island inhabited by Robinson Crusoe, no one actually creates his or her income all alone. They do so under a set of laws and social conventions which regulate the forms of economic cooperation with other people. These laws and conventions are historically specific and may be the legitimate object of moral criticism. Bauer, and every other representative of the counter-revolution in development, condemns laws and conventions which allow people to gain incomes by the exercise of monopoly power or from other sources of 'windfall' profit (Bauer 1981: 12–13, 174). This is the fundamental basis of the counter-revolution's critique of 'rent-seeking' and of Third World governments who create 'rent-seeking societies'. (That critique is discussed with reference to India in chapter 6).

The point which is relevant here is that, whatever the precise criticism, the fact that such criticism is possible and is frequently recognized as legitimate, nullifies the attempt to establish a right to retain income (or wealth, for that matter) howsoever it is come by. The retention of all forms of income or wealth cannot itself be a matter of principle. To attempt to make it so is to adopt the position of the good burghers of Nantes who, in the early 1790s, declared themselves in favour both of the liberal principles of the French Revolution and of the continuation of the slave trade.

Turning now to the pragmatic argument against redistribution, it should be clear that for this argument to be convincing, some quantification is required. The argument is that the costs of redistribution exceed its benefits. This is an empirical question, and cannot be answered by speculation or theorizing. The counter-revolution will have to extend itself to devising new methods of measuring the costs and benefits of redistribution and of weighing costs against benefits. So far it has shown little inclination to become involved in the kind of detailed quantification that would be needed to turn prejudices into policy data.

If both of the *a priori* arguments against redistribution cannot be sustained, it is clear that redistribution between contemporaries, and between generations, remains one of the central dilemmas of development policy. The amount of redistribution that will be worthwhile in any particular time and place will always remain controversial. What is important is that the public ownership of industry can be a useful policy instrument by which a genuinely distributionist government of a developing country can undertake part of the redistribution that is worthwhile.

To say that, however, does not imply that public enterprises in developing countries should be managed slackly or without appropriate economic discipline. If a public enterprise is to be used for planned redistribution by the government, the government must first of all prove itself capable of having the enterprise run with normal economic efficiency. Social purposes served by redistribution should be superimposed on normal efficient working. They can hardly be a justification for industrial anarchy.

Balancing Physical and Human Capital

Physical capital accumulation can out-run people's capacities to plan
and manage its productive use. This simple idea is to be found in many
ideologically diverse contexts, from technocratic discussions of countries'
'absorptive capacity' for foreign capital aid to Marxian analyses of the
socially destructive drive to accumulate capital in capitalist societies.
Whether the end result is social polarization and class conflict in developed countries, or the building of 'cathedrals in the desert' in developing countries, the imbalance of physical capital and human capabilities
is frequently seen as a symptom or a cause of social pathologies.

Development policy looks for remedies to this problem in a number
of different directions. One route is the provision of technical assistance,
training programmes and then the training of trainers. Another route is
the search for appropriate technology, that is, technology specifically
adapted to the level of skills and other resources in the environment
where it is to operate. Both routes aim at finding a closer balance between the physical and the human, between men and women and their
machines.

To the extent to which the new vision of growth is an attempt to
reinforce this familiar endeavour, it is to be welcomed. But, as with the
discussion of public enterprise, the urge to move to more eccentric and
extreme positions on this issue is not long resisted. And in the process,
the niceties of the economic analysis of development problems tend to
get trampled underfoot. Bauer's journey towards an extreme position
has been spectacular on this particular issue.

Bauer's claim that physical capital formation makes a negligible contribution to economic growth rests on some hoary and inappropriate
evidence. This evidence is the sources of growth analyses which were
made for developed countries, mainly the United States, in the 1950s
and 1960s (Bauer 1981: 242, 280, n. 2). These pieces of research are
interpreted as showing that overall economic growth in such countries
has been much greater than can be accounted for purely in terms of the
increases in the volume of 'capital' and 'labour' used as inputs to produce
it. They show an unexplained 'residual' which is said to represent the
major determinant of economic growth.

The aggregate production function is the theoretical construct which
generated these results. The production process of the entire economy
is thereby mathematically specified in exactly the same terms as economists conventionally use for the production of the individual firm. This
leap straight from micro-level analysis to macro-level analysis without
any corresponding mathematical reformulation seemed dubious even to
those who were making it. In his original article on the aggregate production function, Solow disconcertingly announced that he would not

try to justify what followed by calling on fancy theorems on aggregation and index numbers. 'Either this kind of aggregate economics appeals or it does not. Personally, I belong to both schools' (Solow 1957: 213). What helped to give the aggregate production function plausibility was its prediction – admittedly based on a series of highly unrealistic neoclassical assumptions – that the shares of income accruing to labour and capital during economic growth would remain constant, which has been broadly true. But it was pointed out long ago that there are other less unrealistic theories which are also consistent with this result (Salter 1960: 137; Fisher 1969).

Persisting with the aggregate production function approach to growth, one then faces the famous problem of the 'residual', the economic growth that apparently cannot be accounted for by increases in capital and labour. The indestructibility of the residual is more apparent than real. After adjusting for errors of aggregation, price deflation and the definition of capital services and labour, the observed growth in total factor productivity (that is, the 'residual') is negligible (Griliches and Jorgenson 1967: 272; Harcourt 1972: 83).

The original sources of growth analyses cannot simply be accepted at their face value. But even if they could, they do not necessarily bear Bauer's extreme interpretation that capital is unnecessary for economic growth. Everything then depends on what one thinks the residual represents. Solow, for example, thought that it represented technical progress which had to be embodied in each new vintage of capital equipment, a progression of improvements in the design of capital goods. If that were true, it would be impossible to have technical progress and, thus, economic growth, without a continuous process of capital accumulation.

However, ignoring both the question of the embodiment of technical progress and the interactions between sources of growth, Bauer moves on to the conclusion that the residual in growth-accounting exercises represents his own conception of the true determinants of development – the intractable social and psychological forces which each society exhibits. This, of course, is merely a supposition. It is no more a finding of the analysis of sources of growth than is Solow's alternative supposition.

The wasteful character of much investment spending in both developed and developing countries is then brought forward as evidence that investment is not necessary for development. But the truth or otherwise of the first proposition is not logically related to the validity of the latter. If all the investment ever made had been wasteful, it could still be true that some further investment would be necessary for economic development. In the real world, there is not, nor can there be, any guarantee that investment will be productive. Certain very simplified and abstract economic models of long-run equilibrium have the property that investors' expectations are always fulfilled, but we actually make economic decisions in a disequilibrium world. That is why, for national accounting purposes, investment is defined purely negatively: that part of the income of a period which is not spent on goods and services that are 'used up' within the period. These 'left-over' goods and services may or may not generate revenues in excess of their costs in future time periods: there is nothing in this definition that takes a position on their future productivity (Toye 1981: 68–9). And, in any account of the world which takes uncertainty seriously, featuring myopic enterprise managers as well as conservative trade unionists, one thing is certain: a share of investment spending will always be wasted. But that does not imply that development will take place without a continued attempt to invest productively.

If the role of physical capital formation in the process of economic growth is discounted as heavily as Bauer wishes to discount it, a corresponding premium must be placed on other sources of growth, which are conventionally referred to as human capital formation. Human capital can be produced in various ways such as formal education and training and non-formal acquisition of knowledge and skills by actually doing a particular task. Bauer certainly acknowledges the need for basic education services and perhaps an agricultural extension service in his incomplete list of the proper functions of government. But such methods of human capital formation play no part in his explanation of why economies grow. The explanatory weight is borne by 'personal qualities, social institutions and mores and political arrangements which make for endeavour and achievement' (1981: 194–5), or 'people's capacities, attitudes, values and beliefs' (1981: 118).

It is ironical that, as a young economist, Bauer began by criticizing the stereotypes which colonial administrators applied to colonial populations. Not all peasants were lazy, of limited ambition and risk averse, he saw, although his elders largely believed otherwise. But having rejected one stereotype, he quickly settled for another. Whether they have these qualities or not depends on which cultural group they belong to.

There is no scientific basis for linking economic performance with membership of a particular cultural or ethnic group. Bauer quotes his own data on differential output of Chinese and Indian rubber-tappers in 1946. This in itself is precious little evidence for a grand generalization of the kind being propagated. In a recent review of the evidence, Kilby (1983: 107–11) notes that most studies have been cross-sectional in character and that 'when the effect of other variables is accounted for, ethnic and religious factors have had little influence on performance'. These studies have made no attempt to link performance with psychological characteristics. Kilby goes on to question the research design of the existing studies, particularly the difficulty of finding an uncontaminated measure of economic performance. Though convinced that aliens have advantages as entrepreneurs in developing countries, he nevertheless provides no fresh empirical support for that view.

Redesigning Government Economic Controls

The new vision of growth sees government intervention in the economy as a threat, a potential negation of the benefits which privately organized markets bring to a developing country. The implication is that, regardless of what structuralists might say, these markets work normally, that is, advantageously for the society which permits them. Controls on markets that are defined like this are tautologically disadvantageous: they are responsible for distortions and the negation of possible benefits. If statements like these are not to be read as purely ideological utterances, they must be taken as propositions of economic theory. The major economic theory that links market behaviour to gradations of social welfare is welfare economics.

Opinion is divided among the supporters of the development counterrevolution about the wisdom of trying to give it an intellectual foundation in welfare economics. For Lal, welfare economics is 'the one branch of economic theory which provides the logic to assess the desirability of alternative economic policies' (1983: 10). In a much-repeated phrase, welfare economics is believed by most of the development counterrevolutionaries to be the grammar of all arguments about economic policy. It thus comes as something of a surprise to find Bauer trying to finesse the manifold inadequacies and obscurities of welfare economics by brushing aside this entire technical apparatus. 'Whatever insights may be gained from the theory of welfare economics', he declares, 'in fact the literature of market failure has been used largely as a collection of sticks with which to beat the market system' (1984: 30).[7] It has also been used time and again to try and give a pleasing definition to the 'efficiency' which the market system guarantees. There are vested ideological interests on both sides of the debate and always have been. But the vital question is not what purposes has welfare economics been made to serve, but what purposes can it validly serve? By neither asking or answering this question, Bauer implies that welfare economics cannot be salvaged again as a defence of the market system.

His defence strategy is to appeal from economics to politics. Government intervention in markets has unacceptable political consequences, particularly the concentration of economic as well as political power in the hands of politicians and administrators who, being human, will not use it wisely. The concept of 'government failure' is developed to counterbalance those examples from the literature of market failures, which are admitted with disarming frankness. After placing great emphasis on the problem of government failure, it is concluded that the free market is the lesser of two unattractive options.

Thus, when Bauer analyses the impact of government economic controls, he does not do so in terms of optima, distortions and second-best solutions. Instead, his categories are the politicization of economic life, the centralization of political power, corruption, and the erosion of economic and political freedom. All of these essentially political considerations sum up to the evils of totalitarianism, although the word itself has much less salience in his current vocabulary than it did in his vocabulary of the 1950s.

But this libertarian analysis of government economic controls is itself politically inappropriate for absorption into the development counter-revolution. Whatever reforms are attempted on World Bank sponsorship in the economies of developing countries, a wholesale change in the political structure of those economies is very unlikely ever to be acknowledged publicly as an aim. The myth of national sovereignty is still powerful enough to stop in its tracks any new vision of growth which encompassed a desire to influence the basic political structure of a developing country. The Bank has repeatedly said, and must go on repeating, that it respects every country's right to adopt the political system of its choice. Bauer's political approach to the problem of government economic controls lacks operational credibility in the development counter-revolution. A neutral-seeming, technical economic analysis of controls would be much more politically useful for the practical task of getting policies changed.

The Assumption of Perfect Markets

To say that Bauer finesses welfare economics and relies on political analysis does not mean, however, that no economic assumptions are implied in the position which he adopts. On the contrary, inside the political analysis there is an implicit picture of the way in which markets and governments work in developing countries. This picture is revealed by considering an apparent contradiction between two of Bauer's favourite hobby-horses – opposition to government economic controls and opposition to monopoly. Can they both be ridden at once?

Bauer's dislike of monopoly is not in any doubt. It dates back to his studies of colonial marketing boards for exports of primary products such as cocoa, tin and rubber. The soundness of his objections to the machinations of some of these marketing boards at the expense of the peasant producer need not be questioned. But one must ask whether certain economic controls by the state are not necessary to neutralize the effects of monopolies. Clearly this cannot be so in the case, like the colonial export marketing boards, where the monopoly is created and enforced by the state itself. But what about other types of monopoly? The state can directly dismantle state-enforced monopolies, which is what Bauer would advocate. But what of natural monopolies, geographical monopolies or industries whose economies of scale are such that their capital requirements create a massive barrier to entry? Surely the state must intervene here to protect the consumer from high prices and artificial restriction of output?

This contradiction can only be resolved by denying the existence of any form of monopoly other than monopolies created by the state itself. Such a denial is implied by the combination of an anti-state control and an anti-monopoly stance. But, if there are no monopolies to regulate, because all monopolies are state-enforced monopolies which can be abolished directly, the removal of government intervention would make the economy perfectly competitive. Thus, although he avoids discussing welfare economics, Bauer certainly has his own very definite theoretical perspective. It is 'that of the classical *laissez faire* theorist of the nineteenth century' (Desai 1982: 293).[8]

Bauer's unstated and untested belief that economies, if left to themselves by governments, operate in an efficient and competitive manner, turns out to be quite consistent with his admission that the market system has faults. The faults that appear are due to human wickedness. They are fraud, attempts at coercion, contrived scarcities and pressure group operation (Bauer 1984: 29). The market system, as a system, works well and cannot possibly be improved on. For the classical *laissez-faire* believer, like Bauer, 'all state intervention is counter-productive by definition' (Desai 1982: 297). But, on the other hand, no system is so good that it can prevent all forms of human deviance.

Should a government never try to regulate attempts to corner the market, the coercion of competitors or employees and the activities of pressure groups that distort vital economic information? A government that failed to regulate effectively these chronic abuses of the market system would be abandoning responsibility for the health and safety of its citizens on a scale that would surely undermine its legitimacy and weaken its ability to perform the functions of justice, police, revenue and arms. The ultra-liberal argument is contradictory on its own terms. Imagine a pharmaceutical industry operating only under commercial pressures and without government regulation: how many thalidomide tragedies a year could the population expect and how many would it suffer uncomplainingly? What would be the health consequences of scrapping the regulation of animal breeding and food production? or the safety consequences of allowing speculative builders to build without heeding the building regulations? of scrapping the government's health and safety provisions in places of work? How could such an irresponsible government continue in power without resorting to repression of the governed?[9]

It is worth recalling that the nineteenth-century *laissez-faire* theorists themselves were writing at a time when government controls were already, under the influence of Bentham and his followers, a well-established feature of economic life (Sutherland 1972; MacDonagh 1977).[10] The original *laissez-faire* theorists too were praising a system of which they had no experience, but for which they felt nostalgic, a golden age of automatic self-regulation, decentralization and benign outcomes.

Conclusion

The new vision of growth contains some valuable warnings against unthinking reliance on public enterprise, the 'dead labour' of machines and physical structures and the power of government edicts as instruments of development policy. Forty years of development practice have shown that the renewal of such warnings is far from redundant. The new vision, in brief, contains much common sense which in the past has often been neglected by policy-makers in international organizations and in developing countries themselves.

However, it is also clear that it is but a short step from common sense to uncommon nonsense. A close look at Bauer's writing on the three main themes of the new vision of growth provides an opportunity to study how this short step has been taken. A policy of rolling back the public sector to an assumed normal or proper set of government functions is advocated, although that norm is nowhere defined, nor its basis explained. The standard economic arguments to justify government productive investment – the sub-optimality of individualistic saving decisions and the maldistribution of assets and incomes – are not addressed, let alone convincingly dealt with.

Bauer's tendency to move effortlessly from unexciting truths to thrilling absurdities is nowhere more evident than in the slide from the truism that physical capital formation is not sufficient for successful development to the travesty that physical capital formation is not necessary for successful development. In the process, much misinterpretation occurs of the economic literature analysing the sources of economic growth and the formation of investors' expectations in a world characterized by pervasive uncertainty.

Government Failure and Market Failure

On the issue of government economic controls, the relevance of welfare economics is dismissed by Bauer, unlike the advocates of a counter-revolution in development policy whose work is discussed in chapter 4.

All the well-known causes of market failure – including various types of monopoly – are brushed aside as insignificant, while 'government failure', in the form of corruption, centralization of power and loss of individual liberty is brought to centre stage. But the ploy of using government failure to outweigh that of market failure is a shallow one. Apart from the fact that the methods for balancing one kind of failure against another cannot be specified, the underlying assumption that the two types of failure are separate and unconnected is false. All markets are made within some legal, social and political framework of institutions. One of the most familiar causes of market failure, for example, public goods externalities, is precisely an explanation of why this must be so. The particular institutional framework in turn determines the extent of ownership externalities, that is, a producer's inability to charge for certain services rendered or to be charged for certain disbenefits inflicted on others in the course of production. Government success or failure in reforming the institutional framework of economic life determines the extent of this type of market failure.

But just as importantly, the causal link also works in the other direction, from market failure to government failure. Technical externalities are a source of monopolistic behaviour and oligopolistic behaviour. Monopoly or oligopoly firms which are also large can usually exercise considerable political power and influence. This is not just a matter of contributing to political parties' funds. It extends more subtly to other forms of patronage, such as the ability to offer well-paid jobs to former politicians and civil servants, and to disproportionate access to the media through the control of large advertising budgets.

Government failure is not just a matter of bureaucratic inertia or empire-building, it is the outcome of creating organizations to regulate economic activity in the public interest which are then systematically frustrated by the political power of the interests which they have been set up to regulate. The proposition that market failures are small, but government failures are enormous, can make a powerful slogan. But, as a piece of economic and political analysis, it is wholly inadequte in understanding the two-way interaction between market and government failures.

Any willingness to glide over difficult analytical problems to arrive quickly at a convenient slogan will surely have detrimental effects when that slogan is used for the basis of policy-making. Over-simplified 'solutions', resting on little more than the political preconceptions of a distant ideologue, are incapable of resolving the real dilemmas of development satisfactorily.

One 'small earthquake in Chile' that has gone relatively unnoticed was the outcome of the radical measures of economic liberalization undertaken in the 1970s by the Pinochet regime, under the inspiration of Milton Friedman and other free-market economists from the University of Chicago. Their advice to relax controls on product and factor markets was accepted, along with a plan to dampen inflationary expectations by announcing in advance adjustments to the country's exchange rate. The consequences were a shattering financial crisis. As the team of World Bank researchers sent out to investigate reported:

> The outcome was disastrous. By 1982 [Chile] had run through a boom-bust cycle . . . Rates of exchange, interest and inflation moved wildly. Massive amounts of capital moved in – then out, when people stopped believing in the [plan of exchange rate adjustments] . . . In the end, the authorities were forced to abandon the [plan] and to resort to inflationary bailouts or declare their industrial sectors bankrupt.
>
> (World Bank 1986)

The basic flaw in the 'bold economic experimenting' which the Chicago economists conducted on the people of Chile was to ignore the actual structure of the Chilean economy and to assume that the success of economic liberalization policies is not sensitive to the variety of different institutional arrangements exhibited by developing countries. The World Bank researchers discovered – somewhat late in the day for policy-making purposes – that 'as the reforms progressed in Chile, banks expanded the debt of firms affiliated with large industrial conglomerates most rapidly, even though the operating earnings of these firms were poor. Why? Because the conglomerates owned the banks' (World Bank 1986). Those who begin with an unshakeable conviction that monopoly and oligopoly are only created by government controls, and that the interlocking of different markets in developing countries is a curiosity dreamt up by structuralist heretics, are not mentally well equipped to foresee where their brilliant experiments will quickly lead. The way to economic hell is paved with good assumptions.

Notes

1　The concept of the 'vision of growth' seems to be the 1980s equivalent of the old 'strategies' of growth of the 1950s and 1960s. The basic idea is of a course of action determined without sufficient information to permit the calculation of a precise outcome. The differences lie in the overtones: a 'vision' of growth makes us think either of a divine revelation rewarding an initial act of faith; or of the image that an advertising agency strives to create for its products. Both are more in keeping with the public mood of the 1980s than the military metaphor of strategy. For a discussion of how 'visions' and 'strategies' alter, and the role of politics therein, see Leff (1985a: 348–51).

2　Negative economic returns describes a situation in which the value of a domestically manufactured output – say, a car – is worth less at ruling world prices than the imported components which it contains, when these also are valued at world prices. This notion of negative returns does not accord world prices than any normative significance. It merely indicates that if a country discontinued its own car production and imported cars instead, it would actually have additional resources in hand. What is neglected here is the external effects of domestic production, e.g. in training labour and management with more advanced technology.

3 Bauer had himself been influential in making the bridge between academics and politicians during the monetarist revolution of the 1970s. Sir Keith Joseph describes the influence of Bauer as follows. 'I decided to promote what I called "continence" – an effort to get back to less deficits – because I understood from the Alan Walters and Peter Bauers of this world that deficit financing and borrowing were one of the main causes of our troubles, though they in turn were the result of other problems – management, the unions, incompetence . . .' (Keegan 1984: 46).

4 This statement must be qualified in the light of recent concern within the Research Division of the World Bank that, when aid is a substantial contributor to a poor country's balance of payments, it may have adverse effects on export performance. The argument is that aid inflows will raise the real exchange rate, raise labour costs in the traded goods sectors and reduced export competitiveness. This is then made the rationale of aid which is conditional on the adoption of policies of trade liberalization.

5 In the 1950s, totalitarianism was viewed in much the same way as premarital sex. On the one hand, it was irresistibly appealing and, on the other, it was disgusting and repellent. Anti-communism, like chastity, was morally essential, yet almost impossible.

6 This follows from Bauer's rejection of human capital formation, in favour of a belief that entrepreneurship derives from the preferences, motivations and social arrangements of different ethnic groups. There certainly does seem to be something about the topic of entrepreneurship that sends people reaching for their ethnic or cultural stereotypes. Sir Keith Joseph, who acknowledges Bauer's influence on him (see n. 3), claimed, while addressing a public meeting in Swansea, to see some connection between South Wales' economic malaise and the fact that the Welsh language had no word for 'entrepreneurs'. Fortunately, someone in the audience had the wit to shout back: 'What is the English word?'

7 It is one of the many oddities of Bauer's position that his refusal to engage with welfare economics does not prevent him from holding strong and definitive views on the subject of international comparisons of national income (e.g. Bauer 1981: 119–20, 261, 274).

8 Bauer's *laissez-faire* assumptions are also evident from his analysis of the effectiveness of foreign aid. In his view, the value of the maximum benefit to be derived from foreign aid is the difference between the rate of interest charged on aid money and the rate of interest on commercial loans. This could only be true if a perfect capital market existed and everyone could borrow as much as they wished at the market rate of interest. In reality, as T. N. Srinivasan pointed out in his comments on Bauer's approach to development issues:

In particular, the markets of credit and capital goods, [as Professor Arrow] suggested, are most likely to be subject to imperfections or even non-existence. And non-existence or imperfection of even a single market has spillover effects on other markets and can destroy the optimality of competitive equilibrium . . . If markets fail, Professor Arrow argued, other social devices are likely to be invented, such as government intervention, codes of conduct for economic agents, or economic organisations with some power between the neo-classical competitive firm and an all-encompassing government.

(Meier and Seers 1984: 55)

9   Even in the European middle ages, governments came to provide legal remedies for gross exploitation (*laesio enormis*) when detected in the sale of land. The Bologna jurists of the twelfth century, at least, did not believe that the political authorities either could or should ignore examples of human wickedness in market transactions.

10   From the 1830s onward, the UK industrial revolution had the effect of expanding government functions:

This thrusting of a vast and growing body of the population into an economic battleground, this destruction of all vestigial remains of traditional securities and protective devices and this deadly concentration of ill-fed and ill-housed people had great consequences in political and working class history. But they also had great consequences in the history of the state. For it was these that set the problem – or at least rendered more manifest a version of the · problem – for which more collectivised and more centralised social organisation and state regulation had ultimately to provide the answers.

(MacDonagh 1977: 2)

CHAPTER FOUR

The Counter-Revolution Arrives: Lal, Little and Balassa

Development Economics and Welfare Economics

In the 1970s, the press had played an important part in giving the ideas of monetarism a wider exposure and bringing them to the attention of politicians and the public. Peter Jay on *The Times* and Samuel Brittan on the *Financial Times* had been key diffusers of the new monetarism (Keegan 1984: 41). The press has been active, too, in supporting the counter-revolution in development thinking, again against the weight of academic opinion. Bauer's 1981 book was greeted by a flood of academic criticism (Lipton 1981; Colclough 1982; Desai 1982; Sen 1982; Smith 1982; Wylie 1983). His 1984 book, which covered very much the same ground as the previous one, was treated to a signed review by the Editor of *The Times* on 9 February. He found the book 'full of original and profound work . . . implacable in its argument [and] devastating'.

The Institute of Economic Affairs vigorously supported the monetarists' ambition to supplant Keynesianism as the guide to domestic economic policy (Keegan 1984: 38–9; Cowling 1990: xviii–xxii). In 1969, it had published a monetarist pamphlet by the economist destined to become Mrs Thatcher's special adviser on economic policy (Walters 1969). In 1983, it offered another significant pamphlet, this time on the state of development economics, by Deepak Lal (1983a). Its thesis was that 'the demise of development economics is likely to be conducive to the health of both the economics and the economies of developing countries' (p. 109). Its publication was reported twice by *The Times*, under the headlines 'Third World Theories Attacked' (22 August 1983) and 'Third World Theories face a Counter-Revolution' (9 September 1983). Thus the counter-revolution in development thinking finally arrived. It portended some important changes in international policy formation: pressure on developing countries to move towards smaller public sectors and more open economies and the enlarged use of conditional aid as the source of that pressure.

This time the doctrines of the counter-revolution won plaudits not only in the IEA and in the 'quality' press but also in the review columns of one of the most respected fora of the economics profession, the *Economic Journal*. Lal's pamphlet was hailed as a 'major contribution to the literature on the problems facing Third World countries'. It was said to be 'a brilliant display of theory' showing 'an extraordinary mastery of the literature and the facts'. In sum, it was seen as 'perhaps the most comprehensive and powerful statement of the liberal position on development to have appeared', or, if the message is still not clear, 'superb' (Elkan 1984: 1006–7).

Finally, the demise of development economics passed from media and academia on to the political stage. *Newsweek* (13 May 1985) reported that the US representative to the Asian Development Bank had announced that 'the United States completely rejects the idea that there is such a thing as "development economics" ' (Senses 1984: 124, n. 31). As the counter-revolution gathered force, development economics became, in the eyes of the US government at least, an Orwellian un-thing. This was despite the fact that Lal's indictment was less far-reaching than Bauer's.

Whereas Bauer had argued that the old development economics was wrong, politically-motivated and corrupt, Lal describes it as merely wrong and dogmatic. For him, foreign aid does not act, as it does for Bauer, as the great corrupter of academics. On the contrary, aid is the catalyst which makes sound academic advice politically effective. It is worth pausing at this point to observe how comprehensively Lal (1983: 56–7) states the technocratic view of the effects of aid.

> The major benefit the developing countries derive from . . . the multilateral aid institutions . . . is the technical assistance built into the process of transferring the aid money to the recipient countries. Though often sound on general economic grounds, their advice is nevertheless resented for political or emotional reasons. . . . When heeded, the advice has done some good . . . in some instances it may have had an appreciable effect in making pubic policies more economically rational.

In other words, unless academics involve themselves with the aid institutions and technical assistance, their often economically sound advice will never overcome the political and emotional resistances it faces. That would be a pity, since we are overlooking the sometimes unsound advice that also gets passed on in this way.[1] These are the accents of Benthamite utilitarianism, not the continental libertarianism of Bauer.

What may seem a minor difference between two traditions of economic liberalism does have major implications for the manner in which the old development economics is characterized and attacked. It is said to be a dogma, arising from intellectual sloth, generally prejudiced in favour of *dirigisme* and specifically composed of a cluster of economic fallacies. The main fallacies are given as the beliefs that the price mechanism should be supplanted (and not just supplemented); that the gains in efficiency from improved allocation of given resources are quantitatively small; that the case for free trade is not valid in developing countries and that governmental controls on wages, prices, imports and the distribution of productive assets are necessary for the relief of poverty in developing countries. Development economists are further charged with attempting to sustain these beliefs by the invention of a set of theoretical curiosities, that is, perversions of standard economic principles, which are held to be applicable in developing countries only. They are perversions, Lal argues, because they falsely deny the universality of rational economic behaviour and the existence of marginal substitution possibilities, on which standard economic theory relies for its familiar results.

The overarching argument is substantiated in two main ways. The first is to attempt to refute selected examples of the 'theoretical curiosities' which individual development economists have produced. These range over the subjects of trade, commodities, foreign capital, industrialization and planning for redistribution with growth. The second is to draw an empirical contrast between India, as a case study of the bad effects of *dirigiste* economic policy and the newly industrialized countries, particularly South Korea, as a case study of the economic progress which poor countries can achieve with the 'correct' economic policies, defined as free trade, care for microeconomic efficiency and the absence of government controls. The link between these two is the assertion that it is the analytical failures of *dirigiste* development economists which have produced the indifferent economic performance of countries which have been so foolish as to heed their advice. Each of these elements needs to be looked at in turn.

What is the root of this analytical failure? Lal is in no doubt at all about this: the basic failure is the neglect of welfare economics and, particularly, a misinterpretation of the famous 'theorem of the second-best' (Lal 1983: 10–16). There is, after all, as Bentham said, a hedonistic calculus which is relevant to public affairs. But old-style development economists had turned their backs on it, with stultifying results for their usefulness as policy advisers. The reason they had done so was that they had interpreted the so-called 'second-best theorem' in a particular way. It stated that, unless an economy was affected by only one distortion, or departure from the requirements for perfectly competitive behaviour, there was no guarantee that removing the distortion would produce an increase in welfare. Intuitively, one can see that, if there were two or more distortions, their effects could be partially or wholly to neutralize each other, and thus the removal of one of them could make the economy more inefficient than it was before. Given that, in the real world, economies rarely suffer from just a single distortion, the theorem seems to mean that there is no way of knowing whether piecemeal attempts to introduce perfectly competitive markets will raise or lower welfare. The second-best theorem seems to lead to policy agnosticism.

Lal regards this interpretation as 'unfortunate', believing that the theorem provides 'the antidote' to the dogma of *dirigisme*. His major point is that 'no general rule of second-best welfare economics permits the deduction that, in a necessarily imperfect market economy, particular *dirigiste* policies will increase welfare' (p. 16). Again, actual *dirigiste* decisions have often 'led to outcomes which, by the canons of second-best welfare economics, may have been even worse than *laissez-faire*'. Clearly, anyone who is accused of interpreting the second-best theorem as a warrant for policy agnosticism cannot also be convicted of believing that it provides a general rule underwriting all particular *dirigiste* policies. Therefore, the denial of such a general rule hardly scores a major point against the interpretation which is said to be 'unfortunate'. The statement that *dirigiste* outcomes may involve less welfare than *laissez-faire* actually confirms that 'unfortunate' interpretation, because it is itself agnostic about the outcome of particular policy interventions.

It is important to underline Lal's failure to shake the agnostic interpretation of the second-best theorem, because one finds among his conclusions a claim that his text does not substantiate, and which cannot be substantiated if the agnostic interpretation holds. He claims to have 'given reasons rooted . . . in theory, why, of the only feasible alternatives – a necessarily imperfect planning mechanism and a necessarily imperfect market mechanism – the latter is likely to perform better in practice' (p. 106). In fact, there are no reasons in the theory of welfare economics to support this estimate of the balance of likelihood.

This contention is borne out by looking at the appendix guide to 'second-best' welfare theory. The final paragraph of the appendix (p. 112) reads as follows:

> The net effect of an increase in welfare, from closing the initial divergence between the marginal social cost and the marginal social value [for a commodity] and a decrease in welfare, from opening the new 'by-product' divergence (as a result of an indirect tax) cannot be known a priori. If there is a net loss, *it may be 'second-best' (which is all that is feasible) to do nothing.*

This paragraph, the appendix and the whole book thus ends one sentence too soon. Pausing to pursue the logic one more step, one would have had to write: 'If there is a net gain, *it may be "second-best" for the government to intervene, to subsidize the commodity and increase indirect taxes*'. But, if that sentence had been written as the final word, it would have been somewhat harder to keep afloat the idea that welfare economics provides a theoretical presumption *against* government intervention, when in fact it does no such thing.

Bauer's decision not to discuss welfare economics at all and rest all the weight of the pro-market argument on political considerations, now begins to seem more like an obligatory defensive tactic, rather than a surprising personal choice. His enigmatic phrase 'whatever the insights of welfare economics' comes back to mind in this connection.

'Unorthodox Economics'

Apart from the neglect, justified or not, of welfare economics, Lal criticizes development economists for inventing an unorthodox economics that was supposed to be especially relevant to the conditions and problems of poor developing countries. This special kind of economics was needed, it is suggested, in order to justify the very wideranging intervention in economic activity that many Third World governments attempted after gaining political independence. To criticize unorthodoxy as such is not particularly damaging, since it wrongly presupposes the existence of a 'normal' or 'correct' theory. As a mere matter of historical fact, fundamental economic theory has been constantly in dispute, economists being notoriously 'people who take in each other's definitions for mangling'. As Professor Deane (1983: 11) put it in her Presidential Address to the Royal Economic Society:

> The lesson, it seems to me, that we should draw from the history of economic thought is that economists should resist the pressure to embrace a one-sided or restrictive consensus. There *is* no one kind of economic truth which holds the key to fruitful analysis of *all* economic problems, no pure economic theory that is immune to changes in social values or current policy problems.

It is a characteristic of Benthamite thinking to be unable to distinguish between utilitarianism and reason itself. But non-utilitarians have no obligation to let such an inability be transformed into a criticism of their beliefs.

Nevertheless, the charge that old-style development economists have come up with an assortment of fallacies has enough accuracy in it to make one uncomfortable in rebutting it completely. The work of Myrdal, on development planning in Asia, for example, was not entirely free from what one reviewer called a 'show of iconoclasm'. Under self-imposed pressure for radical intellectual originality, genuine insights *have* sometimes been expanded into formal theories which, on a more sustained examination turned out to be partially or entirely defective. Myrdal saw that certain forms of consumption (health services, education, even food) promoted economic growth in developing countries. (He was indeed an advocate of human capital formation, although now regarded by the counter-revolutionaries only as a perpetrator of fallacies.) But he followed this up with the quite erroneous claim that the existence of this type of 'productive consumption' proved that the standard macroeconomic distinction between consumption and investment was worthless for policy-making purposes in developing countries. A useful perception was thus inflated to bursting point.

It would also be hard to deny completely that some development economists have favoured the idea that the analysis of developing countries requires its own separate and distinct form of economic theory. This can be seen in the argument of Dudley Seers that standard neo-classical economics (of the kind favoured by Lal) is applicable to the economies of developed countries, which he regarded as a special case, but not to developing economies, where many different kinds of constraints and bottlenecks inhibited smooth, rapid economic adjustments (Seers 1963). The same dichotomy surfaces also in the modern Marxist or neo-Marxist tradition, where the theory of capitalism is sometimes held to be relevant for advanced capitalism and the theory of imperialism relevant for countries in which capitalism is still taking root. Such crude forms of theoretical dualism are hard to defend, if only because the distinction between developed and developing economies is multidimensional and one of degree rather than one of kind. Thus, the search for a more unified theory is to be welcomed in principle. However, it should not be assumed arbitrarily that unification can come about only in one manner, namely by analysts of development recanting their 'heresy' and turning again to the standard economics of marginal utility which Lal declares to be orthodox.[2]

Lal on Government Economic Controls

At this stage in the argument, it is not necessary to review and comment individually on all the fallacies attributed by Lal to old-style development economists. The question of which ideas of lasting importance are to be found in their work is, however, so important that it must be addressed in due course. For the time being it is sufficient to concentrate attention on Lal's discussion of one of the three key aspects of the new vision of growth, the alleged distortions induced by government economic policies in developing countries.

To avoid any misunderstanding, it should be emphasized at the outset that a general critique of the way that many governments use economic controls in developing countries is often justified, particularly in countries whose administrations are bureaucratic in the derogatory sense. A general critique would point to such failings of controls as:

1 *ineffectiveness* in attaining their policy objectives;
2 *counter-productiveness*, where a control has the opposite effect to that intended;
3 undesirable *side-effects*, where a control has the desired effect, but only accompanied by unwanted consequences of a different kind;
4 *conflict* of controls, where one control is being used to move a variable up, while another is being used to move it down;
5 *excessive cost* of controls, where the redesign of a set of controls could improve cost-effectiveness.

Good administrators of economic policy are constantly alive to the possibility of these sorts of general defects in economic controls, in much the same way that good plumbers are aware of the possibility of low water pressure, metal fracture or the rotting of tap washers. There are indeed some developing countries where the conduct of economic policy is no better than the standard of the plumbing and this is very unfortunate. But none of this constitutes a general case against the use of economic controls, any more than a leaky pipe constitutes a general case against water engineering.

The valuable research done by Little, Scitovsky and Scott (1970) as part of the OECD project on industry and trade in developing countries showed up the extent of poor craftsmanship in their fashioning of economic controls. As one example, the rationing of imports by quantity allocations was shown to have the undesirable side-effect of depressing exports. Governments that attempted to neutralize this side-effect by promoting exports often did so by setting up a number of different schemes that were not properly co-ordinated with each other or with the severity of the restriction of imports. They thus could easily worsen the foreign exchange shortage which the import quotas were initially designed to ameliorate. Many other examples of this kind of tangle were explained and illustrated from case studies.

Lal uses evidence of this kind to make a case against any economic controls and all forms of government intervention in industry and trade. He claims that 'the case for liberalising financial and trade control systems and moving back to a nearly-free trade regime is now incontrovertible' (1983: 32). The Little, Scitovsky and Scott study and its companion volumes is cited as 'an impressive empirical validation of the theoretical case against protection, that, even though *laissez-faire* may not be justifiable, free trade remains the best policy for developing (and developed) countries' (pp. 27–8). But, whether or not nearly-free trade (not defined) is their best policy, evidence of the bungled design and operation of economic controls does not validate the case against protection.

Further, it does not provide the basis for supporting a counter-revolution in development thinking. The idea that development economists approve all forms of economic controls, whatever their defects, and whatever their costs, is a total misrepresentation of other people's views. It is also a foolish one. It can be so easily shown that, for example, Gunnar Myrdal, who is named by Lal as an arch *dirigiste*, published his criticisms of economic controls in India *before* the publication of the OECD volumes and that the details of the criticisms are very similar (Myrdal 1968: II, 916–23). The perversity of Indian economic controls comes close to being a consensus view among development economists (cf. Stewart 1985: 289). It hardly needs an intellectual revolution to secure its place in the profession's collective mind.

Presumably all reasonable people, not excluding old-style development economists, can agree that defective economic controls and irrational government intervention in economic life are harmful. But how does that advance the attack on *dirigisme*? And how does the rediscovery of welfare economics help matters? Not at all, in either case. It turns out that it is not *dirigisme* itself, but only the dogmatic variants of *dirigisme* which Lal wants to denounce. Indeed, 'the real issue . . . is the form and extent of government intervention', not its presence or absence (Lal 1983: 6). And the guidance forthcoming from the attempts to apply welfare economics to the choice of government interventions in specific arenas of economic decision turns out to be no more enlightening than one would expect from such a fragile intellectual construction, even if the agnosticism dictated by the second-best theorem is casually brushed aside.

The whole argument, in fact, does not turn on economic theory at all, although it seems to be important to the counter-revolutionaries to pretend that it does. Lal is really developing a political insight of Keynes, that it is the ineptitude of public administrators that so strongly prejudices the practical man in favour of *laissez-faire* (1983: 108). But to suggest that economic theory either does or should further reinforce such a prejudice is far from correct. The circumstances of poor countries offer much scope for selective, intelligent government intervention. The fact that one can document, as has been done, many examples of intervention that are undiscriminating and insensitive to economic implications comes down to a justification for greater caution in resorting to the use of controls until such time as the quality of public administration can be improved in developing countries. This is a mundane, unexciting argument but, nevertheless, right and important.

The economic theory which would be relevant to the question of whether activities are better undertaken in the private or the public sector is very recent and relates to public ownership rather than public regulation. It is hypothesized that a move from private to public ownership will reduce productivity and raise unit costs, because of the greater divorce between ownership and management in the public sector. The testing of this hypothesis is confined largely to the US and does not clearly confirm or refute it. Experience varies from industry to industry. Since many public sector industries are also monopolies, and/or were placed in the public sector so that they could, as a matter of policy, meet certain social obligations, a problem of interpretation arises. Are observed differences in economic performance anyway attributable to monopoly, social obligation or the fact of public ownership? Even if one abolishes this problem by Bauer's device of defining all monopolies as state creations (and all social obligations, too), the empirical evidence remains mixed and very narrowly based (Millward 1985). But this entire discussion is not one that Lal broaches.

Instead, rather surprisingly, the attempt to wring development policy conclusions out of welfare economics is persisted with. It is surprising because '. . . with a few exceptions, like parts of trade theory or social cost–benefit analysis, there is practically no aspect of development economics which draws upon the existing body of welfare theory' (Lall 1981: 24). This, of course, is the neglect of welfare economics of which Lal complains and which he seeks to remedy. The aim is not to abolish *dirigisme*, but to replace dogmatic *dirigisme* with rational *dirigisme*. The technical instrument to implement rational *dirigisme* is social cost–benefit analysis, which is described as 'one of the major intellectual advances . . . in diagnosing the policy-induced distortions' (Lal 1983: 77).

Little on Social Benefit–Cost Analysis

Social benefit-cost analysis had many exponents in the 1960s and 1970s but, for the sake of simplicity, the methods of Little and Mirrlees (1974) are referred to. This form of analysis grew out of the insight that the value of an investment project which could earn or save foreign exchange was independent of any particular pattern of domestic consumption (because the foreign exchange earned or saved could be transformed by trade into consumption of any type). But it was then found that such a project's value could not be established without knowledge of various other parameters which should influence the government's choice between consumption and investment. (There *is* still a choice between consumption and investment and the discovery of 'productive consumption' or 'human capital formation' does not remove it, just complicates it. The choice must be made by any government which undertakes expenditure now in order to produce consumption benefits in the future.) But, in order to generate the necessary information to value the economy's unskilled labour, the reinvestment rate of the economy's marginal investment project had to be identified. This could only be done if one insisted on the most extensive possible use of cost-benefit analysis throughout the economy. Only a ranking of all prospective investments reveals which one is marginal.

That immediately raises the practical implications of the rational *dirigisme* of applied welfare economics. What began as a method of valuing certain types of project in isolation from the rest of the economy, for the express purpose of sidestepping all the alleged dogma of macroeconomic development planning, was transformed under the pressure of its own internal logic into an alternative method of comprehensive planning. It has had to claim sovereignty not only over public sector investment, but also over private sector investment; not only over tradable production, but also over non-tradable production (Little and Mirrlees 1974: 162–9, 192–203). In practical terms, the economic administration that would be required for this purpose would be no less large and pervasive than exists at present and much more economically sophisticated. These requirements seem even more overpowering than those laid on the public administration by the dogmatic *dirigistes*. Lal insists that 'despite their trappings of modernity, many developing countries are closer in their official workings to the rapacious and inefficient nation-states of 17th or 18th century Europe' (1983: 108). If this is so, or anywhere near being so, the policies of rational *dirigisme* would be at even greater variance from real-world possibilities than the dogmatic *dirigisme* which prescribes (allegedly) economically unsophisticated government intervention. For counter-revolutionaries intent on dismissing development economists as theoretically unsound, the argument from government failure turns out to be distinctly double-edged.[3]

But leaving that aside, there is a more serious problem. Government investment policy centres around decisions affecting non-tradable production: public capital expenditure on the social sector (buildings and equipment for education, health services, personal social services); infrastructure (water supply, sewers, roads, buses, railways, power stations), and internal and external defence (police stations, prisons, military, naval and air installations and equipment). The problem is that applied welfare economics does not have a method which is correct even in principle for estimating the value of non-tradable output in an economy where prices are distorted and where the distribution of income is not initially optimal. The rationality of rational *dirigisme* is the rationality of making use of such opportunities for economic gain through international trade as actually exist. Whether one ought to be rational in this sense in every case and at all points in time is something which needs to be looked at. But it is evident that this rationality does not extend, and cannot be made to extend, to areas of economic activity where trade possibilities cannot impinge. In order to be determinate and applicable, social cost-benefit analysis has to be comprehensive; which it cannot be. Rational *dirigisme* is, therefore, theoretically incoherent.

Revising the Original Problem

The counter-revolution in development theory would appear to suffer from exactly the same distressing tendency of theorizing its insights to destruction as that of which old-style development economists are accused. It started from the quite valid perception that microeconomic allocation problems were unduly neglected in developing countries. It quickly moved to the assertion that microeconomic techniques, pushed far enough, can substitute for macroeconomic development planning. Now that the misleading nature of that assertion has become increasingly acknowledged, the next step of the counter-revolutionaries is to revise the terms of the original problem to which rational *dirigisme* was offered as an answer. Lal's view of social cost–benefit analysis as a tool for diagnosing 'the policy-induced distortions' has been quoted already. This indicates very accurately how the original problem of rational choice in a price-distorted economy is being revised. All those distortions which are not induced by policy, which are not government acts, such as import quotas or investment rationing schemes, are to be magically argued out of existence. The problem will then be simplified sufficiently for rational *dirigisme* to be able to cope with it.

One major non-policy-induced distortion in developing countries is the initial distribution of income. This is important for reasons (originally stated by Little) restated by Stewart: 'If a given income distribution is considered to be wrong then maximising on that basis may lead to a worse outcome than taking a Pareto-inferior decision that leads to a better income distribution. Welfare conclusions . . . cannot occur independently of an assessment of income distribution in the two situations' (1985: 286).

Lal shifts gear from Benthamism to libertarianism to come up with an argument for not doing anything about income distribution. This states that 'we cannot . . . identify equity and efficiency as the sole ends of social welfare . . . other ends such as "liberty" are also valued . . . [and] if redistribution entails costs in terms of other social ends which are equally valued, it would be foolish to disregard them and concentrate solely on the strictly "economic" ends' (Lal 1983: 89). This argument would carry more weight if it did not imply that no liberty is ever worth trading, however great the welfare gains that accrue when redistributive policies are undertaken. Here Lal briefly poses as an extreme libertarian, characterized by a preference ordering of liberty, equality and fraternity which is lexicographic with respect to liberty. But this preference ordering is a value-judgement which many reasonable people will be unwilling to share. And they are less likely to be persuaded to share it when it appears alongside a Benthamite longing for 'a courageous, ruthless and perhaps undemocratic government . . . to ride roughshod over . . . newly-created special interest groups' in developing countries (Lal 1983: 33). This particular juxtaposition of political beliefs reveals the stated objection to redistribution as the classical tactic of counter-revolution: first turn liberty against equality and fraternity, then overthrow liberty itself.

The distortions in the price of developing countries' labour are made to vanish by an attack on Sir Arthur Lewis's famous theory of economic development with unlimited supplies of labour (Lewis 1954). The model is said to imply a perverse preference between income and leisure of rural workers and to be contradicted by empirical evidence of upward-sloping supply of labour schedules in India (Lal 1983: 90–1). The first objection is confused. Whenever the average exceeds the marginal product of rural labour, the transfer of a worker from the subsistence to the capitalist sector allows the income of the remaining subsistence workers to rise. In the short run, everyone benefits from increased income, even without assuming backward remittances from the capitalist sector. Thus no perverse preferences among non-migrants are implied. Lewis's point is that the initial gap between capitalist and subsistence sector rewards is so large and that the pool of underemployed labour in the subsistence sector is so vast, that it will be many years before capitalist-sector wages are forced upwards by lack of willing migrants (p. 7). This seems often to be the case. India, for example, has exhibited near-constant real wages in the organized sector during a fairly long period of capitalist growth (Toye 1981: 217–18). Theoretically, upward sloping short-run labour supply schedules in rural wage labour markets are not incompatible with this state of affairs.

If, despite all the theoretical juggling, distortions in income distribution and the price of labour in developing countries refuse to disappear, and if applied welfare economics provides only an incomplete method of correcting for them in the direction of economic development, what is to be done? Either economic events can be left to take their own course, or governments must have recourse again to familiar techniques of macroeconomic planning to establish the overall framework within which microeconomic choices can be rationally made. In reasserting this conventional wisdom, it is evident that powerful ideological currents can make the obvious sound distinctly heretical But, if it is now the fashion to claim that, although price distortions are endemic in developing countries, the labour market, alone among markets, is functioning competitively, then the appearance of heresy is something to be welcomed. For how can one consistently claim both that labour markets in developing countries work well and that every other price is distorted? The counter-revolution has not yet explained how, in an interdependent economy, that particular combination of outcomes is likely.

The correction of one error must not be allowed to be the opportunity for the introduction of an equal and opposite error. The counter-revolution has done well to insist that the development economist cannot make macroeconomic techniques substitute for microeconomic. But, equally, the substitution of microeconomic for macroeconomic is not possible. Although both types of techniques are inherently limited, they can and should be used concordantly in the fashioning of development policy.

Balassa on the Reform of Trade Policy

Trade theory is the second area of development thinking where welfare economics had been systematically applied in the search for development policy conclusions. It is, therefore, the other obvious arena for the counter-revolutionaries to make their case that the neglect of welfare economics by old-style development economists has led them to support policies which damage economic performance. The work of Bela Balassa on commercial policy in developing countries is complementary with that of Little in giving content to the programme of rational *dirigisme*. It spells out in some detail, and provides justification for, the set of trade policies which we have referred to heretofore rather mysteriously as 'nearly-free trade', which in Lal's pamphlet is sometimes confusingly also called 'free trade'. It is also the set of policies which Little and Mirrlees have in mind when they recommend developing country governments to appraise investment projects as if the government were about to move to sensible trade policies (Little and Mirrlees 1974: 75).

What exactly does rational *dirigisme* in the trade sector or 'nearly-free trade' amount to? For Balassa, it does not mean either the absence of government intervention in the foreign trade sector or the acceptance of the pattern of exports and imports that freely operating market forces would dictate. While criticizing the tariff and quota policies of many developing countries, he accepts the familiar argument of the early development economists, particularly those associated with ECLA (the United Nations' Economic Commission for Latin America), that developing countries ought to check the expansion of their traditional primary product exports, either by an export tax or by an administered unfavourable foreign exchange rate. Also accepted are the infant industry arguments for production subsidies and other subsidies to compensate firms for special cost disabilities, such as a distorted market price for labour, arising for the Lewis-type reasons referred to in the previous section. In addition to such permissible interventions, 'there is some presumption . . . in favour of promoting manufacturing industry in developing countries . . . This can be accomplished by granting a subsidy to the exports of manufactured goods at a rate equal to the tariff applied to the same commodity, or by using differential exchange rates for the manufacturing sector' (Balassa 1971: 186). In all this, two things can be discerned directly. The first is clear agreement with some of the key reasons advanced by old-style development economists as to why complete free trade would inhibit development. The second is an extension of the already-noted requirements for an economically sophisticated public administration, which the adverb 'nearly' does not do much to hint at in the phrase 'nearly-free trade'.

One can also infer from the above quotation from Balassa why such a set of trade policies is also referred to as 'outward-looking'. The intended contrast here is with policies of indiscriminate substitution of imports by domestic production, which are indeed 'inward-looking'. But, if one takes seriously the orthodox economist's view that price changes act as an automatic decentralized adjustment mechanism that continually restores a general equilibrium of markets, policy should be neither 'inward-looking' nor 'outward-looking'. The orthodox economist, in evaluating economic growth, is indifferent between additional income that arises from sales to domestic markets and sales to the export sector. In the same way, a unit of value sold by one domestic sector is taken to be as good as a unit sold by another domestic sector. An outward-looking policy, one of giving special encouragement to manufactured exports, alerts us to the fact that some non-standard assumption is being relied on in the underlying analysis. In fact, it is that 'exports or manufactured goods enable firms to lower costs by employing large-scale production methods' (Balassa 1971: 181). This assumption, the realism of which one can hardly doubt, is actually the centerpiece of the Kaldorian view of economic growth which, because of the huge economies of scale available in the manufacturing sector, but hardly at all elsewhere, makes external demand for the products of the manufacturing sector the regulator of national economic growth (Kaldor 1978: 139–47).

Why does Balassa's use of the economies-of-scale assumption matter? If Kaldor is right, is not Balassa also right? The problem arises only for those who, like Lal, pose as the champions of orthodox, neo-classical economic theory. But arise it does, because the economies-of-scale assumption is a pretty big spanner to drop casually into the neo-classical works. The context in which this spanner has its damaging effects is the attempt by Balassa and associates to move beyond merely describing and prescribing an outward-looking trade policy for developing countries. Specifically, Balassa's contribution to the counter-revolution of the 1980s is twofold. He claims that the anti-export bias of existing systems of trade controls is the main cause of the balance of payments constraint on economic growth in developing countries. He also claims that the right system of incentives (by which he means 'governmental measures that affect the allocation of resources') is that which departs least from 'a neutral state of affairs in which there is no discrimination among economic activities or between foreign and domestic markets' (Balassa and Associates 1982: 9).

Reversing the order of these points, what is wrong with this second claim? To advocate a simplified system of interventions which will effectively reach certain policy goals is one thing. But to justify increasing simplicity by reference to a state of non-intervention whose optimality is clearly implied, if not stated, is quite a different thing. From early Balassa to counter-revolutionary Balassa, one makes an ideological leap, from straight prescription to the attempt to clothe prescription in the language and ideas of welfare economics.

This will not do, for reasons which must by now be becoming familiar. Turning back to the *locus classicus* of the general theory of welfare and distortions, one finds distortions classified into two different categories. The first category includes market imperfections of all kinds and is labelled 'endogenous distortions'. The second includes government interventions of all kinds and is labelled 'policy-induced distortions' (Bhagwati 1971). Balassa's programme for the reform of the system of incentives, in which non-intervention is to be approached as closely as possible, is equivalent to recommending the removal of all policy-induced distortions, while leaving all endogenous distortions in place. The theory of the second-best tells us that such a partial approach provides no guarantee that welfare would improve as a consequence (Salazar-Xirinachs 1985: 10–11). The only recourse then is to claim with Bauer, that all distortions are policy-induced. Then, and only then, would the removal of all policy-induced distortions return us to a neutral state of affairs that would also be optimal.

Balassa, however, is denied such a recourse. At this point, the Kaldorian spanner drops. If one assumes, as Balassa does, significant economies of scale in a major sector of the economy, one is assuming a particular type of market imperfection. Thus market imperfections cannot be willed out of existence without self-contradiction. In this situation, it is unnecessary to dwell on other types of market imperfection which are endemic in developing countries, such as the absence of markets, inequalities of information between market participants, myopia about the future, and so on. It is also unnecessary to spend much time considering whether economies of scale are at the industry level or internal to firms, since it is very hard to explain the existence of firms at all if one denies that scale economies are experienced at the level of firms (Hahn 1981: 131). Market imperfections are indisputably present and to advocate economic liberalization in the presence of market imperfections may well not be a welfare-augmenting policy.

Distortions and Growth: Empirical Evidence

What happens if, Lal's sermons to the contrary notwithstanding, one decides to neglect welfare economics as a guide to trade policy and to advocate liberalization on the pragmatic grounds that existing controls on trade inhibit growth by artificially tightening the balance of payments constraint? In 1983, the World Bank published some statistical analysis in order to show that countries with large policy-induced price distortions enjoyed slower economic growth during the 1970s than countries with fewer or less-severe policy-induced price distortions (World Bank 1983: 57–63). For this purpose, a composite equal-weight index of seven different types of such price distortion was created, only three of which were designed to register distortions in the foreign trade sector; the others concerned factor and product prices. In fact, it was one of the trade sector distortions – the foreign exchange distortion – which proved to be most significantly correlated with the growth rate. The sample size was thirty-one and the distribution of developing countries by area, resource base and political system was quite balanced. This certainly amounts to useful support for a pragmatic approach to dismantling some of the existing types of government control over foreign trade.

At the same time, it is also a convincing demonstration that trade controls are not the major determinant of economic performance. Even if the exercise is taken completely at its face value, it shows that only one-third (or 34 per cent) of the economic performance of these countries is explained by policy-induced price distortions of all kinds. Two-thirds of their economic growth responds to other factors. Before embracing liberalization even on pragmatic grounds, a prudent policy-maker would want to know what these other factors were and whether they would be affected favourably, unfavourably or not at all by the dismantling of trade controls.[4]

Some commentators have also suggested that the figure of 34 per cent may be too high. Because qualitative judgement has entered into the assessment of the degree of distortion, some arbitrariness in scoring has been detected, especially in the case of Chile (Evans and Alizadeh 1984: 43–6). An appropriate correction in the Chilean case would clearly weaken further the overall explanatory power of the hypothesis of price distortions in the trade sector causing slower growth. They have also noted that, for one-quarter of the individual countries, the average impact of price distortions on growth does not seem to hold, and quite a number of spectacular divergences of the actual from the expected relationship between the two have to be explained away by other factors, some economic (large oil exports) and some social and political (unspecified).

This very lack of specification of the social and political structures within which countries' economic policies are conducted is problematic, highlighting questions which the abstracted statistical analysis does not address. The World Bank study, even after allowing for qualifications so far raised by critics, tends to support the contention that states which use trade controls to keep their exchange rate artificially high do inhibit growth by discouraging exports, particularly non-traditional exports. But, because of the neglect of the particularities of social and political contexts, this contention cannot itself be expanded into a justification for rational *dirigisme*, let alone the unrestricted play of market forces and government non-intervention in economic life. Unless the policy-maker has a clear understanding of the way in which state power is being used to further a process of physical and human capital accumulation in the particular context in which policy is being guided, he or she cannot predict at all how a wholesale shift to government non-intervention will affect that growth process.

It is, finally, worth noting that, although the counter-revolution tends to assume an identity between countries with large public sectors and countries with a high level of economic distortions, the World Bank figures do not support this view. The picture is quite mixed, with some socialist countries, such as Ethiopia and Yugoslavia, exhibiting low distortions and some capitalist countries, for example, Nigeria, exhibiting high distortions. Thus privatization programmes cannot be guaranteed to reduce distortions, any more than nationalization programmes necessarily increase them (Mosley 1984: 135).

The Lessons of India and South Korea

Despite all of these complications, Lal brings forward a simple contrast between the growth experiences of India and South Korea as empirical evidence of the superiority of rational *dirigisme* over dogmatic *dirigisme*. From one point of view, to attempt such a demonstration is redundant because no one will argue, or has argued, in favour of badly designed controls dogmatically applied, and by common professional consent Indian economic policies have contained some examples of self-defeating economic controls.

From another point of view, the attempted contrast is of interest because it allows us to examine the view that the rapid growth of the east Asian 'tigers', the economies of South Korea and Taiwan (ignoring here the city-states of Singapore and Hong Kong), can in any reasonable sense be attributed to their flouting of the conventional wisdom of the old-style development economists (Lal 1983: 17–18, 30–31).[5]

It is important to establish at the outset of the discussion that the popular myth of the Asian newly industrializing countries as the triumph of untrammelled private enterprise is quite false. Partly for historical reasons connected with the post-liberation disposal of Japanese assets, the South Korean government owns some important sectors of industry, including monopolies of tobacco and energy production. In addition, there has been, since the founding of the state, an unbroken tradition of centralized government control over the private sector. This control is exercised by the apportionment of official credit, the exercise of veto powers over business appointments in major private corporations and the enforcement of government price controls for many commodities, including foodgrains and fertilizers but, also, many urban goods and services. Private enterprise in South Korea is circumscribed by pervasive government controls, but it is also entrepreneurial and dynamic within these limits (Steinberg 1984: 117–19).

The model of rational *dirigisme*, as proposed by Lal, thus does not fit South Korea. That model is one of parametric intervention with the government setting a few key prices, giving a few key subsidies and, otherwise, letting market forces operate unchecked. This has not been the way in South Korea, where the interpenetration of government and private economic activity has been much more complete than is consistent with the idea of parameter setting. Even in the foreign trade sector, one finds on the import side 'extensive use of made-to-measure tariffs and quantitative restrictions . . . In 1970, out of 1,312 basic items, the import of 524 [was] restricted, and 73 were banned altogether' (Evans and Alizadeh 1984: 34–5). Certain key sectors of the economy are heavily protected, with effective rates of protection in 1978 standing at 135 per cent (ships); 131 per cent (consumer durables); 77 per cent (agriculture, forestry and fishing); 47 per cent (machinery); and 32 per cent (non-durable consumer goods) (Fransman 1984: 50–6). Furthermore, these protective measures were not merely offset by export incentives, to achieve a broadly neutral foreign trade regime, as Little and Lal claim.

Intervention as an Industrial Strategy

On the contrary, the export side of the South Korean economy shows evidence of a significant bias in favour of export industries, deriving mainly from preferential allocations of subsidized credit. This is quite different from the avoidance of bias against exports, which is what the anti-distortion argument recommends. In standard trade theory, welfare losses occur just as much by artificially favouring export industries as by artificially favouring import-substitution industries. It seems, therefore, as if the South Korean government was actually buying, with static welfare losses, some dynamic Kaldorian gains which were substantially greater. But orthodox trade theory unfortunately does not have anything to say on the question of how departures from an optimal trade policy can be expected to influence the growth rate. The counter-revolution has to rely on the World Bank's statistical correlation, which itself has no underlying theory.

In view of the evidence just mentioned of the interventionist policies followed by the South Korean government, both generally in the economy and particularly in the foreign trade sector, the counter-revolutionary description of its chosen paradigm country must be seriously in doubt. There is indeed some acknowledgement of this by Lal, who admits that 'most countries, however, including the East Asian success stories – apart from Hong Kong – retain *dirigiste* spots in their trade policies, and few have seriously attempted the full-scale liberalisation that is required' (1983: 32). Some spots! Some 'tiger'! Could we not after all be staring at a leopard? And can the leopard change its spots?

Rather than simply responding to the pulls of short-run comparative advantage in a foreign trade regime which is 'nearly-free trade', the South Korean government appears to be selecting certain industries with a potential long-run comparative advantage and actively promoting them through and beyond the infant industry stage; and promotion is greater for their exports than for their sales to the domestic market. The government, in other words, is pursuing a particular developmental strategy based on the rapid growth of manufactured exports. Given the success of this strategy, at least in terms of growth, it is rather odd to suppose that the retreat of the state into a purely parametric role would improve, and not worsen, the growth record. It is ironical, too, that although initially the India versus South Korea contrast was put forward to validate the economic liberalization strategy, in the end full economic liberalization is said to be 'required' despite the undisputed fact that South Korea, the great success story, has not followed such a policy.

In all of this argument, as in the World Bank's statistical exercise on growth and distortions, the political and social aspect of the two countries' development is pushed right into the background. The contrast is treated as meaningful entirely within the limits of economics. But, as Evans and Alizadeh (1984) have suggested, every accumulation process has its own social and political context. In South Korea, the state is interested in creating an environment in which national capital can expand, while partly sheltered from the competition of foreign capital. Thus it plays an active and discriminating part in developing the chosen foreign trade strategy and mediates the effects of multinational companies' activities and non-MNC private direct foreign investment. But to support the profitability of domestic capital, in a given state of technology and consumer demand, the state must be able to regulate the level of money wages. Many of its interventions, to set private- and public-sector wages and to control the activities of trade unions, are designed for this purpose. To be successful in this latter task, the state may find it impossible also to be, or become, liberal and democratic. Certainly, both South Korea and Taiwan combined their particular brand of *dirigisme* with a markedly authoritarian polity. It is not indeed the newly created special interest groups among capitalists over whom the authoritarian state rides roughshod, although these are shaped and manipulated paternalistically, rather it is organized labour in South Korea which is treated most repressively.

No contrast between South Korea and India can be instructive until it sets differences in economic performance in their social, political and administrative contexts. It is probably in these areas, rather than in government economic policy narrowly defined, where much more significant and determining differences between the two countries are located.

Development Economists, Policies and Performances

Having convinced himself that he has proved, by the South Korea/India empirical contrast, the link between orthodox liberal policies and superior economic performance, Lal tries to foist the blame for inferior economic performance on old-style development economists. He simply says that they were responsible for the unorthodox, non-liberal policies which many developing countries have at various times adopted. In doing so, Lal places himself squarely in the shadow of Keynes, who at the very end of the *General Theory* made his famous remark that : '. . . the ideas of economists and political philosophers, both when they are right and when they are wrong, are more powerful than is commonly understood. Indeed the world is ruled by little else' (CW VII: 383).

Development economists of both the old style and the counter-revolutionary variety rarely decide by themselves major issues of government development strategy. Thus their effectiveness is almost always mediated by sets of institutions (governmental and other) and by the political conjuncture. Thus development economists should be used to analysing the constraints on development policy advice which institutions and politics impose. By the same token, when the impact of policy advice by development economists is being assessed, the presence of such constraints needs to be taken into full account.

It is naive and superficial to suppose that foolish forms of government intervention can be attributed wholly to dogma, of any form, and to forge an iron link between bad policies and alleged logical mistakes of named intellectuals. If Keynes himself meant to say this, in his famous closing paragraph of the *General Theory*, then Keynes was equally naive. Politicians may sometimes attempt to rationalize their policies by quoting academic names, but that is a very different matter from adopting policies because some famous academic recommended them.

Keynes did not make this distinction and even seemed to be saying that 'the gradual encroachment of ideas' is a process which affects 'practical men' and 'madmen in authority, who hear voices in the air' in exactly the same manner. This is not very flattering to the practical men. There is, however, an important, but sometimes forgotten rider in Keynes's peroration: 'Not, indeed, immediately, but after a certain interval; for in the field of economic and political philosophy there are not many who are influenced by new theories after they are twenty-five or thirty years of age' (CW VII: 383–4). Such a cultural lag would suggest that one should not expect to find the intellectual influences that affected Indian economic policies of the early 1950s later than the 1920s and 1930s. A combination of Feldman and Visvesvaraya would seem to be the latest permissible influences, if one insists on pursuing the search for the originators of 'dangerous ideas' beyond List's 1841 defence of economic nationalism. Certainly, in Visvesvaraya's *Planned Economy for India* (1934), one can find all the dogmatic enthusiasm for indiscriminate import substitution, instant industrialization and comprehensive planning that is attributed by Lal to subsequent development economists. Visvesvaraya, however, was not an economist. He was an engineer.

Nationalism and Non-economists

If we want to analyse the determinants of economic policy and performance in India, or South Korea, or elsewhere, and not merely use them as pictures of vice and virtue in a counter-revolutionary homily, we must dig much deeper than merely asking what academic ideas were available at that particular time and place. Very few societies are so intellectually impoverished or politically or culturally restricted that politicians have no choice between clashing academic ideas. The problem is almost always *why* they chose one set rather than another.

It seems more plausible to attempt to answer this question by trying to work back from the specific modes of involvement by the state in the economy to an understanding of the social character of the state itself. White has distinguished three sorts of social interests that are served by state action: the interests of state office-holders as an autonomous group; the interests of a hegemonic class or class coalition; and the interests of the nation itself *vis-à-vis* other nations (1984: 98–9). In India at the relevant time the dominant interests seem to have been those of a class coalition and those of the national interest as understood by the political representatives of that coalition.

Thus, even if all the historical evidence had been destroyed, it would strain credulity to believe that the post-Independence economic policy was derived from the writings in the early 1950s of a few development economists, such as Singer, Prebisch and Nurkse.[6] By that time, the demand for a nationalistic economic policy had been a key element in the Congress anti-British struggle for over forty years and for a Congress government to abandon it in the moment of victory would have been politically unthinkable, whatever the contents of the current economics journals (cf. Toye 1981: 21–38).

But we do, in fact, have some interesting evidence of the impact of outside advice on the trajectory of Indian economic planning in the 1950s. Responding to the scarcely veiled suspicion of, among others, Bauer, that India was acting under the ideological sway of the Soviet Union, Soviet advice to India in the 1950s has been carefully studied. It emerged that the tenor of the Soviet advice was to proceed much more cautiously towards organisational change and planned economic transformation and that this advice was ignored (Clarkson 1979).

The advice of Western economists to India in the 1960s has also been studied. A representative example is Morton Grossman, a Ford Foundation economist in India between 1959 and 1967. Of him it is said that:

> To the extent that his advice was asked, he favoured policies by the government to use India's resources in an economically rational manner to maximise growth rates: to reduce controls that inhibited efficient use of resources, to reduce restrictions that discouraged efficient entrepreneurial behaviour by Indian businessmen and peasants and to set prices that reflected the real scarcity value of India's resources, including foreign exchange, rather than to subsidise inefficient production or consumption.
> (Rosen 1985: 98)

At the time such advice was not much heeded, but in the 1970s and 1980s, with constant repetition and a process of gradual learning through time, it has had an increasing impact on Indian policy-making.

One very salient fact is usually omitted in the attempt to link early Indian planning with old-style development economists – that the nationalist consensus on the goal of rapid industrialization was given its technical form by leading planners who were not economists of any kind. Mahalanobis was a statistician and Pitambar Pant was a physicist. The role of economists, both Western and Indian, was to try to inject some greater economic sophistication into a conception of planning that owed much to politics, statistics and engineering, but which was largely innocent of all types and varieties of economics. This was a pretty unrewarding task, particularly for foreign economists trying to avoid charges of political interference. The obvious temptation was to accept the underlying goals and assumptions of Indian planning of the 1950s and just give to them a little more technical economic finesse.

This is what many Western economists working in India at the time did. Little, now a doyen of the development counter-revolution, took this path. In 1958–9, Little was writing highly theoretical papers to support the policy of raising the level of development expenditure for the Third Indian Five Year Plan (Rosen 1985: 117). His views prevailed. The technical methods whose prestige was used in these policy debates are, unsurprisingly, those which are now being attacked by the counter-revolution as defective. An alternative path was taken by Singer, whose advice to the Indian Planning Commission was to avoid the problems of an overvalued foreign exchange rate (private communication). His advice was ignored. He is however, publicly pilloried by Lal as one of a small group of old-style development economists who were responsible for encouraging India to adopt a faulty development strategy.[7]

Notes

1 An illuminating example of the kind of advice which USAID officials were ordered to give to poor countries in February, 1985 is provided by Killick (1986: 101–2). US Secretary of state George Schultz sent a telegram to USAID officials which included the following general instruction:

> Policy dialogue should be used to encourage LDCs to follow free market principles for sustained economic growth and to move away from government intervention in the economy. This allows the market to determine how economic resources are most productively allocated and how benefits should be distributed. To the maximum extent practical governments should rely on the market mechanism – on private enterprise and market forces – as the principal determinants of economic decisions.

2 The obvious alternative route is for orthodox neo-classical economists to recognize that many of the factors which development economists originally identified as specially relevant to economic performance in poor countries actually have a much wider relevance, and that they also significantly affect the economic performance of the rich and developed countries. Important among these factors are uncertainty, absence of information, dynamic disequilibrium, learning curves, entry barriers to markets and non-economic motivation and behaviour in households, firms and government bodies.

3   The real-world disjunction between widespread acceptance of social benefit-cost analysis (SBCA) in principle, and failure to use it widely in practice, has been singled out for discussion by observers.

> At best, SBCA is used to select projects in the intra-sectoral competition that ensues after the key investment choices have been made. In fact, in many countries, the contrast between prescriptive theory and actual practice is even starker. Little or no use is made of SBCA to select projects; and designation of individual sectors for high priority is the major conceptual determination of investment choice.
>
> (Leff 1985a: 337–8)

The explanation of this disjunction offered by Leff is, in summary, the following: 'The complexity and uncertainty that affect investment choice in developing countries make this an area where decision-makers find heuristic decision rules especially attractive' (pp. 343–4). Investment choice in line with a 'strategy' is thus an example of H. A. Simon's 'bounded rationality'.

4   It would, however, be naive to take this exercise at its face value. It should be obvious that, since prices are used to aggregate physical output into an index of national product, countries with severely distorted prices will also have severely distorted indices of national product, i.e. misleading economic growth rates.

5   Apart from South Korea, the performance of Taiwan has been assessed, from the counter-revolutionary perspective by Little (1979: 448–507). An interesting comparison is between Taiwan and the People's Republic of China, where the historical and cultural background is similar, but the styles of social organization and economic policy notably different. Whereas Taiwan grew at 4.4 per cent (1950–75), the PRC grew at 3.5–4 per cent per annum (1957–75). This is hardly a major difference of performance (Little 1979: 448, 463n. 42). The PRC has also built up a large industrial sector and done well in meeting the basic needs of its huge population. But in the whole of the Maoist period (1949–76), it did not follow the development policy prescriptions of the counter-revolution. Since 1976, however, the desire to gain access to Western technology has led to foreign direct investment receiving active official encouragement. A more recent study of government controls in Taiwan is Wade (1990). This fully documents the departures from the free-market model in Taiwan. See the Introduction to the Second Edition for further comments on Wade's findings.

6   The attempt to link economic outcomes in India with the work of individual economists is made as follows:

> India . . . ended up by pursuing import substitution and export promotion without reference to economic costs, guided only by the belief that 'India should produce whatever it can and India should export whatever it produces'. The inefficiency, waste and corruption that the Indian trade control system has engendered are incalculable. But, at least for *this* Indian, it stands as a lasting and appalling monument to the ideas of Nurkse, Prebisch, Singer, Myrdal, Balogh, *et al.*
>
> (Lal 1983: 31)

This muddles up two distinct issues. They are: (1) whether to set up a foreign trade regime which departs from orthodox liberal 'nearly-free trade' and (2) whether to do so by means of a bureaucratic allocation system. The fact that India did both these things does not mean that they are logically indistinguishable, or that other countries did not succeed in separating them, or – what is relevant here – that the five named economists favoured the bureaucratic allocation system which Lal quite rightly criticizes. This passage does nothing 'to illumine the logic of the alternative views on development and in particular the role of government to promote it', which Lal declares is his 'primary concern' (p. 2). For further discussion of policy choices for foreign trade, in the context of India's experience, see chapter 6.

7   Hirschman, as so often, is deep where the counter-revolution is shallow:

> The effect of new theories and ideas is much less direct than we often think: to a considerable extent, it comes by way of the general impetus that is given to a certain field of studies. As a result of a few contributions, that field suddenly becomes alive with discussion and controversy and attracts some of the more intelligent, energetic and dedicated members of a generation. This is the indirect, or *recruitment*, effect of new ideas, as opposed to their direct, or *persuasion*, effect . . . The importance of the recruitment effect explains, among other things, why the influence of new ideas is so unpredictable and why it is so difficult – and often ludicrous – to assign intellectual responsibility for actual policy decisions, let alone for policy outcomes.
>
> (Meier and Seers 1984: 110–11)

CHAPTER FIVE

Political Economy of the Left and the New Right

The Counter-revolution and the Left View of the State

The coming of the counter-revolution in development theory was widely ignored by those who analyse development issues from a left-wing political perspective. In an atmosphere of general complacency about the solidity of a left-of-centre consensus on development, the portents of change were missed. So much was taken for granted that the available intellectual energy on the left was channelled primarily into fierce debates on moot points of theory. Often it required deep immersion in Marxist polemics for even the sympathetic outside observer to understand the nature of the point at issue in these debates. What little empirical work was stimulated by them frequently turned out not to resolve the point at issue. Meanwhile, the resurgence of diagnoses and policy prescriptions believed on the left to be discredited beyond all hope of recall continued unobtrusively, but powerfully.

Precisely because the strength of the counter-revolutionary tide was not foreseen or correctly appreciated, the left's defences against it were much too casual in manner and too porous in their effect. It is important for those on the left to be clear where their defences were tested and found wanting in the early 1980s, if their thinking about development is to be turned in directions more relevant to the policy dilemmas of the real world of poverty and power.

It is argued here that the left's usual view of the role of the state as the guardian of vested social (class-based) interests is too limited and too static to counter the policy proposals of the development counter-revolution effectively. The new right has constructed its own political economy of the state, rooted in individual self-interest, which taps just as deeply into popular distrust of state action to promote national well-being. It is further suggested that more attention should be concentrated on those conditions under which Third World nationalism can have a progressive impact, although recently the left has lined up with the counter-revolution in glossing over this possibility. The linkages between these three lines of argument can best be brought out by looking at each of them in greater detail.

Chapter 4 showed the heavy emphasis which the counter-revolution in development theory has placed on welfare economics and its application to the two specific policy areas of project investment and foreign trade. Among the criticisms of the application of welfare economics to project investment were the suggestions that it presupposed the existence of an ideal type of rational bureaucratic state, and that it did so in an even greater degree than did previous conceptions of macroeconomic development planning. Again, in discussing the counter-revolution's proposal to apply welfare economics to trade policy, the point was made that the empirical justification for the removal of trade distortions (in terms of good consequences for economic growth) is made entirely without reference to the differing social and political structures of the countries concerned. Both of these criticisms are consistent with the left's view (and that of some political economists not on the left) that the role of the state is of pivotal importance in analysing development policies.

The Class State

There is, however, a fundamental difference between insisting that social and political analysis is an essential part of economic policy-making and jumping up with stock pieces of social and political analysis to answer that need. It has been characteristic of many development economists who rightly accept the former proposition also to allow themselves the indulgence of resorting to the latter. How is this done? On the left, the general form of the stock argument is this. What the counter-revolution identifies as the gross errors of domestic economic policy-making in developing countries are not errors, when their sociopolitical context is properly understood. If they are mistakes, they are deliberate mistakes, designedly made to favour those who are socially and politically powerful.

For example, the counter-revolution holds that an over-valued exchange rate is a serious error made by developing country governments. Development economists from the left would respond that it is probably not an error at all, in the sense of an act of oversight or intellectual confusion which the doer would want to correct, having properly understood its implications. An over-valued exchange rate has predictable results for the distribution of income. It favours importers of goods and services (and, depending on how the primary importers price for resale, the users of imports). It disadvantages exporters and those selling their products to exporters. These economic consequences, in turn, have to be seen not just abstractly, as economic indicators moving up and down, but in their concrete political impact on a particular society.

If Ghana is our object of study, an important group of disadvantaged exporters will be cocoa farmers in the rural areas, whose own consumption of imports is relatively modest. The favoured importers will be urban consumers with well-developed tastes for foreign consumption items; and industrial enterprises, many in the public sector, which rely on foreign-made capital equipment. If political decisions in Ghana are, as they were for many years after independence, heavily influenced by urban consumers and public sector employees and little influenced by peasant farmers, the persistence of an overvalued exchange rate seems to follow from a policy design, and not a policy mistake.

This simplified example from Ghana could evidently also be interpreted as an example of 'urban bias', as defined by Lipton (1977). The stock explanation by left development economists bases itself on the political economy of social classes. It does not see these as necessarily conforming to locational cleavages, such as the rural-urban divide. But, like the political economy of urban bias, it does postulate a social system which is biased against the poor: '... the system is biased in favour of those who control the major means of production (the 'rich') and discriminates against those who do not (the 'poor') ... [Policy] measures may appear wrong-headed to the uninitiated, but be perfectly sensible from the standpoint of a rural or urban bourgeoisie that profits from (them)' (Griffin and Gurley 1985: 1123). If this is true, the left can take comfort from the fact that the counter-revolutionaries have undertaken a hopeless task. They have to persuade the political leadership of developing countries not only to remove economic distortions but, *ipso facto*, to remove their own political underpinnings.

There is something eminently plausible in all of this. We have escaped from the arid description of policy as the rational calculation of welfare gains and losses, abstracted from embodiment in persons, places and time. We have arrived at a world whose plausibility we recognize, a world in which rationality is used by the powerful, but not necessarily respected by them. It is a world which, therefore, has a hidden aspect, which may provide clues to help us understand what is superficially puzzling – the persistence of ill-treatment and injustice, the resistance to obvious changes that would benefit the many who are exploited or neglected.

At the same time, it has been a standing temptation for developmentalists on the left to make themselves too comfortable inside this kind of explanation. This intellectual cosiness has sapped their ability to resist the challenges posed by the development doctrines of the new right. The stock explanation is too general and too static to provide a satisfactory resting place. It concedes, by implication, if not expressly, too much of the counter-revolutionary case.

One obvious implication of the standard left view of the role of the state in developing countries is that the counter-revolutionary view of appropriate development policy would be correct, if only the vested interests of the politically dominant class could be abolished. To argue that current policies are wrong-headed by design is to concede that they are wrong and, thus, that their designers should be removed and correct policies – presumably social cost–benefit analysis and nearly-free trade – instituted instead. This is not very strong ground on which to confront the counter-revolutionary rallying-call, for 'courageous, ruthless and perhaps undemocratic government [in developing countries] . . . to ride roughshod over . . . newly created special interest groups' (Lal 1983: 33).

It only seems to be strong ground because the standard left view contains the assumption that a rural or urban bourgeoisie which has captured state power in the developing world cannot be ridden over roughshod, and its vested interests cannot be abolished by anything short of a social revolution. But this is a peculiar and unreliable assumption to make. It is crudely economistic; it is static; it is even politically unhelpful from a left perspective. Yet it is at the heart of the left's stock riposte to the counter-revolution.

The Stability of Class Rule

The relationship between politics and economics has been formulated in many different and inevitably controversial ways. But to assume that the form of a state derives directly from the prevailing mode of production seems to rule out much of the evident variety and autonomy of political regimes in developing countries. Is it sensible to try and explain the political careers of Ferdinand Marcos, Rajiv Gandhi, and Ayatollah Khomeini in terms of subtle differences in the underlying capitalist mode of production in the countries that they formerly ruled? However closely we were to study the economies of the Philippines, India, and Iran, would not such explanations of political developments there always seem narrow and mechanical? Intuitively, something less economistic and something more capable of capturing the mutual interaction between politics and economics seems to be required. But once the possibility of interdependence is admitted, the immutability of politically dominant classes is placed in doubt.

The standard left view is a static one. It assumes that current policies which minister to the vested interests of a rural or urban bourgeoisie are sustainable indefinitely. If there is any sense of dynamic, it is of a dynamic of continuous reinforcement, with accumulating wealth strengthening the bourgeoisie's grip on political power. But it was not lack of wealth that finally undermined the regimes of Jean-Claude Duvalier in Haiti and Ferdinand Marcos in the Philippines, nor did gold and diamonds in abundance save Emperor Bokassa, or priceless Persian carpets the Shah of Iran. Political legitimacy can be eroded by extravagance, luxury and corruption, as well as bolstered by them. External factors, as well as internal factors, can turn out to be crucial to the survival of regimes.

To cover the counter-examples mentioned, the standard view is sometimes qualified. The belief by some on the left in 'a special providence that guides the hand of statesmen, so that their actions inevitably coincide with the objective requirements of expanded reproduction' is seen by others for the absurdity that it is (Brewer 1980: 15). It is then admitted that the state will not necessarily succeed in its 'task' of preserving the existing social system: 'circumstances may overwhelm it, and the historic role of stupidity and error should not be underrated' (Brewer 1980: 15). Stupidity and error are defined here as actions that are irrational in relation to the imputed class objective.

This is still unsatisfactory because the nature of the overwhelming circumstances (which are presumably something other than the social revolution whose force the standard view acknowledges) are still unclear. More seriously, if we give rulers' stupidity and error a significant role in history, what is left of the theory with which we started out? Has it not become a tautology, according to which the state preserves the interests of the socially dominant class (and its own ability to continue to act in this way), except when it fails to do so – because of ill-defined circumstances, its own stupidity or error? Suddenly, the theory is no longer mechanical and narrow, it is vacuous instead. Either way, it is not well placed to neutralize the counter-revolutionary case on development policy.

The counter-revolution believes that, in the long run, certain types of current development policy are not sustainable. Even if developing country governments want to pursue the 'wrong' policies – overvaluation of the exchange rate, emphasis on heavy industrialization, an extensive public sector, neglect of incentives for agriculturalists and so on – they will eventually find themselves unable to do. Eventually, they say, reality will break in, the bad consequences of 'wrong' policies will make themselves felt and the party will be over. 'Wrong' policies are here defined as actions which are irrational because contrary to the assumed dictates of second-best welfare economics.

This is another economistic argument. It says that economic forces – investment, inflation, employment, the exchange rate and availability of adequate supplies of appropriate consumer goods – will ultimately determine the fate of political regimes, even though political manoeuvring can delay the arrival of that fate for a while. The doctrines that retribution for 'wrong' policies can be postponed but not escaped, and that postponement only makes retribution more severe in the end, both serve tactically to persuade developing country governments of the urgent need to adopt policies of structural adjustment. It is also, therefore, a self-fulfilling prophecy. If enough governments believe it, it is true.

From the perspective of the left, it serves to pose an important question, specially for those embracing an equally economistic view of politics. Are the dominant bourgeoisies living on borrowed time? Is the persistence in 'unsound' policy measures itself gradually removing their political under-pinnings? While it may be ideological to insist that this is happening (since to do so is speaking with certainty of an unpredictable future), the standard left view is also ideological, if it is arguing that all policies, however wrong-headed, are certainly sustainable without limit.

Ironically, this popular left view does not do much to support the kind of political action that is diagnosed as progressive. On the one hand, it attributes the exploitation and oppression of the poor to the domestic government and its social supporters. This attribution agrees exactly with that of the counter-revolution and must have the effect of making such governments more vulnerable to international interventions of various kinds 'in the interests of their own peoples'. International interventions are not notorious for favouring political and social revolutions. With a few exceptions (for example, India's intervention in East Pakistan in 1971), their aim is to restore the *status quo ante*. On the other hand, the frozen political economy of bourgeois vested interests depicts the domestic working classes and the peasantry merely as the passive victims of an all-powerful master class. Can such an analysis help to form an appropriate revolutionary psychology?

The standard left view may have the political advantage that it identifies clearly the oppressed and the oppressors, the method of oppression and social revolution as the remedy (Staniland 1985: 154). This helps to offset the two distinct political disadvantages just referred to. But, from the viewpoint of logical coherence and intellectual interest, that is, as a theory, rather than just as a political position, the inadequacies of the standard view should by now be obvious.

The State at a Political Structure

Perhaps its most serious theoretical inadequacy has been the failure to see that the political structure of the state is a significant independent influence on development performance. By 'the political structure' of the state is meant the specific organizational forms of the legislature, executive, judiciary, military (including paramilitary and police) and the state's ideological arms. The term also includes the specific links or articulations between the different types of state institution. Political structures not only differ between developing countries but different structures impose different constraints on policy. They are not unalterable, but they are relatively durable, so that alterations take time and involve risks.

Economic policy performance is mediated by the political structure. In particular, economic performance is influenced by how authoritarian the political structure allows the government to be. This has not been entirely ignored on the left. Before the counter-revolution gathered its strength, the link between development and a 'strong state' was appreciated, for example by Myrdal (1970: 227–42). But the strength of a state was seen by Myrdal as its ability to rely on social discipline or on the social tolerance of compulsion. The weakness or 'softness' of states in developing countries was thus interpreted as a problematic absence of the right cultural context for development planning. It was not focused on differences in political structure that permit a more or less authoritarian stance by governments in a given cultural context. So it was largely brushed aside as an expression of Myrdal's Nordic puritanism, a regrettable ethnocentricism embarrassingly close to Bauer's linking of development prospects to the cultural characteristics of ethnic groups.

The suggestion that there exists a trade-off between economic performance and the coercive capability of political structures is an uncomfortable one for the left, whether it be the liberal left or the Marxist left. The liberal left is committed to the belief that all good things, material and spiritual, go together all the time, while the Marxist left is nervous about believing anything which could be used to re-label it as Stalinist. Both lefts hold that the real problem is not the weakness of the state in poor countries, but the class-serving purposes to which its strength is put. To have to say that in the short and medium term (the time horizon with which policy-makers and planners are mostly engaged) there appears to be a choice between pressing ahead rapidly on the economic front and operating a relaxed and humane political arena is to present the left with the sort of dilemma which it is most reluctant publicly to acknowledge.

Imperialism: Interpretations of the 1980s

Until 1989, an unresolved conflict on the left continued between the standard formula on the state already discussed, which envisages a strong state, well entrenched socially within a dominant class, carrying out self-strengthening policies at the expense of neo-classical economic rationality, and a puppet state with multinational enterprise and developed country governments pulling most of the strings. Analyses based on 'class logic' stood side by side with analyses based on 'capital logic'. The latter provided the backbone for most theories of imperialism and neo-imperialism.

The capital logical approach takes a worldwide canvas, rather than focusing on the question of the political economy of a chosen developing country. It emphasizes worldwide economic linkages and the insight that the investment of capital in developed, fully capitalist countries acts as the 'motor' of an entire world system, with economic, political, social and cultural aspects. Thus the capital logic approach is also economistic in character: 'Radicals argue that economic factors either loom large in the foreground or are grey eminences in the background of almost all useful theories of imperialism' (Griffin and Gurley 1985: 1102).

The use of capital logic did nothing to undermine the cherished belief on the left that the state in developing countries was strong. After all, it was argued, if the domestic circumstances of the bourgeois state in developing countries should, for any reason, make it politically vulnerable, it could turn to its international bourgeois allies. They would be able to bolster it by economic and, if necessary, military assistance. They would be able to isolate diplomatically its political opponents and even destabilize them by economic and covert military pressures. Thus, although academic political sociologists were unhappy about the non-integration of the class logic and the capital logic approaches, they told the same story in the end; that embryonic or fragile political structures in developing countries are not significant, because their effects could always be compensated for through the mechanisms of neo-imperialism. The ending of the cold war has by now discredited this line of argument very effectively.

Warren on 'Pioneering Imperialism'

But, even as the counter-revolution in development theory gained ground, the capital logic approach to imperialism was in any case being blunted by reappraisals undertaken from within the left. By 1980, the retreat from earlier left positions on imperialism had gone so far that 'the most intrepid defence of . . . the post-war industrialisation effort in the Third World came . . . from an English socialist in the tradition of Marx's original position on the problem of backward areas' (Hirschman 1981: 19). Hirschman's reference was to Bill Warren's work on imperialism.[1] Warren's arguments mirror, in an extreme form, views that were widespread on the left of the spectrum of development opinion at the moment when the counter-revolution began to win its ideological victories.

It was indeed an extraordinary state of affairs. At the precise moment when the subtleties of a vigorous Marxist scholarship might have provided a bulwark against the beguiling simplicities of free-market ideology in the development field, the doctrine of 'progressive capitalism' was published with great acclaim. It is not in the least surprising that this doctrine was then taken as an illustration of 'the congruence of Marxism and other neo-classical doctrines' (Seers 1979a). Although the avowed intention of the doctrine of progressive capitalism was to draw in deeper measure on the inspiration of Marx, the result was a statement of views which, once the Marxist vocabulary had been stripped away, could easily be confused with panegyrics of capitalism from the extreme right of the political spectrum.

Warren's starting-point was to quarrel with Lenin. He saw imperialism not, as Lenin did, as the last throw of a decaying, moribund or parasitic capitalism. Rather, imperialism is the force in history which blazes the trail, or pioneers, for capitalism in the Third World. Imperialism creates conditions in which Third World capitalism will eventually blossom. Critics of imperialism who deny this 'actually reverse the views of the founders of Marxism, who held that the expansion of capitalism into pre-capitalist areas of the world was desirable and progressive' (Warren 1980: 3). Lenin's about-turn on imperialism was motivated by the wish to ally nationalist groups in colonies and semi-colonies with the working class in developed countries. But the maintenance of this reversal in the post-1945 world of colonial liberation places, according to Warren, the working class in developing countries in the political control of the nationalist middle class; teaches that capitalism is about to succumb from its internal economic weakness; and encourages episodes (like the cultural revolution in China or the rule of Pol Pot in Kampuchea) in which political groups attempt to achieve socialism regardless of their objective economic and social circumstances.

These unfortunate effects were attributed to the great strength of nationalism in the post-colonial world. Latin American formulations on the development of underdevelopment and dependent development were stigmatized as the 'mythology' produced by, and reinforcing, Third World nationalism. Dishonourable mention was also given by Warren, as by Bauer, to the radicalized intelligentsia of the developed countries who have propagated these myths of nationalism. He claims that they mistook the second-generation problems of economic development – underemployment, hyperurbanization and land scarcity – as evidence of global polarization rather than of successful public health policies of the previous generation.

Such a crisp and comprehensive contribution came as a gust of fresh air to the debates on development prospects and policies that had engaged the radicalized intelligentsia of the West in the late 1960s and early 1970s. The archetypal Western radicalized intellectual, who at that time dominated development thinking was Andre Gunder Frank, the orthodox Chicago economist who abruptly became a Latin American revolutionary figure (compare Frank 1958 and 1972). Much of what Warren says is instantly understandable if read as a vigorous rebuttal of theses associated with Frank. In particular, the denial of the thesis of global economic polarization is designed to undermine the idea that the development of the West was only possible because of a concomitant process of 'underdeveloping' other, peripheral parts of the world, an idea which had gained wide popular currency at that time. The stress on the benefits of colonialism, combined with arguments that colonialism did not force its subject territories to specialize in primary products in the international division of labour, was aimed at discrediting the uncompromisingly anti-imperialist stance which Frank and his associates had adopted. In these circumstances, Warren finds himself developing certain themes in common with the coming development counter-revolution. He also relies on the authority of the same arguments as Bauer and Little, which have already been discussed in chapters 3 and 4 (compare Warren 1980: 177–8, 183–4, 191, 217, 225).

The Devaluation of Latin America's Contribution

Warren was not aware that his own theory of imperialism was first formulated in Peru in the early 1920s; and that the development debate in Latin America is not exactly the same as the one in which he was participating in the UK and North America. Less than a decade after Lenin's *Imperialism: The Highest Stage of Capitalism* was published, and while the Bolshevik revolution in Russia was still a recent event, the Peruvian writer Haya de la Torre considered the implications of Lenin's analysis for Latin America. He noted that, as far as Latin America was concerned, imperialism did not appear as the last stage of capitalism, but rather as the first experience of capitalism – or the pioneer of capitalism, in Warren's phrase. Consequently, the working class was weak and submerged and quite unable to play a leading role in an anti-capitalist struggle. From this, he concluded that opposition to capitalism in Latin America would have to be conducted under an anti-imperialist banner, drawing on the political force of the middle class and the intelligentsia. An alliance of anti-imperialist Latin American states would be in a position to set the terms for the entry of capital, to facilitate good and necessary inflows and to exclude unnecessary and dangerous inflows (Hirschman 1971: 277–8).

Haya is remarkable not only because he anticipated the substance of Warren's quarrel with Lenin. He is remarkable also because he used that insight to forecast two of the features of developing countries whose existence Warren is at pains to prove – the mass of anti-imperialist writing on the one hand and the growth of Third World control over foreign stocks and flows of capital on the other (Warren 1980: 2–3, 171–5). But unlike Haya, Warren does not manage to connect the two as cause and effect. He believes that increased economic independence in developing countries is simply an illustration of the progressiveness of capitalism and that anti-imperialist views are dogmatic and superficial propaganda obstinately refusing, despite the authority of Marx, to acknowledge this progressiveness.

In the course of the recantations on the left in the 1970s, something else was lost besides the Latin American origin of the view that imperialism pioneers capitalism. The search for Marxist purity, in pursuit of which these recantations were conducted, seriously undervalued the structuralist economics of the UN Economic Commission for Latin America, better known by its English acronym ECLA, or its Spanish acronym CEPAL. It also seriously undervalued the political sociology of F. H. Cardoso, which, even if it remains theoretically questionable, represented a valuable antidote to the prevailing sterility of left political economy.

If indeed imperialism is the pioneer of capitalism, the middle class in Latin American society would have to face the ambiguous responsibility of mediating the impact of foreign capital on that society. How would it mediate? Would it be biased in favour or against foreign capital? Would it support the lower strata against capitalist exploitation, or would it betray them in order to secure its own interests? On the one hand, the economistic approach of ECLA did not, except in the odd publication on social development, bear on this question. On the other, Frank's version of dependency simply denounced the betrayal by the lumpenbourgeoisie of national and proletarian interests and the imposition under neo-colonialist pressures of policies of lumpen development. But writers like Cardoso and Faletto rejected Frank's approach as vulgar and mechanical, placing their emphasis on the need to examine social and political struggles over the forms of external linkage in their historical concreteness (Cardoso and Faletto 1979: 13–21; Cardoso 1984: 117–25).

This more sophisticated discussion of dependency thinking rejected the idea that the whole discourse could be abstracted from, and formalized as a theory. The rejection was re-emphasized by the claim that dependency constituted not a theory but a framework for analysing situations of dependency (Palma 1978). The analysis was to consist of historical studies displaying the links between economic policy, ideology, politics and class position in a variety of real cases, in the minor Marxist tradition of the *Eighteenth Brumaire*. Instead of resting satisfied with Frank's denunciation of middle-class betrayal, Cardoso wants to use concrete historical analysis to identify specifically those classes and groups which strive to maintain dependency; to anticipate the emergence of new forms which dependency might take and, ultimately, to inspire social movements that will implement realistic alternatives which the analysis has identified. That Cardoso and Faletto cannot always carry through successfully their research and action programme is true and to say so is fair comment (Staniland 1985: 132–40).[1] Simply to ignore the programme and its partial success, as Warren did, was misleading as well as culturally insensitive.

In several ways, the reformist strand of dependency theory, represented by Cardoso and Faletto, was the most fruitful enterprise by political economists of the left prior to the counter-revolution in development thinking. They never lost sight of the conflictual nature of development, arising from the fact that late developers have to develop within a pre-existing global nexus of economic and political power. At the same time, they did not claim that all the possibilities for national development are determined by external factors. The development experiences of countries varied, depending on the balance between domestic and foreign capital in the structure of production, and in civil society and politics. Their approach was, therefore, neither crudely deterministic nor economistic (in principle). It also avoided a rigid pessimism about the prospects for development. Unlike Frank, they did not tell a despairing story of an ideal national development that could be unblocked only by a comprehensive social revolution. Certain forms of productive development were possible, albeit with costs to the coherence of civil society. Authoritarian rule (such as the military dictatorships in Latin America from the 1960s to the 1980s) was, however, seen as problematic. In this they differed, both from economists who viewed political arrangements as neutral in impact and therefore irrelevant to development, and from those counter-revolutionaries who were later to beg for authoritarian rule as positively essential for development. They analysed the costs of authoritarianism in terms of the increasing marginalization of vulnerable social groups, defined both economically and ethnically.

From the perspective of the 1990s, all of these features make the Cardoso–Faletto approach an attractive one. In particular, it foreshadows the current willingness to look at the relations between internal and external influences on development without strong prior belief in the determining character of one or the other. It also prefigures contemporary understanding of the need to see economic policy issues in their broad social and political context, rather than as simple technical issues with standard solutions. The genuine commitment to poverty alleviation and a more democratic polity strongly resonates with the more consensual development policy which international institutions like the World Bank have tried to foster from the late 1980s onwards. For all of these reasons, the associated-dependent approach to development still commands attention and some admiration.

That admiration does not imply an inability to see its intellectual flaws. Perhaps the most glaring is the tendency to treat historical interpretation as unproblematic. Economic history is presented as a given, whose conclusions are obvious, not as a set of hypotheses, always provisional and needing constant revision. Another manifest difficulty is the failure to integrate convincingly economic and political explanations. While politics are allowed to make a real difference in history, certain economic structures are assumed to remain quite impervious to politics. Precisely why and how this can be so is not properly resolved. The theorizing of the approach remains at an early stage, its open-mindedness sometimes remaining too open, and sometimes too arbitrarily closed off. Indeed, opting to describe the enterprise as an approach or a framework for analysis, rather than a theory, may have been a mistake, if that implied that an analytical framework does not itself have to possess its own underlying theoretical coherence.

Those seeking a full and balanced evaluation of the Latin American contribution to development theory can now find it in the work of Kay (1989). Apart from rejecting Frank's underdevelopment theses and his revolutionary romanticism, Kay stresses the need to theorize class and civil society more adequately, and to test a new theoretic with empirical micro-studies. In particular, old views of the role of the state in development need to be redefined. Kay detects in both structuralists and dependency writers a tendency to idealize the state and its potential to deliver development, either as national industrialization or as socialism in the Cuban style. The political economy of the left should, he suggests, become much more aware of the limits to state action in overcoming the basic situation of dependency in the world economic system (ibid: 206–8). But this new circumspection does not extend to abandoning either the project of national development, or government intervention (of a selective and intelligent kind) in attempting to advance that project. Kay's re-evaluation is manifestly much less radical in scope than the doctrine of progressive capitalism, which in the guise of true Marxism, attacked economic nationalism, state-promoted development and the fundamental idea of development as a conflictual process.

It is interesting to take a brief look now at the idea of progressive capitalism as an example of 1970s neo-Marxism. The point in doing so is not to dispute whether this idea or some other is the *real* true Marxism. Rather, it is to understand how it was possible to construct a version of Marxism which entirely lacked any notion of contradiction, opposition, conflict or antagonism in the development of social formations, and which instead presented a harmonious history of capitalism as an instrument of social and economic advance. In concentrating on one author of this doctrine, Warren, we see it in an extreme, even an absurd, form. But its significance was much wider than one person's view. Rather it was part of a more general transition, which saw both Marxists embracing capitalism and the counter-revolution taking over a quasi-Marxist critique of the state.

Progressive Capitalism: Marxism as Liberal Optimism

The doctrine of progressive capitalism, which Warren was advancing as the counter-revolution arrived, is that the expansion of capitalism into pre-capitalist areas of the world [is] desirable and progressive' (Warren 1980: 3, 25). This doctrine was presented as being 'the traditional (or classic) view of Marxism'. Whether this claim to Marxist authenticity is justifiable is a matter of opinion.[2] Without a long disgression into Marxist scholarship, the weight of the claim cannot be properly assessed. Suffice it to state here that the doctrine dramatically lacks one key characteristic of Marx's own thought, namely, its dialectical quality. Few would deny that Marx's view of history was explicitly dialectical. That is to say, history was seen as a process embodying antagonistic contradictions, which progressively increase in intensity until a postulated future final transcendence – the social revolution which will destroy the capitalist mode of production.

This view in general proposes that human development progresses between one historical epoch (and one mode of production and exploitation) and another, later epoch (and another superior mode). (Even this statement needs some qualification, in the light of Marx's comments on the superiority of ancient classical culture.) This, however, does not commit him to the view that progress takes place *within* a given historical epoch, such as capitalism. Many of his analyses suggest that culture, morality, politics and scholarship had retrogressed during the capitalist period. Although Warren dismisses such analyses as 'mere propaganda' by Marx, they cannot be treated in this cavalier fashion without destroying the dialectical character of Marxism. Progress between epochs plus progress within epochs equals just another simple history of progress. The dialectic of history disappears. Intellectually, we are back with the post-revolutionary liberal optimism of de Condorcet (1955: 175–9; compare Bury 1955: 207).[3]

Marx's own thought synthesized three themes. The romantic theme was a conservative criticism of capitalist society for its destruction of individual freedom and organic communities. The Promethean theme celebrates man's unlimited powers for collective self-creation, particularly as embodied in the industrial proletariat. The theme of Enlightenment rationalism provides a 'scientific' theory of the developing crisis of capitalism, turning on the dynamics of capitalist competition and the tendency of the rate of profit to fall (Kolakowski 1978: I, 408–16).

Unfortunately for the doctrine of progressive capitalism, Marx was absorbed into late-nineteenth-century Marxism primarily as the rationalist economist who had uncovered new laws of motion of society. As Marxism became codified at the time of the Second International, it was as a 'scientific' analysis of economic history and of the mechanics of intensifying economic crises, leading to the final collapse of the capitalist system. In this version of Marxism, the crises and collapses of capitalism cannot be seen as mere complexity or superficial unevenness in the working-out of man's unlimited powers of self-creation. They become the pith and substance of the doctrine, the premises upon which alternative political strategies have to be debated.

However, to restore some of the richness to Marx's concept of human progress is not thereby to endorse it. In particular, whether Marx's account of the transcendence of capitalism is consistent with the political aspiration of the contemporary poor in the Third World is a large question which those on the left do not seem to think requires much discussion. Marx's reference to 'a great social revolution' describes it as mastering 'the results of the bourgeois epoch, the market of the world and the modern powers of production', and as subjecting them 'to the common control of the *most advanced* peoples' (Marx 1973c: 324–5). The implication that the apotheosis of human development would leave the world market and all the forces of production in the control of the most advanced peoples does surely raise the question of the position of the least advanced people after a great social revolution. How liberated would they be?

Marx's politics were internationalist, a fact which is rightly emphasized by Warren. Notwithstanding the powerful element of romantic conservatism in his thought, Marx was never a nationalist.[4] The social revolution to which he looked forward was not a nationalist or anti-colonial one. He was sufficiently of his own time to make unquestioning assumptions about the cultural superiority of Europeans and their duty of stewardship on behalf of less advanced peoples. Ethnocentrism and paternalism permeated Marx's thinking. When these assumptions are put alongside the doctrine of 'progressive capitalism', one is constructing a 'Marxism' that the development counter-revolution might itself find half acceptable.

The current dominance of the 'new right' in the field of development policy rests partly, as was argued in chapters 3 and 4, on its willingness to over-simplify complex issues of welfare theory and governmental practice. But it also rests, to a greater extent than has yet been generally recognized, on important intellectual failures in the competing tradition of Marxian political economy. The list of its failures includes taking positions which explicitly or implicitly concede agreement to errors, and the neglect of intellectual resources which the counter-revolution in development thinking is itself unwilling to tap.

In the 1970s, the Marxian political economy writers frequently failed in both of those senses. Admittedly, they were trying to solve problems accumulated from the 1960s when the tradition had absorbed wholesale draughts of strident nationalism and populism, exemplified by Frank's 'development of underdevelopment' theses. But the solutions arrived at as a result of this internal dialogue turned out to be a poor defence against the external onslaught of the development counter-revolution.

The attempt to give underdevelopment theory a more substantial grounding in a class analysis of the state in developing countries produced only a static, economistic view of the state, in the main. The standard left formula of the bourgeois state concedes that the development policies of the counter-revolution are correct, but denies that they will be implemented. This denial itself assumes that the dynamics of the bourgeois state are self-stabilizing, which is empirically doubtful.

Rejection of the wilder and more strident nationalism of underdevelopment theory was necessary, no doubt. But rejected too were valuable contributions to development policy made by the Latin American structuralists and to action-oriented political analysis made by Latin American political sociologists. Just when the world economic recession was proving very dramatically the disadvantages of being part of a structurally dependent country, previous first-hand attempts to explain those disadvantages were being devalued, by development economists on the left.

The Political Economy of the New Right

Up to the middle 1970s, commentators of the new right concentrated their efforts on analysing errors in government economic policies and on advocating 'settled conclusions' derived from welfare economics which would eliminate these errors of policy. The essence of their project was a rationalistic explication of economic 'truth', as that truth was perceived by enthusiasts for the unconstrained (or hardly constrained) operation of market forces. That erroneous policies had identifiable beneficiaries emerged clearly enough, and that these beneficiaries therefore had an obvious interest in the continuation of the policy mistakes which benefited them. But these insights did not yet occupy a central place. The policy prescriptions were addressed to governments, on the assumption that governments could, and eventually would, wake up to their mistakes and do better.

At the heart of this approach lay an important contradiction, which emerged in the discussion of the usefulness of social cost–benefit analysis (SCBA). SCBA was a method of rational analysis of investment choices, which ideally could be used to select investments which maximized economic (and in one variant, social) benefits from a given resource budget. It proceeded by estimating shadow prices, representing true resource scarcities, and used these for investment calculations, rather than the actual prices, which had been distorted by policy errors. Critics were quick to ask the following question. Under what circumstances would a government which had adopted policies that distorted actual prices be willing to insist on shadow prices being used for its investment choices? A number of possible answers suggested themselves. The government might be 'schizophrenic', unable to co-ordinate the different branches of economic policy. Or it might be economically rational, wanting to remove price distortions, but weak in its capacity to push forward rapidly with such a reform. A third answer was that the government had no real intention of reforming price distortions, and used shadow pricing methods only to give a spurious scientific validity to investment choices that were, in fact, made on quite different grounds from rational economic calculation.

This third answer drew the debate on to new ground. Interpretations involving state schizophrenia, or well-intentioned feebleness, retained the underlying assumption of a benevolent government, willing – though hardly able – to accept the economist's rational advice for change. The third answer breaks with this view, and posits a government with its own non-economic agenda, willing to manipulate economic advice in furtherance of quite different ends. As we have already seen, the political economy of the left had already seized on this answer, and described the non-economic agenda as one of class-based power: the state, it held, formed its policies to support, reinforce, and promote the strength of the dominant class or classes. But instead of rejecting this description completely and comprehensively, the new right, while rejecting much of it, finally came to accept one very significant part. The class analysis was set aside unceremoniously: whatever was exercising power, it was not a social class. The beneficiaries of economic distortions might be a set of interest groups, but these groups did not overlap or coalesce to form any greater social entity – all that was cloudy nineteenth-century sociology. In addition, the sociological method of analysis was itself rejected. Here one is inevitably reminded of Margaret Thatcher's dictum that 'there is no such thing as society'. The individual has to be the bedrock of all analysis, and individuals must be taken as they are found, their tastes and preferences and their inherent capabilities already given. This is the doctrine of methodological individualism. It follows from this that interest groups themselves have to be derived from the interests and behaviour of the individuals which compose them.

The significant element of the left view of the state which was finally absorbed by the right was the idea that the state was not benevolent, but malevolent. The good faith of the state in seeking the welfare of the society which it governed could no longer be accepted. That something was rotten in the state of developing countries, an uncontroversial proposition, was transformed into the belief that *everything* was rotten in these states. The task of the new right in the 1980s was to construct a political economy to substantiate that belief using the methods of microeconomic analysis instead of the old Marxist generalities about classes. Thus some exponents of the neo-liberal economic philosophy of the 1980s set to work as creators of a whole new social scientific paradigm based on the application of the methods of economics to the study of politics in developing countries. This new political economy of development (henceforth NPE) used the assumptions of neo-classical microeconomics – methodological individualism, rational utility maximization and the comparative statics method of equilibrium analysis – to explain the failure of governments to adopt the 'right', i.e. neo-liberal, economic policies for growth and development. In this way, neo-liberalism constructed not merely 'a body of settled conclusions immediately applicable to policy', but also, in the form of the new political economy, an account of *why* its own prescriptions had, over forty years of the practice of development, found so little political favour. At their most ambitious, the neo-liberals attempted the unification of economics and politics – both in normative and in positive modes under the banner of rational choice theory.

Although a vast and quite variegated literature has accumulated which might be packaged with the label of 'the new political economy', no attempt is made here at a comprehensive survey. However, the reader will need to know some of the examples of the NPE literature which are taken as especially representative of the genre. Its flavour is well conveyed by both Buchanan, Tollison and Tullock (1980) and Collander (1984). Surveys of results from the work in the NPE vein can be found in Bhagwati (1982) and Srinivasan (1985). The relevance of the NPE to developing countries is asserted enthusiastically by Findlay (1989); its limitations in this regard are stressed by Meier (1989).

The NPE is characterized first of all by a profoundly cynical view of the state in developing countries. To say, as exponents of the NPE do, that people in political positions are typically motivated *only* by individual self-interest is, and should be, shocking. It is shocking because it denies and disparages all the norms and values of political life no less dramatically than those ancient philosophers who pretended they were dogs in order to demonstrate their scorn for the ideals of the Greek polis. However one defines the public interest, and however much scope one grants to the protection of private interests as part of the definition of the public interest, the unbridled pursuit of self-interest by rulers belongs to the pathology of politics – to tyranny or dictatorship or, ultimately, to anarchy.[5] To attribute individual self-interest as their exclusive motive to politicians in developing countries is to deny their sincerity, their merit and, ultimately, their legitimate right to govern. While this is appropriate criticism for particular rulers or regimes, in the developing no less than in the developed areas of the world, as a general characterization of the state in developing countries, it is breathtaking in its scope and pretension. The NPE is not merely saying unflattering things about Third World politicians – that they are misguided, myopic, or cowardly. Its claims are much more extreme: that their unbridled egoism makes them constitutionally unfit for any political role whatsoever.

Why so extreme? The NPE contrasts its negative view of the state with the assumption of the benign or benevolent state which underpinned the early literature on development planning and, (as argued here) the 1970s debate on SCBA. That assumption has at times proved obviously misleading and unrealistic, especially when used in combination with another assumption frequently implicit in those discussions of planning – that the state was also omni-competent, i.e. it had access to all the information and policy instruments that it needed to achieve its objectives, whether benign or otherwise. But it would have seemed wiser for the neo-liberals to challenge the myth of the omni-competent state in developing countries, rather than the myth of the benevolent state. Given that the prescriptions of neo-liberalism are represented as the true embodiment of the public interest of developing countries, it would have been more logical to doubt politicians' competence, while suspending disbelief in their good intentions. Then at least one would not have produced a theory where prescription and description are so seriously at odds as they are in the NPE, where the body of settled policy conclusions is so readily (too readily, in truth) to hand, while the political process is damned as incapable of serving *any* conception of the public interest.

The political hypotheses of the NPE are too cynical, too extreme, and it is this extremism (the reason for which we will speculate on later) which creates the second major feature of the NPE, its pessimism. For the major prediction of the new political economy in its positive mode must be that significant changes towards the 'right' neo-liberal policies will not, or will hardly ever, take place. Where the interests of rulers and ruled conflict, personally self-interested politicians will not make arrangements which secure the legitimate interests of citizens. In the absence of a natural harmony of interests, rulers serve themselves better by using their power to exploit others, and political arrangements which limit rulers' pursuit of self interest are the only constraint on this exploitation. If such arrangements do not exist or have been subverted – which is the scenario in developing countries, according to the NPE – then the adoption of 'good' policies becomes an impossible dream. An inherent inability to implement policies that are taken to be obviously socially desirable amounts to more than just gloom about the prospects for reform. It is much more deterministic and much more pessimistic than this, as has been recognized by Grindle (1989: 31–2), who states that:

> while the new political economy provides tools for understanding bad situations and for recommending policies that will engender better situations, it provides no logically apparent means of moving from bad to better ... Locked into an ahistorical explanation of why things are the way they are and the notion that existing situations demonstrate an inevitable rationality, it is hard to envision how changes in such situations occur.

In an interdependent world with an unequal distribution of political power, it is only to be expected that some of the dynamics of policy changes in poor, developing countries will be international in character. But the NPE typically pays much less attention to international influences on public policy in LDCs than to national influences. Its frame of reference for analysis is the individual developing country. This is either analysed as a unitary entity, as in theories of 'the predatory state' (or 'the Leviathan state') which has its own rational self-interest; or as an arena in which outcomes result from the pursuit of rational self-interest by individual LDC politicians, bureaucrats and other actors. In the best examples of the NPE, for example Repetto's analysis of irrigation projects (see Moore 1991), other actors do include international influences like multinational construction companies and international aid agencies. But this is not usually the case. The international actors are kept typically beyond the framework of analysis. Ironically, in view of the new right's heavy emphasis on international trade and investment, the NPE usually takes a very 'closed economy' approach to policy-making in developing countries. This in turn renders it particularly defective for illuminating actual policy changes in the 1980s, when the demands of foreign creditors and internationally sponsored structural adjustment programmes were responsible for so much of the policy change that did – NPE pessimism to the contrary notwithstanding – occur in developing countries.

The Economic Analysis of Politics: a Flexible Friend

Why are a profoundly cynical view of Third World states, a rigid pessimism about the prospects for reform and a country-focused analytical framework such prominent features of the NPE? The answer to this riddle, it will be argued here, is to be found not in the intellectual sphere, but in the realm of rhetoric. The NPE is an economic theory of politics, and uses the assumptions of neo-classical microeconomics. But nothing in those assumptions, or in the economic theory of politics as such, requires or determines the three major features of the NPE that have been identified. In the transposition of the economic theory of politics from its earlier reference to developed countries (and particularly, the United States) to its present reference, via the NPE, to developing countries, a number of significant component parts have been removed and replaced with something significant component parts have been removed and replaced with something different. Such flexibility of the content of the economic theory of politics emphasizes that neo-classical microeconomics is not so much a doctrine as a method. It is a particular brand of logic, within which a great variety of different models of reality can be constructed, but not *any* model of reality. It is even more like a set of Lego than the 'tool-kit' with which it is usually compared. It is worth noting just how flexible the economic theory of politics has been over the years, in order to avoid the mistaken view that the conclusions of the NPE can simply be read off from its neo-classical starting points. Three examples are discussed here, concerning the nature of interest-group pressures in the political process, the origin of social rigidities and the optimal size of the government sector.

Originally, the pressures of interest groups in the political process were evaluated positively: they were a good thing. Interest group pressures were interpreted as equivalent to a competitive process in the political arena. The political need to achieve a broad consensus for the government's programme of measures ensured that extreme demands would be moderated by compromises, while the reasonable expectations of minorities would be respected in the process of coalition-building. The political competition of interest groups thus served not only to protect, but actually to construct the public interest. In the NPE, all this has changed. Interest-group competition has become *destructive* of the public interest (identified with liberalization policies) and symptomatic of a political fragmentation which occurs when politicians and administrators (illegitimately) as well as ordinary citizens (legitimately) pursue their individual self-interest (Grindle 1989: 13).

An even more dramatic change has occurred on the question of the origin of social rigidities, because here the shift of emphasis occurs between the earlier and later works of the same author – Mancur Olson. In the revised edition of his path-breaking *The Logic of Collective Action*, Olson summarizes its key finding as follows: 'even if all of the individuals in a large groups are rational and self-interested, and would gain if, as a group, they acted to achieve their common interest or objective, they will still not voluntarily act to achieve that common or group interest' (1971: 2).

This finding, that paradoxically rational individuals will not organise themselves to achieve their common interests, is then used as a critique of writers in the pluralist tradition who assumed not only that interest group pressures were benign, but that they would indeed manifest themselves. It was not the benign nature of interest group pressure which Olson questioned in 1971, but the logical inconsistency of assuming that self-interested individuals will voluntarily sacrifice in order to promote group aims (ibid.: 126). But a decade later, the story line has been completely reversed. In *The Rise and Decline of Nations* (Olson 1982), notwithstanding the difficulties of group collective organization, such groups are argued, not only to exist, but also to 'reduce efficiency and aggregate income in the societies in which they operate and make political life more divisive' (1982: 47). Interest groups' activity is then used to explain the relatively slow growth performance of Britain, India, China and the South African apartheid system. Not only have interest groups changed from being unproblematic to being the critical source of socioeconomic ills, but the logical flaw which Olson originally spotted in interest group theory has dropped progressively out of sight.

A third example of the changing content of the economic theory of politics concerns the role of government. Anthony Downs, the pioneer of the economic theory of politics, used the theory to argue that the government sector would be inevitably *under*-extended (1960: 341–63). His argument turned on the cost to citizens of acquiring information about remote dangers which could, if they occurred, cause massive damage, and which the government could potentially prevent. His example was the possible threat from improved Soviet space capability. Today, environmental problems, such as CO_2 emissions and global warming would be a much clearer illustration. However, by the 1980s, the NPE is concerned exclusively with the *over-extension* of government. The argument used is the power of interest groups to vote themselves increases in public expenditure while diffusing the resultant costs through rises in general taxation.

The purpose of indicating these three major *voltes-face* in the content of the economic theory of politics is not to pass an opinion on whether the early version is better than the later one, or vice versa. Two points are relevant to our argument about the NPE. One is well put by Hindess (1988: 20–1), who remarks 'how radically different conclusions can be generated from the same set of abstract principles' as a result of different and essentially arbitrary assumptions about the conditions in which they are supposed to apply. The other is that all three changes are consistent with each other. They together represent a dramatic shift away from a pluralist, participatory ideal of politics and towards an authoritarian and technocratic ideal based, not on big government, but on small and highly efficient government. In the longer perspective, they signal the return in the 1980s to dominance of the non-participatory strand of Western liberal political theory (Hexter 1979: 293–303).[6] One can argue that the neo-liberal economists of politics are absorbed in the technical ingenuity of their models, so that their work merely reflects the larger shift in the political mood that occurred in the 1980s. They may not have been aware how conveniently their new conclusions suited it; and there is certainly no evidence that they deliberately altered them to gain political favour with the new right. But it is not necessary to claim this. All that is necessary is to make the negative point that there is nothing about the practice of the economics of politics which inevitably generates the cynicism, pessimism and contracted domestic focus of the NPE.

Nor, when one comes right down to it, is there anything about the theory of rent-seeking which drives one inevitably towards these features of the NPE. The original analysis of government economic controls did not provide a new political economy. Its author, Anne Krueger, explicitly declined to draw any political conclusions from her discussion of rent-seeking (1974: 302). Its significance in the doctrines of neo-liberalism was economic, not political. It was aimed at showing that trade controls are much more costly in terms of economic welfare than they had previously been taken to be. Empirical estimates of the size of the loss inflicted by the use of trade restrictions have, over the years, normally been small. Typically, the gain in efficiency to be derived by the removal of trade controls has been estimated to be around 3–5 per cent of GNP – an amount equivalent to one year of growth in the case of many developing countries. If governments of LDCs believed that trade controls could be used to improve their growth rate in the medium and long term, they might well be willing to trade off static efficiency losses of this kind of size against their expected increase in long-run growth. Trade liberalization as a policy was handicapped because its pay-off was stated, even by its own advocates, to be relatively small. Krueger's rent-seeking theory was an attempt to address this problem, in the belief that the true economic costs of protection must be higher than had previously been calculated.

Krueger identified an additional source of static welfare loss from protection, namely the resources which are used up by economic agents in competing for an allocation of administratively allocated import licences. Such resources produce nothing and, at the limit, could equal in size the economic rents which the licensing regime creates. Thus the *potential* costs of using quantitative restrictions on imports were shown to be much greater than had previously been considered. This was a fundamental neo-liberal insight and it has not been gainsaid. But its implications for political economy remain to be fully assessed. They are not at all as straightforward a confirmation of the tenets of the NPE as it might appear at first blush.

The additional welfare losses arising from a QR regime result from an unproductive, but resource-consuming, competitive scramble for import licences that bring windfall gains to those who acquire them. For these additional losses to be realized in practice requires such a process to exist. But does it exist? It does not exist when the competitive scramble which we actually observe in developing countries is conducted by those who would be otherwise unemployed; clerks who fill in forms, leg-men who stand in queues at government offices are consuming largely their own time and effort, and it is often sadly true in developing economies that these do not have any alternative productive use, and therefore no economic value. But more importantly for the NPE, a competitive rent-seeking process does not exist when licences are al-located by a process of pure patronage of the sort which self-interested political leaders use to reward their cronies. When a military ruler instructs officials of the Foreign Trade Ministry to issue import licences to his chief henchmen and lieutenants, there is *no* competitive process and *no* resource cost involved. This point is usually overlooked. In neo-liberal discussions of 'the politicization of economic life', the scramble for spoils and patronage are lumped together as if they were slightly different aspects of essentially the same phenomenon, whereas for the purpose of gauging the real significance of rent-seeking theory they have diametrically *opposite* implications.

The cynical view of Third World states, that self-interested state rulers, lacking much in the way of institutional constraints, maximize their own welfare at the public's expense fits most easily with the scenario of patronage, rather than with that of the competitive scramble for spoils. The competitive scramble theory assumes that rulers are indif-ferent about the identities of the winners of the spoils. If this were true, it would be difficult to explain why the authorities would continue to oppose an auction of import quotas. An auction, after all, captures the rents of the import licences for the ruler's own treasury, while eliminat-ing their dissipation on unproductive activities. Its crucial disadvantage, from the self-interested politician's viewpoint, is that it also abolishes clandestine political control over the distribution of unearned benefits. And, on that criterion, the competitive scramble is no different from an auction.

It is difficult to argue, in the light of these considerations that it is the logic of the theory of rent-seeking that has produced the characteristic features of the NPE. The theory of rent-seeking has no specific theory of political economy built into it, and, to the extent that it is based on the idea of impersonal competition for rents, stands at some distance from the cynical account of Third World rulers' behaviour which the new political economy offers. (It also has some surprising implications for standard neo-liberal prescriptions of trade policy – concerning the policy ranking of QRs, tariffs and domestic subsidies – but these would take us too far from our present theme to explore here.)

The NPE and the Uses of Rhetoric

An important hiatus thus exists between the neo-classical roots of the NPE (whether in the economic theories of politics which existed before 1980 or in the original theory of the rent-seeking society) and the actual form and content which characterizes the NPE of the 1980s. To elucidate the NPE solely in terms of its genealogy in economic science would be inadequate and confusing. The rhetorical uses of economic theory must also be brought in to any explanation of why the NPE is as it is. Economic theorizing always taken place within a specific changing historical context. Our assumption here is that two-way interaction can take place between economic theories and their changing context. Larger-scale change in the political mood, such as occurred in the 1980s, can affect what is theorized and the substance of the conclusions of theory. Influence can also flow in the reverse direction, as theorists deliberately seek to alter the stances of public policy-makers. If these assumptions are valid, one should not expect to be able to confine the intellectual history of the NPE just to its lineage in logic: there may well be strange logical leaps of the kind which have been noted above. We need to turn elsewhere to investigate why one kind of intellectual tool is produced from the tool-kit at one moment, and another kind of tool at another time, or why the same tools produce opposite policy conclusions in succeeding periods.

It may be worth emphasizing a corollary of the assumption of two-way interaction between theorizing and its historical context. It is that the economic theory of politics (of which the NPE is an off-shoot) itself rests on too narrow foundations. 'To take account of the role of ideas (influencing, and being influenced by, public policy) must require, at the very least, a more complex model of the individual actor than Downs and the public choice school appear to offer' (Hindess 1988: 22). Although this chapter does not offer a detailed critique of the internal logic of the NPE, this is one major point which such a critique would have to include.[7]

But leaving that aside, what was the historical context of the emergence of the NPE, and what were the extra-scientific factors that shaped its development? These are large questions, and what follows is the merest sketch. Let us start from one further puzzle of the 'new political economy': its title. Why does the NPE refer to itself as 'new'? The standard answer to this is that it is new because it rejects the naivety of the development economists and others who in the 1950s and 1960s believed that the state was an agency that promoted social welfare – the assumption of the benevolent or do-gooding state. But this is to respond to one naivety with another. To suggest that all that was needed to give birth to the NPE was a process of gradual disillusion with the benevolence of the state in developing countries has the same simple-minded quality as the benevolent state assumption has itself.

One could put another case. It is that rather few development economists forty years ago actually believed that the state in developing countries was concerned unreservedly to maximize social welfare. Quite a lot of economic work is technical and requires no particular view of the state. The assumption of the benevolent state, when it appeared without qualification, was usually more a matter either of pure diplomacy or of 'reformist hope'. It is vital to recall that the development economists of that time were largely foreigners to the developing countries, where they operated with either explicit or implicit sponsorship of their home governments. They wanted to assist their adopted country in their capacity as professional 'improvers', but not to get entangled with local politics. As professional economists seeking to promote reforms, they assumed the existence of certain institutions and attitudes, as it were trying to coax them into life while aware that they were often not in fact there. *Saying* that they were not there in public would, however, have been easily interpreted as a political act. The benevolent state assumption in developing countries was thus a convenient myth for those in a false position, not their firm belief. Many felt morally uncomfortable in their inability to explore openly the reasons for their professional frustration, but most of these loyally respected the diplomatic imperative.

What the orthodox could not acknowledge publicly in the 1950s and 1960s surfaced as dissent. Specifically, it appeared in the neo-Marxist political economy of development. In the work of Paul Baran (1957; 1973), this combined a cynical view of the state in developing countries with strong and critical emphasis on the role of foreign capital in frustrating rational development. Gradually this tradition bifurcated, with some neo-Marxists retaining the stress on the determining pressure of foreign capital ('capital logic') and others locating the source of distorting pressures in the domestic class system above all ('class logic'). The class logic version of the Marxian political economy of development is morphologically almost identical with that version of the NPE which concentrates on the problematic role of interest groups. Both have political processes which guarantee economically irrational outcomes. The only important substantive difference is that the former attributes the pressures for economic irrationality to an exploitative class, while the latter attributes it to the activities of self-interested groups. And both, of course, keep out of sight the international pressures which a capitalist system generates on developing countries. It is thus highly misleading to ignore the influence that neo-Marxism exerted on the NPE. The success of neo-Marxism in discrediting the assumption of the benevolent state paved the way down which the new right moved triumphantly in the 1980s. The NPE is new specifically in succession to the 'old' political economy of neo-Marxism.

The decisive events in ensuring this succession took place, as usual, in the sphere of high politics. Some time at the end of the 1970s, at the end of McNamara's time as President of the World Bank, diplomacy no longer seemed to require tact and tongue-biting, but instead a justification for a much more active intervention in the local politics of developing countries. Neo-classical economists, many of whom were then still producing project appraisal manuals with shadow prices and income-distribution weights, went back to the box of Lego and produced instead various sanitized versions of neo-Marxian political economy, sanitized in that they were deducible from individual rational self-interest rather than anything so unorthodox as 'class'. (The neo-Marxists were having sufficient difficulty with class themselves![8])

The move from the 'old' neo-Marxism to the political economy of the new right can be traced both in academic discourse and in practical affairs. Among academics, some have simply abandoned the conceptual vocabulary of neo-Marxism in favour of that of public choice analysis, on the basis that the latter furnishes a more consistent and powerful set of hypotheses about the political economy. Others have tried to blend neo-Marxism into rational choice theory, analysing long-term historical developments in terms of a predatory state acting under constraints of bargaining power, transactions costs and discount rates (Levi 1988). This is essentially an attempt to modernize a Marxist analysis of the autonomy of the state that goes back to Engels's *Origin of the Family, Private Property and the State*.

In practical affairs, one classic study in the switch from Marxism to the NPE is the trajectory of David Stockman, who was responsible for putting the supply-side revolution in US economics on the conservative political map, and was President Reagan's Budget Director during his first term. His early student Marxist politics; his discovery of a 'Grand Doctrine' in the corruptions of the welfare state, if post-FDR America could be so called; his conviction of the high moral quality of a thorough-going anti-statist revolution; and his bitterness at the 'triumph of (US) politics' which defeated that revolution as soon as it had produced a Republican electoral victory – all of these things mark him as a bell-wether of a generation that succeeded, but only briefly, in foisting on conservatism an ideological position. The transition from the old to the new political economy found in David Stockman its representative figure (Stockman 1985). Many similar conversions from Marxism to the new right of the 1980s also occurred in the UK (Cowling 1990 (1963): xxxviii–xli).

The re-vamping of the neo-Marxist class logic story with the aid of methodological individualism left its major rhetorical features unaffected. The introduction of rational self-interest as the sole motive of politicians and bureaucrats did not change the neo-Marxist view of the state as an entity merely pretending a real concern for the public interest and national welfare. Like neo-Marxism, the NPE makes strong normative claims, essentially taking it as obvious that a certain set of social and economic arrangements is right. The conjunction of a cynical view of the politics of existing regimes and strong normative claims leads both to produce a bleak and deeply contradictory pessimism about the possibilities of progress. But the aim in both cases is not so much to interpret the world as to change it, and for that purpose cynicism and pessimism are powerful ideological instruments of persuasion – if they can be combined with a vision of a liberating crisis. The NPE found in the profound economic shocks of the 1970s a catastrophe that served as a surrogate revolutionary crisis. The liberation was to be provided, not by classless intellectuals, but by international economic experts. Dudley Seers who postulated (1979a) 'the congruence of Marxism and other neo-classical doctrines' provided the clue to these and other parallels. For in both neo-Marxism and the NPE, what is attempted is no less than the unity of theory and practice.

On this interpretation, it makes no sense at all to try to refute the cynicism and pessimism of the NPE about the governments of developing countries by pointing to current examples of successful reform pro-grammes in Africa and Asia (as Grindle (1989) does). For it is here that the economic catastrophe has taken place, and the international economic experts of structural adjustment have arrived. Most of the empirical evidence from the 1980s on policy reform is contaminated (from a scientific point of view) by the very rhetorical success which the NPE theorists have achieved in underwriting international action in support of liberalizing reform. The appearance of contrary cases represents failure for the scientist, but signals success for the soothsayer. But the com-parison here of the new political economy with the neo-Marxism and the indication of the strong soothsaying element in both should not be taken to imply that the intellectual achievements of the NPE have been negligible. Apart from Krueger's theory of rent-seeking, the NPE has provided enlightening explanations of how microeconomic incentives can sustain particular types of projects and programmes which are meant to be, but are not in fact, developmental. These may look oddly similar to the now despised 'vicious circle of cumulation causation' theories of the past, but they are welcome because they are more thoroughly grounded in the analysis of individual behaviour. It is the large-scale analyses of the NPE which are flawed – by exaggeration, self-contradiction and *arrière-pensée*.

Conclusion: Making Sense of Nationalism

What changes are needed if our thinking is to be released from these flaws? The NPE is one of those branches of modern economics which, in the words of A. K. Sen (1984: 7), 'seems indeed to be based on the corset-maker's old advice: "If madam is entirely comfortable in it, then madam most certainly needs a smaller size." ' The assumptions of methodological individualism are painfully restrictive (Meier 1989: 20–2). Social, political and indeed economic *structures* have to be re-introduced into the analysis. In doing so, however, it is very important – and this is one other vital legacy of the NPE – not to do so to the exclusion of individual agency and the single person's power of self-determination. A structuralism which treats people *only* as determined by structures is no less objectionably reductionist than an individualism which treats society, polity and economy *only* as the aggregates of self-determined individual action. A consensus is now emerging that agentless structure versus structureless agency is a false dilemma and that this long-standing dualism has now to be set aside in favour of theories that permit reciprocal interaction between the individual and the social setting. The argument here is owed to Giddens (1984), but many others, including Lawson (1985), Hodgson (1988) and Dearlove (1989) have endorsed it.[9]

By way of illustration, let us consider the problem of nationalism. Nationalism, the denial of legitimacy to regimes where political rule is not coextensive with one language or culture, presents difficulties of explanation both for the economic theory of politics and for neo-Marxism. It seems to be such a powerful force in the modern world – whether we look to its First, Second or Third incarnations. Yet both neo-liberalism and neo-Marxism, if they do not ignore it altogether (in the manner of Olson, whose book on *The Rise and Decline of Nations* is innocent of any index entry for nationalism), represent nationalism simply as a product of economic interests, either individual or class interests. The individual economic interest route collapses in self-contradiction for the same reason as does the analysis of voting in terms of rational choice: there is a paradox of national identification exactly analogous with the paradox of voting. The fate of the nation is so little affected by the moral or material investment of a single nationalist in its well-being, that no nationalist would make that investment (Berry

1970: 45–6). The class economic interest route collapses when called upon to explain the persistence of nationalism in officially classless societies like the USSR and Eastern Europe in the period of state socialism (Kolakowski 1978: 103–5).

Any explanation of nationalism, its growth and its consequences, must have recourse to certain *structural* features of the social world. These features may include class, but are not restricted to class as neo-Marxism might claim. Relevant structural features of social life for an analysis of nationalism would be the pattern of social stratification, the form and functions of the education system, the level of literacy, the degree of secularization and the nature of migration and other contacts with more developed countries (Gellner 1983). In that long run in which we are all dead, it is the changes in these features of society which produce the rise and decline of nations. But in the short and medium run, they act as the parameters of individual choice. Any individual is free to choose to become a revolutionary nationalist hero or heroine. He or she is equally free to renounce the nationality of birth and to assimilate to an alien culture. Nothing prevents some people from deciding to do *both* of those things (witness those English *émigrés* who have become leaders of the IRA). Finally, nothing prevents other people from deciding to do neither, perhaps because they agree with Santayana that 'nationality is . . . too implicated in our moral nature to be changed honourably, and too accidental to be worth changing'. Even in the short run, the existence of structural determinants does not abolish individual choice.

It is important to insist also that choice is not necessarily exercised only after a process of economic calculation. 'In the growth of nationalist feeling and agitation, there is no need to assume any conscious long-term calculation of interest on anyone's part . . . It would be genuinely wrong to try to reduce these [nationalist] sentiments to calculations of material advantage or social mobility' (Gellner 1983: 61–2). As Barry (1970: 45) has put it, national identification leads to certain kinds of actions which lie outside the framework of economic calculation, and the most useful response is to work out the circumstances in which it does so. Yet the fact that nationalism lies somewhere beyond rational calculation should not permit neo-liberalism to brush it aside, as of little significance. After all, the 'erroneous' domestic economic policies which the NPE attributes to the cynical self-interest of LDC rulers, are also frequently interpreted as the policies of economic nationalism (Burnell 1986: 37–9). If that were true, one would surely want to be equipped with a form of political economy broad enough to analyse nationalism and its economic policy impact, in the variety of shapes in which it appears in different developing countries. The realization by the international financial institutions that structural adjustment has a 'missing political dimension' may be a reflection of their own previous willingness to view economic liberalization through the prism of the NPE, when this boldly excludes, by assumption, the considerations which might make economic nationalism intelligible.

If a renewed emphasis on social structure is accepted, then the institutions of political life take on an expanded significance.[10] They are no longer seen merely as a set of constraints (unchanging and unexplained) within which individual politicians and bureaucrats rationally maximize their utility. Their role in conferring legitimacy, authority and power on those who participate in them can be understood, as can the associated concept of institution-building and institutional decay. If the problem is that self-interested behaviour by rulers of developing countries has increased, one must enquire how structures have changed to weaken the institutional constraints on opportunistic self-aggrandizement in the realm of politics. One could go further and argue that the real problem is the inability to re-construct institutional constraints in some developing countries once the externally imposed colonial institutions were swept away, and once traumatic external interventions have de-stabilized old societies. Politicians have responded to this empty institutional space in many diverse ways. Some, like President Mobutu of Zaire have become a by-word for rampant corruption. Others, like Flight-Lieutenant Jerry Rawlings are not corrupt, but are driven by a (sometimes violent) messianic puritanism to save their country. In some cases, such as Pol Pot and the Khmer Rouge in Kampuchea, chiliasm turns atrocious: the rulers do not accumulate wealth, only the piled-up human skulls of the killing fields.

It is impossible to discuss how different politicians in the Third World react to what Lucy Mair (1965: 34) once called 'the breathless speed with which historical circumstances have extended the room for manoeuvre' without addressing the moral factor in politics – its absence in certain instances of anarchy or tyranny; the particular kinds of constraints which are imposed on politicians and bureaucrats in hypocritical regimes, where considerations of political 'visibility' become important, and the instances where, *mirabile dictu*, rulers of developing countries actually are benevolent, although possibly also misinformed about how best to tread the road paved with good intentions. Thus the re-introduction of structuralist ideas is not just a device to revert to the assumption of benevolent LDC governments, which as has been argued, was in any case previously advanced with considerable mental reservations even by those who espoused it. It is a proposal to inject into political economy a much richer and more refined analysis of politics than the NPE permits. It is also an invitation to apply a more refined understanding of politics not only to governments of developing countries, but also to the international actors in political economy.

As for the validity of the NPE's 'body of settled conclusions immediately applicable to policy', the reintroduction of structures and institutions to the debate helps to explain why an automatic presumption in favour of free-market solutions may not be warranted. Markets themselves are institutions. Markets for agriculture often have to be developed, that this is costly and that the costs often have to be borne by the state. The cutting back of state activity may, in plausible circumstances, actually hinder the desirable goal of greater scope for economically rational pricing of rural inputs and outputs. Essentially the same lesson applies to the growth of small-scale industry. One can argue from an inherent imperfection in labour contracts to the need for institutions to moderate the welfare losses inflicted by authoritarian managers of work: the growth of these labour unions is rarely encouraged and often actively discouraged by neo-liberal advocates of economic liberalization. Yet their healthy development is necessary both to protect employees from exploitation and unfair discrimination and to contribute to pluralism in the political arena. Women as a gender are exposed to widespread and persistent discrimination and devaluation, which their access to the labour market does not itself dissolve. Women must have strong grassroots organizations to confront these persistent disadvantages, and that the key issue is how they can harness some of the power of the state to sustain their struggle for appropriately equal treatment with men.

What the state can do to promote rural markets, to foster small-scale industry, to respond intelligently to the pressures to labour unions and womens' organizations and to address a great range of other legitimate tasks of development depends upon how well the government's own institutions are working. Why insist, with the neo-liberals on minimal government, if better government is a possibility? Government budgeting institutions are crucially involved in any agenda for better government. Yet even those who recognize the need for *more* government expenditure, lack a clear vision of how the selection and management of rational expenditure programmes can be institutionalized. On the revenue side of the budget, neo-liberal emphasis on fees and user charges diverts attention from the reconstruction of progressive tax systems.

Finally, international institutions can help or hinder the government's attempts to address the tasks of development. This is true in two particular senses, discussed in Chapter Seven. If the policy prescriptions of the IMF or the World Bank are too standardized and are attempted to be pressed home without due consideration for local institutional variations, the effects will be unhelpful. At the same time, there is no innate requirement that the international financial institutions should always behave in this Procrustean way. They, too, are a terrain for learning and innovation. The innovations of the 1980s have been significant, though not all of them have delivered what their inventors believed that they would. Much scope remains for further learning and new institutional departures that will provide a better combination of incentives and disciplines for developing country governments than has been achieved so far.

Notes

1   'It is to the methodology of Cardoso and Faletto that we must look for an adequate account of Latin American history but . . . their substantive account is in need of radical amendment', according to Roxborough (1984: 4). He adds that the reasons for the neglect of the Cardoso-Faletto volume are unclear, but would be interesting to explore from the point of view of the sociology of knowledge. In the case of Warren, the English translation did not appear until 1979, after his death. Since Cardoso is cited only in the English translation, one must infer that Warren did not read Spanish or Portuguese.

2   The whole notion of 'Marxist authenticity' is in any case a confused and dubious one. Marxism was sometimes disowned by Marx, who denounced certain French 'Marxists' with the words: 'As for me, I am *not* a Marxist' (McLellan 1975: 71–2). The simultaneous adulation and revulsion which Marxism has always received sabotages agreement about what it actually is.

3   It was Condorcet's merit that in his vision of history as a sequence of types of society, each arises logically and necessarily from the preceding one, and each inevitably carries within itself the seeds of the next one to come . . . Progress . . . was not for Condorcet a purely intellectual or technological matter. On the contrary, it was progress above all in morals and in happiness, precisely because knowledge aids the growth of virtue . . . Everywhere around him, Condorcet could see colonialism and slavery breaking down, inequality between nations and within nations being lessened . . . [He forecast that] life expectancy will rise and even man's mental powers will be improved, in part by education and, in part, perhaps, genetically.

(Pollard 1971: 90–2)

4   One might have expected the romantic motif in Marx's thought to have been accompanied and sustained by a nationalist motif. On the contrary, Marx's idea of community always lacks a concrete context. His own Jewish background is only mentioned once in all his writings, along with many critical and offensive remarks about Jews. Isaiah Berlin (1979) comments: 'Extreme German chauvinism had taken pathologically anti-Semitic forms in the years before Marx's birth. This occurred in the Rhineland no less than elsewhere in Germany, anti-Jewish feeling was not confined to religious intolerance . . . it was openly racialist' (p. 262). Therefore:

The baptised Jewish intellectual, still regarded as racially a Jew by his fellows, could not hope to be politically effective so long as nationalism remained a problem for him. It had somehow to be eliminated as an issue. Consciously or not, Marx all his life systematically underestimated nationalism as an independent force . . . This is one of the major weaknesses of his great synthesis.

(pp. 279–80)

I am indebted for this reference, and for discussion on this point, to Len Mars.

5   It may be of interest to explain why the statement that 'politicians and bureaucrats are motivated only by individual self-interest' is shocking. First, it is assumed that the proposition is not tautological, that is, it does not mean that whatever these actors do must be self-interested in some sense, because otherwise they would not do it. Second, if the statement is not empty because tautological, it means that these actors when faced with any conflict between their own individual interest and the interest of any other person will infallibly prefer the former. Third, it is assumed that conflicts of interest do occur, and that a natural harmony of individual interests does not prevail. When conflicts of interest occur between individuals in *economic* life they are arbitrated in the market place by the 'invisible hand' of the price mechanism which, on given assumptions, can achieve an 'efficient' reconciliation of conflicting interests. But even Adam Smith did not suppose that market-generated outcomes could be efficient without an over-arching framework of law and regulation to maintain the sociopolitical parameters within which markets can work efficiently. Now if the politicians and bureaucrats, who are responsible for enacting laws and enforcing regulations, use their *political* power to advance personal and private interests when they conflict with the public interest, they betray their duty to the general public and that is, and ought to be shocking. The application of the neo-classical self-interest assumption to politics is, therefore, something much more fundamental than the simple 'extension' of a behavioural assumption from one arena of social life to another.

6   The participatory strand in Western political theory starts from Aristotle and runs through Machiavelli and Guicciardini, Harrington, Ferguson and Rousseau. The non-participatory strand starts with the Stoics and runs through the Roman legists, Magna Carta, Coke, Blackstone, Bentham and James Mill.

7   For an earlier attempt to discuss the basic logical difficulties of certain economic theories of politics, see Toye (1976). A good recent discussion is Dearlove (1989), as well as Hindess (1988).

8   In this regard, they follow closely in the footsteps of Marx himself. The *Communist Manifesto* speaks of two classes, bourgeoisie and proletariat, but in his other writings three-layered and other multi-layered models of class structure are to be found; and when Marx discusses class in what was later to become Volume III of *Capital*, the manuscript breaks off before the definition has properly begun (Prawer 1978: 146–7).

9   Strictly speaking, it is the recent revival of this argument that is owed to Giddens. It has long been a commonplace of the anthropological literature. Malinowski (1926: 56) wrote that 'the savage is neither an extreme

"collectivist" nor an intransigent "individualist" – he is, like man in general, a mixture of both'. The anthropological discussion has focused on the question of how, if society is continuously re-created by the transmission through socialization, education, etc.) of social roles (husband, parent, teacher, judge, ruler), social change can occur. Emmet (1960) suggested that change was the product of individuals deciding (rather in the manner of an actor's ad-libbing) marginally to reinterpret their roles. (The recent absorption of some of the anthropological literature by students of Third World politics, especially in France, has led to the reappearance of the theatrical metaphor as a key to political understanding).

10   Bates (1989) also emphasizes the importance of institutions, but from inside the methodological individualism tradition. His argument is that while rational individuals should constitute the unit of analysis, 'they compete within a set of political institutions; and the structure of these institutions shapes their interactions so as to determine the outcome that will hold in equilibrium' (ibid.: 10–13). While criticizing market-based theories of politics, he advocates further work in the same tradition as the literature on the theory of committees and elections.

CHAPTER SIX

The New Political Economy Applied to India's Development

The New Political Economy and Competing Paradigms

The counter-revolution in development thinking has produced a new kind of political economy. The analysis of the welfare effects of government intervention has been extended to generate new theories of the state in developing countries, and even of the type of society in which the state operates. This new style of political economy has been developed in a way that supplements both welfare economics analyses of government economic controls and Bauer's more general strictures on 'the politicization of economic life'.

In the first instance, an evaluation of this new political economy must proceed at a rather abstract and general level. In the previous chapter, our questions concerned its internal logical consistency and its congruence with widely accepted facts and theories of development. Empirical examples were brought into the debate as and when they were relevant, but necessarily could not be pursued in depth. That is part of the problem with arguments conducted at such a high level of generality. But, since one important criterion of a new perspective is whether it can inspire fruitful research at the level of detail that is required for policy-making, a second stage of assessment is now desirable. Does the new approach succeed in explaining how individual developing economies and societies change better than the existing alternatives? This question can only be tackled by means of a more thorough case study of one country.

In this chapter, India has been chosen as the developing country to be studied in greater detail. Although undeniably the choice of one country from the Third World, which is heterogeneous and becoming increasingly more so, has an element of arbitrariness in it, there are justifications. On any reckoning, India is important within the Third World, because of its huge population (690 million in 1981) and the very low levels of consumption available to the great majority of them.

Although, in the light of the arguments of chapter 1, India cannot be described as typical of the Third World, it is a country which the development counter-revolution has very explicitly claimed that its analyses fit. It is used as a prime example of the alleged failures of interventionist development policies. Thus it cannot be said that the decision to focus on India unfairly biases the terms of the debate against the viewpoint of the counter-revolution. Additionally, India has forty years of development experience, and the quality of basic information about India is relatively good by Third World standards. At the very least, one could suggest that if the perspective of the counter-revolution does poorly in explaining the political economy of Indian development, it will need some rethinking and reworking.

Before looking at the contribution of analysts who have used 'the new political economy' to elucidate India's development, it is worth noting that political economy itself is a very loosely defined field of knowledge, or research methodology. Political economy is an attempt to specify some relationships between economic and political behaviour.[1] But such a relationship can be conceptualized in a wide variety of different ways. The adjective 'new' tells us only that methodological individualism is the NPE's basic axiom.

One useful distinction to bear in mind when looking at theories of political economy is based on the direction of causation which the theory adopts. Are economic forces interpreted as 'causing' the political outcomes, or are political forces interpreted as 'causing' the economic outcomes? In the former case, the theory is said to be 'economistic', while in the latter case, the theory has been described by the term 'politicist' (Staniland 1985: 71, 96–8). Clearly, economism and politicism are two extreme types of political economy, where a single line of causation is assumed and the causal direction of one is the exact reverse of the causal direction of the other. But it can be illuminating to ask how closely actual theories of political economy approximate to either of these ideal types. Economists like the development counter-revolutionaries, who spend much time specifying their economic models correctly, must also acknowledge the need to consider the formal structure of their political economy models.

The contemporary analysis of India's development can, in a rough and ready fashion, be split up between three competing paradigms of political economy. The first is the neo-classical paradigm, which represents the contribution of the counter-revolution in development thinking to our understanding of India. The second is a form of classical

political economy which gives central analytic importance to the opposition of interests between town and country. The third is a political
economy of class opposition among dominant social classes in the
Marxian tradition.

Each of the paradigms has been fuelled by empirical research by
economists on different aspects of the Indian economy. The neo-
classical version has been based on empirical studies of government
intervention in trade and industry and the varied effects that such policy
actions in India have had. The classical version has focused on rural–
urban and agricultural–non-agricultural distributions of assets and investments. The Marxian political economy has been focused around
the problem of industrial stagnation and the dynamics of state expenditures. It is difficult to say whether these areas of empirical work
were all inspired by the paradigms in the first place. Perhaps they were.
But in all cases the empirical economic groundwork was established in
the 1970s fairly solidly, while the erection of theories of political economy
in the 1980s has gone ahead with rather less assurance and success.
The narrowness and separateness of each set of empirical foundations
has been a major reason for this.

A look in turn at each of the three competing 'political economies'
of India which are currently on offer should help to bring into sharp
relief the strengths and weaknesses of the counter-revolution's new
political economy. How much new insight has it brought about Indian
development and how comprehensive is that insight? Should the new
political economy be accepted as a replacement for all its competitors?
Should it be accepted as complementary to existing insights? Or should
it be rejected altogether as completely misconceived?

The first step in answering these questions is to state in some detail
what the neo-classical position has had to offer. As representative examples of this position, the work of Bhagwati and his collaborators,
of Krueger, of S. Roy and of P. S. Jha is considered. None of these
choices is questionable, except perhaps that of Jha's work. The latter
pays lip service to the ideas of the Polish economist Michal Kalecki,
who was not a neo-classical thinker. It is, however, primarily about the
social and political consequences of Indian government economic controls and, as will be argued, the patina of Kaleckian ideas is very
superficial.[2]

Indian Controls and the Economics of Rent-seeking

India was one of six countries used as case studies in the OECD Development Centre's large research project on industrialization in the
late 1960s, the others being Brazil, Mexico, Taiwan, the Philippines

and Pakistan. The general conclusions of this study, as set out by Little, Scitovsky and Scott (1970), are the basis of the neo-classical approach to development policy. The fundamental difficulty about post-war industrialization in developing countries was identified as the failure to pursue economic growth single-mindedly. Considerations of national self-sufficiency had also been a major influence on governments in developing countries and industrialization was actively promoted by them, both for reasons of economic growth and for reasons of national self-sufficiency. The result of government intervention to promote industry 'in the national interest' was a series of tariffs and quota controls on imports which protected domestic industry and kept the domestic currency overvalued in terms of what it could purchase abroad.

The overvaluation of the currency discouraged exporting, both by the protected domestic industry, which could not achieve all potential economies of scale, and by the agricultural sector. Investment in the agricultural sector was thereby discouraged, although it was not import intensive and made relatively efficient use of the resources which it did command. The inefficiently small domestic industries were encouraged to become both import intensive and capital intensive to an excessive degree, but because they had difficulty importing raw materials often under-used their productive capacity.

The situation could be even more tangled than this. Whether it was so depended on the exact design of the government's controls over imports and industrial investment. If entitlement to scarce, and therefore precious, imports was pro rata to industrial capacity, it might create an incentive to try and corner licences for industrial investment, by keeping such capacity idle or grossly under-used, while reselling the imports on the black market. If licences to invest or import were given at bureaucratic discretion, however minimal, rather than auctioned or allocated by lot, various kinds of corruption could enter the system. They might be demands for 'speed money', to do what the rules required but more quickly, or contraventions of the rules in return for financial or other favours. The desire to control corruption sometimes added to the checking and counter-checking at each stage of the bureaucratic procedure. This created additional delays and increased the willingness to pay speed money, or to short-circuit the whole process by bribery on a grand scale.

The OECD country study of India by Bhagwati and Desai (1970) provided evidence that India's trade and industrialization policies had produced the general set of economic distortions catalogued by Little, Scitovsky and Scott. It is possible, as the case of South Korea shows, for a developing country to undertake state-promoted industrialization without using an overvalued exchange rate for the purpose. But India had not exploited this possibility. Bhagwati and Desai calculated the rates of effective protection on Indian industrial goods (that is, the protection afforded not just by the tariff or quota on the imported finished product, but the protection given by the overall tariff/quota system, including the protection on intermediate goods and raw materials used to manufacture the same product domestically). They found very high rates of protection of domestic value added across a wide range of industrial goods. Import-substitution within industry appeared to be indiscriminate rather than selective.

But in addition to the economic distortions caused by an overvalued rupee, the specific methods adopted by India to restrict imports and to regulate new investment in the protected industrial sector caused extra problems. Using the reports of official committees of enquiry into the operation of the Indian control system, a qualitative picture was built up of long-winded and dilatory administrative procedures. These had gradually lost a clear sense of their original economic purposes and, moreover, were constantly being further complicated by the attempt to avoid bureaucratic corruption. Apart from the official anti-corruption measures themselves, there was much circumstantial evidence to indicate that corruption in India was a real problem.

It is important to insist on the distinctness, and separability, of three quite different things, even when, as in India, all are found together. One is a policy of state-promoted industrialization. Another is the use of an overvalued exchange rate as the instrument for state protection of industry. A third is a bureaucratically discretionary method of restricting imports and sanctioning investment in industry. The new political economy of the counter-revolution characteristically lumps all three together, speaking of a single syndrome of '*dirigisme*' or 'interventionism'. Although they certainly can be found together, as in India, they can also be found separately. The OECD country study of Pakistan, for example, showed that there, although the economic distortions from an overvalued exchange rate were greater than in India, the problems associated with the use of direct controls were significantly less. The governments of developing countries thus have a series of choices to make after opting in principle for some form of industrial intervention.

The new political economy of India has grown out of the findings of Bhagwati and Desai and later work by by Bhagwati and Srinivasan (1975). Ironically, this was not because either work offered much by way of political analysis of India. Their political focus was the narrow one of political influences inhibiting economic liberalization programmes. Their treatment of this was both brief and naive. Rather, the origin of the new political economy was in the implications that were drawn out of their economic analysis of the consequences of bureaucratic controls.

India was taken by Krueger (1974) as one of the two empirical cases (the other was Turkey) from which could be developed a theory of 'rent-seeking societies'. The allocation of government licences to import, where the value of the imports in domestic currency is much greater than the domestic currency which has to be surrendered to acquire the foreign exchange to pay for the imports, was presented as an archetypal government control that creates windfall gains, or 'rents'. Such rents are the rewards of the partial monopoly power which licences or permits confer and which in a control system the state can bestow selectively. Thus, as Bauer has acknowledged, 'the general proposition that incomes . . . are . . . not taken from others, is subject to partial qualification. The incomes of some people are augmented by the exercise of monopoly power . . .' (1981: 12–13). In the case of import and investment restrictions, the source of such monopoly power is the state.

A theory of how people can compete in order to acquire these gains ('rent-seeking') was then developed, embracing both legal means (increasing capacity, if imports are allocated pro rata to capacity) and illegal means (bribery and corruption of government officials who administer import controls). This theory is said to be far more generally applicable than merely to import controls. Although rents from import licences were calculated as 5 per cent of India's national income in 1964 and two-thirds of all 'rents' of this kind in India, other government controls – on wages and interest rates, for example – were said also to operate to stimulate competitive rent-seeking activity. This hint opened the door to more grandiose extensions of the idea of competitive rent-seeking, in which the marginal nature of rents from controls in relation to aggregate economic activity was no longer so clear.

Krueger correctly notes the fact that rents created by economic controls face the developing country government operating them with a set of choices. But none of the choices it faces are attractive. It can limit the competition to acquire available rents, and then be seen as favouring particular classes or groups, or it can allow competition for rents to proceed and risk a general collapse of confidence in the market as a mechanism for allocation, or it can allow competition for rents subject to additional, new controls, which, by creating their own rents, establish a political 'vicious circle' (Krueger 1974: 302). When the choices are presented in this bleak fashion, the case for economic liberalization is made by default. However, a policy device like the auctioning of licences to the highest bidder can help the state to capture the rents it has created, without favouring any particular class or group.

With appropriate disciplinary modesty, and despite the reference to political economy in the title of her article, Krueger refused to venture 'beyond the competence of an economist to evaluate the political impact of rent-seeking' (p. 302).

India as a 'Rent-seeking Society'

In the 1980s, some of Krueger's key concepts and terminology were adopted and extended without her own self-restraint with regard to political conclusions. It was an easy move from the theory of competition for rents to a political economy which labelled India as a 'rent-seeking society'. It would have been more exact to label India as a society with a rent-creating government, since, on neo-classical assumptions about economic motivation, all individuals will be rent-seekers. But the phrase 'rent-seeking society' has passed into common currency, despite this inexactness.

S. Roy, who has contributed a quite recent Institute of Economic Affairs pamphlet on the Indian economy, attributes to rent-seeking the many defects which he sees in the development of Indian society. He states that 'if the basic and commonsensical lessons of political economy had been acknowledged early on in the history of the Indian Republic, we might have found today a much more prosperous economy and a much healthier body politic than is the case' (1984: 14). Although Roy's overt purpose – like that of neo-classicals generally – is normative, to reveal the lessons which must be learned from political economy for economic policy, like them he is also putting forward a particular explanation of how the current, pathological situation has come about. That explanation, in turn, has implications for whether the normative lessons can actually be learned, or whether there is some structural block or inhibition in Indian society's channels of learning.

One crucial shaping force which is identified by Roy as the cause of India's present discontents is 'an attitude of statism', the polar opposite of the correct attitude of taking responsibility for one's own well-being. This attitude is traced back to Moghul times, whence it blended with British imperial paternalism. Lasting into independent India, it is said to have been 'reinforced by the social and economic policies pursued by successive governments' (p. 31). Roy is here trying to ride two explanatory horses at once. If the attitude of statism had been as ubiquitous and durable in India as is claimed, it could hardly have required much reinforcement from the socioeconomic policies of the planning period. The thesis that failure to understand political economy in 1947 was critical is undermined by insistence on the historic durability of the alleged statist social psychology of Indians.

If that insistence is, therefore, ignored, Roy's theory collapses back into Krueger's. That is, that the misguided adoption of certain economic policies, especially import quotas, itself creates a society with certain kinds of economic irrationalities such as permanently under-utilized industrial capacity, a corrupt administration and a political structure dominated by interests fed financially by windfall gains. This latter feature is important because, almost by definition, it rules out the possibility of achieving the reform which neo-classicals are seeking, at any rate in a democratic polity like India. Roy is quite unequivocal about this central point. 'Even a limited liberal agenda [for India] would appear doomed to be still-born. Incumbent politicians, government officials and the public-sector unions in general would vigorously oppose any reduction in government intervention in the economy for fear of losing the rents and sinecures of the status quo' (p. 67). Thus, while India must learn the common-sense lessons of liberal political economy, it cannot. According to Roy, the foolish spree of government intervention in the planning period has effectively locked India into an equilibrium of unhappiness from which only an external shock can possibly dislodge her.

Bearing in mind the previously noted distinction between economistic and politicist variants of political economy, it appears that Roy's basic model is a highly economistic one. Leaving the logically flawed account of statism aside, the crucial determinants are seen as economic – the system of incentives which, when once distorted, produces a polity which then defends and protects the distorted incentives that have created it. In this, it displays an analytical similarity to the equally economistic theory of the state in vulgar Marxism.[3] Here the bourgeois class controls the power of the state, using it to entrench the class interests of capital and to maintain the exploitation and misery of the proletariat (for example, Kurian 1975: 85–113). Roy's version of the new political economy, along with vulgar Marxist political economy, can be designated as an economistic hypothesis of equilibrium unhappiness (or, for brevity, an EHEU theory).

Roy's pessimism about the prospects of reform in India never makes quite the impact which it should because his (unattainable) ideal arrangements lack credibility. Despite much preparatory fiddling with the norm by comparison with which distortions can be clearly identified as distortions, it remains completely bifurcated. The neo-classical picture of free markets for private goods plus government provision of public goods is painted, though with some blanks (for example, merit wants) and some blurring (for example, how the concept of public goods is made operational). The problem is the gap which yawns between the assumptions made about people's economic motivation and their political responsibilities.

On one page, 'men are concerned almost wholly with . . . living their own lives as best they can' (Roy 1984: 16). Two pages later, 'where [freedom] exists but people are too apathetic, ignorant or busy with their daily lives to exercise it, public life soon becomes self-deceptive and absurd' (p. 18). But how could a republic of narrowly self-interested householders be expected to do anything other than to allow 'its public agents to become brokers and entrepreneurs – trading not only in the products of government-controlled industries, but also in an array of positions of power and privilege, all in the name of directing a common endeavour to help the poor' (p. 28)?

Thus the assumption of very narrow self-interest of householders which Roy uses to justify the freedom of markets from government intervention explains all too easily the difficulty of maintaining an appropriate boundary between the private and the public domains. If an appropriate private/public boundary is the central objective of the new political economy, fundamental assumptions which put the objective totally beyond the reach of policy surely need to be looked at again.

Roy's version of the new political economy is more concerned with highlighting specific alleged anomalies of Indian government policy (such as discrimination in favour of scheduled castes and tribes in education and employment, badly thought out family planning campaigns, legal delays, the absence of proper flood precautions) than with improving the overall coherence of liberal political economy. Even when these 'anomalies' can be logically connected with the broad theme of the political economy of rent-seeking, the connections are not made. Better insight into the links between economic controls, rent-seeking, official corruption, the demand for higher education and the conflict over scheduled caste constitutional provisions is to be found in competing paradigms (for example, Bardhan 1984: 50–3). But how the political economy of rent-seeking has been integrated into a much more comprehensive approach to the political economy of Indian development is a question which leads us ahead slightly too fast. It is one that will be answered when Jha's version of the Indian rent-seeking society has been compared with Roy's.

Political Economy of Stagnation

As noted at the end of the first section of this chapter, P. S. Jha rather confusingly clothes his account of the political economy of Indian development with the terminology of Kalecki. In the early 1960s, Kalecki wrote half a dozen slightly obscure pages on 'intermediate regimes' in developing countries. Jha adopts this term to denote the rise to political dominance in India of 'an intermediate class or stratum consisting of market-oriented peasant proprietors, small manufacturers, traders and other self-employed groups' (Jha 1980: vii). The relation of this intermediate class to rent-seeking is that it was the beneficiary of the rents from Indian economic controls. 'Since this class had benefited from economic controls it tried, not unnaturally, to perpetuate and even strengthen the regime of shortages' (p. viii). In turn, the strengthening of government economic controls during the Second Plan and after is given as the reason for 'the onset of economic stagnation in 1966'. What is being proposed is a sequence whereby controls generated a shift in political power to a 'new class' of self-employed rent-seekers and the debilitating economic consequences of that shift.

This is not at all what Kalecki was describing. He saw the interests of the lower middle class in developing countries gradually amalgamating with a dynamic form of state capitalism (1972: 163). He saw the dominance of the intermediate class as being vulnerable primarily to pressure from foreign capital or from feudal elements, rather than internal repression or the self-defeating nature of their economic strategy. Jha is proposing, in stark contrast, to outline a political sociology of economic controls – something which Kalecki never even mentions in his very brief essay. That is why it is preferable to group Jha's ideas with those of Roy, who also interprets India as a rent-seeking society. Both alike respond to the analysis of controls by Bhagwati and Desai, denying however that the documented failures are inadvertent and instead asserting that they have deep social and political causes (Jha 1980: 94).

What follows this, in Jha's case, is more of a journalist's report than an academic's thesis. His excellent access to primary sources of information is not fully matched by the ability to process and model the abundant data to hand. The economic vignettes concern the quick profits made by traders in soap, vanaspati and rubber tyres as a result of poor administration of government price controls on these products during the inflation of 1972–4. The parallel economy based on tax evasion, smuggling, real estate transactions and other forms of illicit trading is also presented in circumstantial detail. This usefully fills out Krueger's claim that import controls are by no means the only source of rents in India. Price controls can also create windfall profits for holders of stocks of the controlled commodity. They can also stimulate the growth of unofficial markets where transactions take place at prices other than the controlled price, leading on to evasion of tax on these transactions and the search for uses for untaxed money. It is, needless to say, in the nature of illicit activity that estimates of its quantitative significance are highly speculative.

The increase in black-market profiteering and other flows in the parallel economy is linked by Jha to certain observed changes in Indian politics. Particular emphasis is given to the 1968 ruling that outlawed business donations to political parties, without providing any alternative legal method of financing political parties (p. 114). Money from the parallel economy has been increasingly used for this purpose. This boosted the prospects of the Jana Sangh and similar petit bourgeois parties in the 1960s, as well as forcing the Congress Party into more populist attitudes and more dubious electoral practices. Roy linked the prospects for a prosperous economy with those of a healthy body politic. Similarly, Jha attempts 'to trace the effects of economic development on the distribution of political power and the results of shifts in the latter on the future pattern of economic development . . . thus [achieving] a true political-economy . . .' (p. ix).

Limitations of the Rent-seeking Approach

In its programme, then, Jha's approach is less purely economistic than Roy's, in that political change reacts on economic change at the second round of analysis. Formally, there is more genuine interdependence of economic and politics in Jha's work. However, when it comes to the lessons to be learned for future development policy, the perceived interdependence of economic and political constraints on growth is given a strange twist. On the economic front, an alternative economic strategy is recommended along Gandhian lines, despite the boost that this would give, if successful, to self-employment, the economic status of the intermediate class.[4] The abolition of most price controls is also recommended, although the prescription for existing controls over foreign trade and industrial investment is never made clear. On the political front, Jha is much less pessimistic than Roy. He believes that the state funding of electoral expenses will purge the bulk of the existing political corruption. He also believes that a government which reflects the interests of the dominant intermediate class could carry out such a measure, because the intermediate class itself 'may come to the conclusion that the very forces of economic stagnation which have increased their power and prosperity will eventually destroy them altogether' (p. 278).

The attempt of the new political economy to construct a convincing social theory on the basis of the economic analysis of rent-seeking, as exemplified by the work of Roy and Jha, has a number of limitations. There is disagreement about the nature of the vested interests that are created by economic controls: are they the rich peasants and shopkeepers/traders of Jha's intermediate class, or are they bureaucrats and public sector employees, as seen by Roy? This is partly a difference of view arising out of focusing on price controls rather than foreign trade and investment controls, but there is an unresolved question in both accounts of how precisely the salaried officials relate to the prosperous private sector self-employed. Who is exploiting whom? Is one group parasitic on the other, or is there, as Krueger has it, just a general competition for unearned gains conducted according to a fairly elastic set of rules?

The contrast in policy advice for India arising out of the new political economy is also striking. The deep pessimism of Roy about the prospects for liberal reform could hardly be further removed from the utopianism of Jha. What can one say of a learning effect – appearing as a *deus ex machina* on the penultimate page – designed to explain why a class, which had hitherto been as narrowly self-interested as Roy's neo-classical assumption requires, should in future take a longer view of its interests, and allow its wings to be clipped for its own good? To say the least, it is not intellectually satisfactory in itself, apart from the doubt it throws on whether the descriptive insights of the new political economy provide a useful framework for the discussion of policy-making. But since the notion of usefulness is always relative to available alternatives, the discussion can best proceed by investigating the major competing paradigms of the political economy of Indian development.

A Competing Paradigm: the Rural–Urban Divide

Unlike Bhagwati and Desai (1970) and Bhagwati and Srinivasan (1975), who merely provided the Indian empirical analyses on which the theory of rent-seeking was built, Lipton (1977) both provided empirical evidence on the rural-urban divide in India (and, of course, many other countries) and constructed a sociopolitical theorization of it (see especially chapters 3, 4 and 14). The Indian empirical evidence was strongly challenged by Byres (1979), as part of an overall critique of Lipton's thesis of urban bias as the cause of 'maldistribution with growth'. After this dramatic initial clash, surprisingly little has been done to explore further the validity of urban bias analysis in the Indian context. Africa, where in any case urban bias was claimed to be more powerful than in India, has had more attention from subsequent researchers (for example, Bates 1981).

Lipton (1984) revisits the debates which followed the publication of *Why Poor People Stay Poor*. On the empirical size of urban bias in India, Byres's suggestions of various possible measurement errors are rejected as invalid or irrelevant, and the claim of substantial, though probably diminishing, urban bias in the Indian political economy is firmly reasserted. Nevertheless, and without regard to any previous criticisms, it does seem that the level of urban bias in a given developing country is not very easy to measure. The reason is that, although one can define the idea of 'bias' without resorting to the full apparatus of welfare economics, when it comes to measuring it, a definite numerical statement of the unbiased norm is needed. That can only rest on a welfare economics foundation.

The neutral state of affairs against which urban bias has to be measured is the ideal general equilibrium of markets, with a neutral impact of government interventions. Actual measures of urban bias turn out to be better or worse approximations to that ideal. The usual method, in the tradition of Lewis (1968), is to use world prices, or border prices, as the indicator of neutrality and to compare domestic prices with world/ border prices to get the gauge of bias or distortion. The urban bias paradigm borrows the neo-classical approach to the measurement of economic distortion.

The problem with it is that world or border prices do not have the normative significance with which they are invested. A calculation of the difference between the world and domestic prices of a representative Indian farmer's output, combined with the difference between the world and domestic prices of the inputs he used to produce this output, is obviously sensitive to changes in the world prices of agricultural outputs and inputs. Such changes occur for a wide variety for reasons, including government policies and cartelization in developed countries. The measured level of urban bias in India can thus be altered by a board decision of a large US multinational wheat trading company, or an EC directive to run down sugar stocks. Nothing at all need have changed within India itself.

This important point tends to get relegated to the footnotes accompanying the respective calculations. For example, a recent World Bank estimate of price distortions in agriculture contained the following instructive footnote. 'We recognise that the general equilibrium effects of removing price distortions on a global basis would alter border prices and, therefore, alter the magnitude of the distorting effects. However, it is extremely difficult to estimate "shadow free market prices" in a first-best world . . .' (Bale and Lutz 1979: 14, n. 3). Apart from the changing degree of distortion which is present in world/border prices, other fluctuating distortions are reflected in the official exchange rate that has to be used to convert prices in domestic currency to border prices, or vice versa. Thus numbers purporting to quantify the level of urban bias in India should be treated with caution.

Although the facts of urban bias are generally furnished by neo-classical methods, this is not sufficient reason to regard the urban bias paradigm as a minor variant of the new political economy. This is because Lipton correctly distances himself from the counter-revolution's exclusive explanation of the cause of economic bias or distortion in terms of government intervention. Departures from the ideal neutral state occur for many reasons, and domestic cartel activity within India has to be included, along with overt actions of the Indian government (Lipton 1984: 161, n. 17). Lipton implicitly criticizes the work of Bates on African urban bias for 'appearing at times to imply that urban bias processes operate only through state "intervention" in otherwise unbiased market processes' (p. 161, n. 12).

The urban bias paradigm also differs from the new political economy in that it does not take the usual economistic approach to causation. It attributes independent power to a so-called urban class which, in India as elsewhere, is said to engineer and to benefit from urban bias. The theory of an urban class which is controlling and shaping economic outcomes into a predictable, urban-biased pattern is both a differentiated theory of political economy and a 'politicist' theory, in Staniland's sense. Sociopolitical forces are in charge, determining economic outcomes. There is no suggestion that these forces were somehow created by a prior economic policy decision, such as the use of direct controls.

The sociological claim that an urban class exists in India is a crucial part of the urban bias paradigm. In this connection, it is noteworthy that the term 'class', although it is defined precisely, nevertheless is used interchangeably with other sociological categories. The term 'urban class' appears to be synonomous with 'urban elites', 'urban alliance', 'urban group(s)', 'urban ruling groups' and 'the urban bias coalition'. At different points, the exposition focuses on the small, interlocking elites in the urban areas and on a more comprehensive grouping including 'the permanently urban poor'. Sometimes the urban elites are said wholly to incorporate the bureaucracy and sometimes they are said to be able to be 'partly autonomous'. At times, the rural elites within the urban class are seen as being incorporated by the urban elites; at times they are said to be brought off by them; at other times again, they are described as 'urbanizing' themselves. Such an elastic description of the urban class is no doubt designed to improve the theory's power of generalization. But it necessarily weakens its testability in any particular location, such as India. There may lie the partial cause of its disappointing performance as a research paradigm for political economists of India in the early 1980s.

Whether or not urbanites constitute a class, they must at least operate as an interest group, if the theory of urban bias is to succeed. Moore (1984: 20) has noted an important omission in the political economy of urban bias: the absence of 'examples of *how* the [urban] class alliances . . . have actually operated politically'. Thus, although the model of political action is recognizably 'Indian', with its emphasis on government intervention in markets for foodgrains and inputs to foodgrain production, we seem to lack evidence linking the political activities of the urban class with specific decisions on this kind of intervention. It is generally agreed that the mere fact that a class benefits from certain government policies does not by itself establish that this class is operating effectively as an interest group. More case studies of political action over budgetary allocations of investment, as well as over pricing policy for foodgrain output and inputs are necessary to fill this important lacuna.

Typical studies of the politics of smaller cities (for example, Pune and Agra), even when looking at their budgetary processes, will not pick up much that is relevant to these processes. Instead, they typically concentrate on questions of party performance and ethnicity (for example, Rosenthal 1970). It is at the level of state governments that these processes ought to be particularly visible, but so far they have eluded the researchers' prying eyes. Studies of state finances in India are usually technical studies of public finance in relation to development planning, which yield only the occasional flash of political information – such as that Madhya Pradesh MLAs lobby loudly and successfully for minor irrigation schemes (Wallich 1982: 56). The result is not only that the political economy of the rural-urban divide in India still provides a political economy without politics, it is also that a politicist version of political economy, in Staniland's terms, lacks a substantial account of the political forces which are said to be in the driving seat of urban-biased economic growth.

In these circumstances, the realism or otherwise of the development policy which emerges from the urban bias paradigm remains an open question. At a very general level, the policy recommendation is to alter the existing allocation of public resources in favour of agriculture and the rural sector. Since with hindsight it can now be seen that India's growth trajectory had become unbalanced by the middle of the 1960s, it is widely agreed that a correction in favour of agriculture was necessary. But this agreement has been influenced substantially by aid agencies, other international organizations and foreign development economists, like Lipton, who made the pro-agriculture case effectively at the time, and without any of the benefit of hindsight. The anti-urban-bias coalition which Lipton called for, to include rural organizations, urban trade unions, government officials and political parties, as well as foreign agencies has been a much more uncertain affair in India. In 1977, a pro-peasant central government came to power under very unusual circumstances, but it was swept away in 1980 after a brief and largely ineffective tenure of office.[5]

Another Competing Paradigm: Dominant Propertied Classes

Apart from the urban bias paradigm, the paradigm of dominant propertied classes provides an alternative view of India to that offered by the new political economy. It does not, however, provide a complete alternative. What it attempts to do is no less than to integrate both the analysis of rent-seeking and the analysis of urban bias into a more comprehensive overall framework of ideas. The wider framework is a sociology of conflict between three classes which are identified as between them dominating Indian society. The issues raised by Krueger, Roy and Jha, on the one hand, and Lipton or Mellor (1976) on the other, are then reinterpreted and reconciled within this more comprehensive vision.

Bardhan (1984) is a skilled exponent of this ambitious scheme. His work is certainly a minor masterpiece of compression, which is achieved at little cost in either clarity of outline, or richness of detail. Bardhan starts from trend growth rates in agriculture and industry, then connects the slowdown in industrial growth with the deceleration in public investment after 1965. His next endeavour is to 'put these economic-technological factors in the political context of the class alignments and the constraints they imply on state action' (p. 61). The class alignments are the relations of the dominant proprietary classes (industrial capitalist class, the class of 'rich farmers' and a class of bureaucrats). State action derives from 'the professionals in the public sector', an autonomous bureaucracy which may be overdeveloped as a result of colonialism, but which might even be a legacy from Moghul times (compare Roy's 'statism').

The conflicts between these three proprietary classes (for the bureaucracy is classified as proprietorial) are held to determine India's economic trajectory, as well as its political prospects. The analysis of these conflicts by Bardhan is schematic but undoubtedly ingenious. The first type of conflict is the rural–urban divide. It is played out 'between the urban industrial and professional classes on the one hand and the rural hegemonic class of rich farmers on the other' (p. 54). The conflict centres on the issue of the prices paid by the government to procure surpluses of wheat, rice and sugar for the public (mainly urban) food distribution system. The second type of conflict is the conflict over bureaucratic 'rent' creation and distribution, with the public sector professionals at odds with the industrial capitalists and, to a lesser extent, with the rich farmers on the issues of public regulation and public production.

> The majority of businessmen who do not have the clout or the money power of the conglomerates have to approach these [bureaucratic] dispensers of permits and licences essentially as supplicants ... The bureaucracy impinges somewhat less on the interest of rich farmers, even though in matters of administered prices, procurement, restrictions on grain movements and trade, and distribution of credit and fertilizers, it has numerous powers to exercise and favours to dispense.
>
> (pp. 58–9)

Thus by dividing the three dominant propertied classes along two different lines of cleavage, Bardhan is able to subsume both the new political economy of the rent-seeking society and the paradigm of the rural–urban divide.

To understand how Bardhan applies this sociology of class conflict to more detailed problems of India's development, it is necessary to comment first on previous analyses of the vicissitudes of India's development performance and policy. Toye (1981) showed that the mid-1960s deceleration of industrial growth was not a general phenomenon but one concentrated in the capital goods industries and to a lesser extent in the intermediate goods industries. It was also much more in evidence in the metal-using industries, like transport and electrical power, than other types of industry. Since the public expenditure statistics revealed immediately preceding cuts in investment expenditures, a case could be made that it was a dramatic policy shift – specifically, the abandonment of the policy of state-promoted capital accumulation which characterized the Second and Third Plans – that caused the slowdown in industrialization. It did so at first directly by stepping down the production of machines to make machines, then indirectly, when the absence of certain machines, such as railway wagons and electrical generators, had its effect on other types of production.

There has been independent support for this explanation. Srinivasan and Narayana (1977) are credited with its 'first detailed exposition' by Bardhan (1984: 23, n. 1). Ahluwalia (1983) has also documented the changing role of public expenditure and its effects on real value added in manufacturing. However, despite these confirmations of the economic explanation of India's industrial slowdown, the political explanation of the sudden policy shift against state-supported industry needed further elaboration. Wade suggested that the political forces at work would be found in the dynamics of the Congress Party's increasingly acute 'need for legitimacy' (1984: 441). These dynamics concern the eroision of the Congress Party's ideological supremacy, as memories of the Congress's independence struggle faded; the requirements imposed on the party by the electoral cycle; the emergence of a new leadership skilled in party administration and organization; and their need to bargain (with public resources) for the votes managed by state and local leaders, who were increasingly from the rural areas, which is where, in India, the great majority of the votes are still to be found. Wade showed that these features of Indian political life were consistent with key facts of public finance in India. They helped to explain the divorce between central development goals and actual resource allocation; the increasing decentralization of public expenditure decisions; the preference for consumption over investment spending and the difficulty of increasing official public savings.[6]

In terms reminiscent of Wade, Bardhan presents a picture of the Indian government as managing class conflicts by expanding subsidies on food, agricultural inputs and public-sector-produced inputs with little regard for their impact in raising productivity.[7] This expansion is seen as driven by the rising stakes in electoral competitions and the rise of 'gangs led by a large number of MLAs and MPs, political middlemen who over the years have specialised in the profession of brokerage services' (Bardhan 1984: 66). The weapon, the motive and, indeed, the culprits themselves, are again identified by Bardhan in the mysterious case of the disappearing capital formation.

But what then are the implications for development policy? In a country characterized by such conflicts between its dominant proper-tied classes, what room is there to manoeuvre towards a superior development path? Indian democracy, at least until the eve of the period of emergency rule (1975–7), is said to have 'provided a subtle and resilient mechanism for conflict management' (Bardhan 1984: 77). But since that time growing stresses and strains on the democratic system have been evident. Bardhan is tempted to go beyond Wade to speak of a 'crisis' of Indian political legitimation, which moreover is continuing to worsen. Although the outcome of this crisis is necessarily uncertain, it does leave some scope for a better and happier state of affairs to emerge. Bardhan does not, however, offer any substantial advice on how the government could resolve the legitimacy crisis on its own terms. Its only option appears to be 'to streamline the administration, to clamp down heavily on the permissive polity, repressing labour unions and disciplining dissent.' By implication, that is a course of action not regarded as desirable.

The Counter-Revolution and Indian Political Economy: a Verdict

To reach a verdict on the competition between the counter-revolution's new political economy of India and the other paradigms described above, one first needs criteria for judgement. Three commonly used criteria are consistency, power and usefulness. Consistency means the absence of serious self-contradiction within the logic of the chosen paradigm. Power means the ability to explain satisfactorily perceived puzzles within the subject matter to which the paradigm is applied. Usefulness means relevance to real choices or decisions that have to be made, or apparently have to be made. These are the criteria that will be adopted here.

In terms of consistency, the theory of rent-seeking appears to run into problems at the point where it ceases to be purely economic in content, and starts to cohabit with political sociology. In Roy's account of the rent-seeking society, there is a clear fracture between the description of Indian politics – based on the economist's assumption of myopic self-interest – and the prescription for it, concern for liberty and the political good. In Jha's account, there is a descriptive contradiction not dissimilar to this. It is between the ability of his intermediate class to gain economic, and then political, power by causing stagnation and slow development, and its subsequent sudden ability to learn to moderate its demands on the system.

The competing paradigms seem to fare better on the test of consistency. If the measurement of urban bias is rightly regarded as a second-order problem, a major consistency problem arises only with the vague and apparently shifting composition of the urban class. This is no worse than the vagueness that surrounds the concept of an intermediate class in the new political economy.

The theory of dominant propertied classes is not quite immaculate in its internal logic. It raises a similar kind of question to that raised by the counter-productive behaviour of the intermediate class. If the conflicts of the dominant propertied classes do produce economic results which are inferior to those which could be produced in the absence of conflict, why do the three classes not work together for their common benefit? The suggested resolution of this puzzle draws on the economics of coalition-building. It is that the incentives for collective, rather than individual class action are too weak to induce class collaboration. Social rigidities stand in the way of superior outcomes, of reasons elaborated by Olson (1982).

The adequacy of this resolution must be in some doubt. It tends to explain too much, though, rather than too little. The underlying premise, that market imperfections such as public goods and other externalities create monopolies and cartels independently of government intervention, can be readily granted. The difficulty arises when this essentially microeconomic analysis is transposed into macrosocial contexts, and huge classes are treated as if they were rational calculating individuals. Moreover no one has yet devised an indicator of the degree of social rigidity, so that the link between social rigidity and slow economic growth remains a heuristic one only. In fact. Olson's theory has been used to explain the stagnation of the Indian economy in the late nineteenth century (1982: 178–80). Contemporary 'stagnation' is rapid economic growth by the standards of a century ago. Does the same theory really 'explain' both these situations?

Returning to the question of the explanatory power of the three paradigms judged overall, the theory of dominant propertied classes appears to have a commanding advantage. Because it incorporates its rivals wholesale, it must have at least equal explanatory power to either of them taken singly. Neither the new political economy nor the urban bias paradigm sees itself as a suitable victim for the Moby Dick of Marxism. But they are ill equipped to resist that fate, in their present condition. The new political economy has made very little headway in developing any credible political sociology. In a sense, one has, in the

Indian case, to sweep the theory of the intermediate class up with the new political economy in order even to have something to discuss. The urban bias paradigm is much more plausibly equipped with a sociological perspective. But it is ambivalent about the relation between the bureaucracy and the urban class and, thus, not very strongly placed to contest the proposition that India has three dominant propertied classes.

This conception is not only more powerful because it constructs an encompassing framework around its competitors. As has been pointed out previously, the new political economy, as represented by Roy, has been weaker in the light it has been able to shed on the details of Indian social struggles over bureaucratic recruitment, higher education and constitutional safeguards for the victims of social discrimination. This may not be totally attributable, however, to the power of different paradigms. It may be partly connected with their particular champions' abilities and insights.

The new political economy carried with it very strong claims of usefulness for development policy in the sense that it provides a detailed agenda of liberal reform. The agenda ranges widely across the field of national policy. It covers foreign policy and education vouchers, as well as the central policy issues of the development counter-revolution – the abolition of foreign aid, ending of foreign trade controls, privatization of public-sector industries and a return to free-market pricing (Roy 1984: 60–7). At the same time, it purports to explain why 'even a limited liberal agenda would appear doomed to be stillborn' in India. The economistic nature of the underlying political economy model generates an EHEU theory which undercuts the motivation of would-be liberal reformers at the same time as it presents them with a very detailed blueprint for political change. The theory of the intermediate class has a Gandhian blueprint for change and an economistic political economy model with second-round learning effects, but these are minor differences. The overall effect remains one of unreasonable precision of policy prescription yoked to unreasonable pessimism or optimism about the prospects for political change.

The urban bias paradigm, although not satisfactory in its analysis of social and political processes, has proved useful for policy-making because it could formulate a coherent and realistic strategy. Coherence was achieved by a primary focus on the rural/agricultural sector, which clearly had been neglected, and dangerously so, by the previous Indian development strategy. The relevance of agricultural development not only to the desired industrial growth, but also to unsolved problems of underemployment and poverty could then be demonstrated. This strategy was realistic, to the extent that the technical means of agricultural change were available and the institutional difficulties, although recognized under such headings as the need for decentralization and the constraints of international politics, were not taken to be insuperable. Through the 1970s, the anti-urban-bias strategy actually made some impact on the nature and goals of Indian planning.

Although it scored well on explanatory power, the dominant propertied classes paradigm does not advertise its immediate usefulness for policy-making purposes. This is only partly because its advocates wish to distance themselves from the developmental activities of governments. It is also partly because the explanatory power of the theory is much greater with reference to social structures than it is with reference to social processes.

What we still need to know at the economy-wide level is how the dynamics of the dominant class conflicts work themselves out. At present, this question falls between two stools. One of these is the rich history of Indian development, its economics and its politics, threaded on to a single historical contradiction – between the transformational goals of development planning and the conservative forces of Indian democratic politics. This is essentially the approach of Frankel (1978). At the other methodological pole is an account, like Bardhan's, of the Indian social structure maintaining itself by means of a (deteriorating) mechanism of conflict management. Somewhere between these two is a scheme of periodization of recent Indian history whose transitions can be shown to respond to the dynamics of dominant class conflicts.

Something of this kind was sketched by Rubin, who produced a periodization of India's political economy since Independence, which not only describes each episode but tries to identify the pressures which generated the transition from one episode to another. These pressures are grouped into positive ones (growth of capital formation, tax revenues and the availability of foreign resources) and negative ones (growth of defence expenditures, public consumption expenditures and inflation). Instead of simply arguing (with Wade or Bardhan) that since 1965 the Congress Party's need for legitimacy has favoured consumption instead of investment expenditures, Rubin shows that the positive and negative pressures have come together in different combinations during different historical episodes (1982: 173–222).

For example, the continuation of economic growth in the 1962–4 period occurred because the negative factors of increased defence spending and inflation were countered by positive factors of increased tax revenues and greater foreign resources. In the 1965–71 period, greater public consumption was not offset by increased tax revenues, while foreign resources fell away sharply. During 1973–4, while public consumption was cut back, inflation had accelerated rapidly and the level of foreign resources remained low. In the Emergency, falling inflation and improved foreign resources allowed government capital formation to recover. The examples are simplifications. Nevertheless, 'at various times and under various conditions, democratic politics had *different* effects on investment in the public sector' (Rubin 1982: 207 emphasis added).

One obvious supplement to this more dynamic approach to political economy is to focus still more sharply on the role of inflation in the dynamics of India's political economy of development. There is now some interesting new empirical work available, appearing to validate cost-plus pricing as the theory of industrial prices in Independent India (Chatterji 1986). The interaction of industrial and agrarian price movements could, therefore, be modelled to give a new theory of the dynamics of Indian inflation. Such a model might provide fresh clues to changes in the incidence of rural and urban poverty, and to the rise and fall of political movements among those most exposed to the ravages of inflation on their already pitiably low standard of consumption.[8] Most ambitiously, its predictions could be tested against an independently derived periodization of the history of Indian development. This would be political economy in the spirit of Michal Kalecki, but Kalecki the analyst of financing development in a mixed economy, rather than Kalecki the commentator on intermediate regimes.

In the first section of this chapter, it was asked whether the political economy of rent-seeking should be substituted for previous perspectives. Our conclusion mush be that it is by no means sufficiently robust for that to be possible, however popular it might be in some quarters. At best, the new political economy seems to have established itself as a part of a much more comprehensive picture of class conflict in contemporary India. But it seems that this picture, too, is not as full or enlightening as it might be. Paradoxically, after so much study, from so many different viewpoints, our understanding is still poorest of the dynamic aspects of Indian society and economy – the very sequences that are 'development'.

Postscript: India's New Economic Course

India's move in 1991 to a programme of economic liberalization is an important postscript to this discussion. What had seemed so unlikely over forty years of Indian development plans – a move away from indiscriminate import substitution, public-sector-driven industrialization and self-defeatingly complex administration of economic behaviour – has now been accepted as government policy and begun to be implemented. This change on the one hand confounds the pessimism of those who, like Roy, predicted that such a change would be impossible, or who, like Jha, believed in a spontaneous enlightenment of the intermediate class in India. On the other hand, it might appear to vindicate the broader counter-revolutionary position that the strategy which India followed for four decades would ultimately have to give way to much more orthodox liberal economic policies.

Since at the time of writing (late 1992), India's reversal of her development strategy is so recent, it is very difficult to give a definite interpretation of it in the light of the political economy theories just laid out. But external pressures evidently were an important cause. One clear example of this was the pressure on India in the early 1980s to rely less on concessional official borrowing (or 'aid') and more on commercial borrowing at market rates of interest. The old development strategy had kept India out of the debt crisis that had engulfed most of Latin America by 1982. Her international creditworthiness was good, and increasing use of commercial lending appeared unproblematic. But it exposed India (as it does all borrowers) to a 'whiplash effect'. Creditors continue to offer new loans until the real economy begins to deteriorate. Then, not only are new loans cut off, but pressures for the reduction of past loans become acute. This occurs at precisely the moment when the country's capacity to service its debt has decreased (Lipton and Toye 1990: 36–7). The pressure to adjust the real economy, and have recourse to official flows from the IMF and the World Bank on whatever terms can be obtained is, at this point, very powerful indeed.

Another important external pressure was the disintegration of the former Soviet Union, in the aftermath of the revolutions in Eastern Europe of late 1989. The old development strategy not only had recognizable similarities with the Soviet model of development, but also relied on the Soviet Union both for barter-based trade and as a political counter-weight to United States influence. The crumbling of a major international ally undermined the long-established Indian strategy of balancing between the pressures of the two superpowers in its foreign and domestic policy.

These various external pressures were not the whole explanation of the move to economic liberalization, however. During the 1980s, control of the public finances was allowed to become lax. This allowed a resurgence of inflation, which apart from a brief episode in 1974–5 had otherwise been kept down to very low levels by developing country standards. Accelerating inflation (from 4.4 per cent in 1985–6 to 13.7 per cent in 1991–2) eroded the country's trade competitiveness. By 1990–1, a balance of payments deficit of almost $9 billion had emerged, while foreign exchange reserves had fallen to less than the value of one month's imports. Such a situation was evidently unsustainable without a change of policy and a new source of foreign exchange inflows.

Internal economic mismanagement was a consequence of the broader political and social crisis that had been sketched by political economy analysts like Bardhan. The overwhelming support which the electorate had given to Rajiv Ghandhi in 1984 after the assassination of his mother, Indira, had all but evaporated by 1990, when Rajiv also was assassinated during the general election campaign. His Congress Party barely clung to office, and the government of his successor, P. V. Narasimha Rao has had to launch its new economic course from a precarious political position. It is sustained largely by the fact that rival parties are not yet ready to mount a fresh electoral challenge.

During this period, some genuine progress has been made in stabilizing the economy and taking steps towards liberalization more significant than any previously attempted, such as the move to a dual exchange rate. Inflation has fallen and the balance of payment deficit has been reduced, while foreign exchange reserves have been rebuilt to a much healthier level. The budget deficit has been brought under better control, as some important subsidies have been reduced or abolished. A more liberal treatment of foreign investors has been promulgated. In the 1992 budget, plans have been announced for the progressive liberalization of the foreign trade regime. The proposed sequencing of the reforms appears to be feasible from a technical point of view. However, the liberalization strategy remains in its early stages. Many of the important decisions, with major consequences for India's politically important classes, remain to be implemented. In particular, the dismantling of fertilizer subsidies and public procurement of food-grains at official prices will be resisted by the farm lobby, while retrenchment of workers in public-sector industries will be resisted by the trades unions. Already some tinkering has occurred in these two sensitive areas, but there is still much hesitation about moving to full liberalization of these key sectors. The political limits to India's new economic course have, therefore, yet to be clearly established.

The provisional conclusion from the latest events in India seems to be that there is nothing inevitable or pre-ordained about the collapse of the previous strategy of development. The external environment for India, as for many other developing countries, worsened markedly in the decade of the 1980s. At the same time, a complex of sociopolitical problems, which had long been gathering, reached its crisis in a period of serious economic mismanagement at the macro-level. That immediate crisis has now been passed. But it is still far from certain that the radical change to an economic liberalization strategy will succeed in resolving the deep-seated social and political problems which initiated India's new economic course.

Notes

1   Hirschman has teasingly suggested that the 'prestige of social silence . . . may owe much to the *lack* of integration and communication among the

individual disciplines of economics, sociology, political science and so on' (1981: 266). More seriously, he has also argued that the attempt to formulate an abstract, general theory of the link between economics and politics can lead only to 'banality or frustration' (quoted by Staniland 1985: 193). Political economy is thus an area of enquiry from which different types of political-economic linkages may be theorized, depending on the particular problem being studied.

2 Seers argued that Marxism and neo-classicism share the values of faith in 'science', historical progress and technology; internationalism; and distaste for moral endeavours to eradicate poverty and exploitation. He called them doctrines suitable for defending the interests of the elites of the USSR and the US respectively. See Seers (1983: 1–45).

3 See discussion on pages 119 to 123. For the standard collection of Kalecki's essays on growth and development in socialist and mixed economies, see Kalecki (1972).

4 The link between opposition to price controls and Gandhian economic policies may not seem overwhelmingly obvious to students of the *khadi* subsidy. Some additional light is thrown on it by the following recollection of Colin Clark, in Meier and Seers (1984: 63):

> Gandhi (nobody will believe this) proved to be a convinced free-market economist, strongly critical of the price controls, rationing and compulsory purchase of farm crops which the Nehru government was then introducing. The right solution, he said, was to raise the price of food, then everyone would have to work harder. The source of India's troubles was that the people were thoroughly idle.

5 The circumstances were Indira Gandhi's decision to seek electoral ratification of nearly two years of Emergency Rule, combined with another decision to allow the election to proceed in much the same way as pre-Emergency elections. Such a combination is surely very unusual in political history. The Janata government, which briefly followed, acted as if it never really recovered from the shock of its victory in March 1977.

6 The preference for consumption over investment spending does not follow with complete logical strictness from the hypothesis of a legitimacy crisis in the dominant party. After all, even investment spending can be used for political bargaining purposes and, apparently, has been in Nigeria, for example. The economic significance of investment spending depends on whether it is merely investment according to definitions in the national accounts, or investment in the sense of purchasing assets which will actually be productive of income streams more valuable than the assets' cost, when suitably discounted. It is hard to say whether political motives render investment unproductive, or merely redistribute investment that would in any case have been unproductive. (I owe the Nigerian example to Douglas Rimmer.)

7 The consequence of this can be seen in the gradual rise of the capital/output ratio over the period of planning in India. This phenomenon cannot be explained by the increased technological sophistication of investment in India, because it is to be found across the board and not merely in the

technologically sophisticated sectors of production. It could be argued that it was dismay at rising capital/output ratios which caused the dramatic policy shift against the strategies of the Second and Third Plans. This seems a rather over-rational account of what happened, implying highly developed economic management skills even in a period of political turbulence and diffident leadership. Bardhan, at least, has politics as the cause and rising capital/output ratios as a result.

8   In this connection, it is worth noting that Indian governments since Independence have, notwithstanding repeated claims of reckless resort to deficit finance, been unusually responsive to signs of accelerating inflation. 'Budgetary deficits at least until the 1980s have been kept to a very small proportion of GNP . . . Indian governments unlike many in the Third World are very sensitive to inflation and react fairly quickly to suppress it' (Joshi and Little 1986: 2–3). Does this responsiveness derive from the self-interest of the bureaucracy? This seems doubtful. '. . . if the bureaucracy is powerful enough to induce political action to restrain inflation in its own interests, then it is surely powerful enough to see to it that its own salaries are indexed [to the rate of inflation, which currently they are not]' (p. 8). Joshi and Little also find the relation between Indian democracy and the dominant party's conservative attitude to inflation 'rather obscure', while suggesting that India's toleration for inflation has been rising the 1980s. Clearly this whole subject area is ripe for further study.

CHAPTER SEVEN

The Counter-Revolution in Aid and Trade Policy

The Defence of the Old International Economic Order

The chief stimulus to the debate on international aid and trade policy in the last twenty years has undoubtedly been the demands of developing countries for a 'new international economic order' (NIEO). This demand was spelt out by one of the periodic Conferences of Non-Aligned Countries, held in Algiers in 1973. It was to involve a fundamental restructuring of the international economy for the benefit of the nations of the 'South', that is, all those not in North America, Western or Eastern Europe, Soviet Asia and the eastern Pacific rim, including as honorary 'Northerners' Australia and New Zealand. This call was followed up in May 1974 by the adoption by the UN General Assembly of a Declaration of Principles and a Programme of Action designed to put North–South economic relations on to a basis of 'equality and co-operation'.

These resolutions coincided with the first of the two major oil shocks to the West (and other oil-importing countries), as a result of OPEC's decision to triple the price of oil in the space of a few months and its ability to make this decision effective in the market place. In this dramatic context, probably South and North alike suspected that the South might have the power to alter the terms of international cooperation markedly in its own favour, regardless of the outcome of negotiations over the demands for an NIEO. It was certainly known to leaders of both North and South states that, within the North, opinion was divided on the merits of the call for an NIEO, with some powerful voices welcoming it as a move towards greater international justice.

In the event, much less structural change has occurred than was generally expected. A brief price boom lifted revenues from non-oil commodities in 1973–4. But the combination of a high oil price with deflationary policies in much of the North after 1980 has kept commodity prices for non-oil commodities generally depressed. By 1986, the oil price itself, as a result of the world recession of the early 1980s and specific energy-saving policies of consumers, had fallen back to approximately the same level, allowing for inflation, as it commanded in 1973.

But the threat of an NIEO, particularly one imposed by the South and supported on moral grounds by influential opinion in the North, acted as a strong spur to the counter-revolution in development policy. It has mounted an effective defence of the existing international economic order. Its reaction to demands for an NIEO can be seen in two different forms. The first of these was to publicize a number of 'anomalies' – odd and undesired outcomes – that would be likely to arise from the adoption of an NIEO. In polemical fashion, these were then ridiculed, with the purpose of discrediting the whole idea of an international redistribution of resources through aid or trade. The second reaction was a more judicious one, which concentrated on examining the intellectual basis in moral and political philosophy for global redistributivist strategies like the NIEO.

The game of 'hunt the anomaly' has been played most vigorously by Bauer. In trade policy, his opposition to monopolies and cartels led him to question the prominence accorded to international commodity agreements (ICAs) in the programme for an NIEO. Why should this particular device be regarded by the South as one of the centrepieces of an NIEO, although ICAs are likely to do very little for the alleviation of poverty in developing countries? After all, if an ICA requires that a developing country restrict its supply of a particular commodity, how is that supply restriction usually brought about? The frustrated producers are too often the less-well-endowed small-scale producers. By contrast, the large, established private companies or public sector corporations are able to lobby effectively for a good share of the available quota. And if an ICA effectively raises a commodity price, rather than just stabilizing it around a market clearing level, it will penalize consumers, at least some of whom will be poor people in poor countries (Bauer 1981: 156–62).

In aid policy and practice, it proved easy to locate similar kinds of anomaly. It is theoretically possible, for example, for official aid to have a regressive impact on world income distribution. 'Many taxpayers in donor countries are far poorer than many people in Third World countries where, moreover, aid often benefits the prosperous rather than the needy and where the governments who demand international redistribution do not practise it at home' (Bauer 1981: 116–17). This highlights another anomaly of aid, that attempts to ensure that aid is used for the relief of poverty in the recipient country might well be resisted by the recipient country on the grounds that such attempts infringe its sovereignty. A third anomaly is that aid-giving for the relief of poverty may ignore hostile acts by the recipient country and, thus, the donor's citizens could have been taxed for the benefit of an unfriendly state. These are the three most serious of the many anomalies that the counter-revolution culled from the theory and practice of aid-giving. Clearly, the existence of these possibilities, and evidence that they have indeed occurred at some time or other, must have the effect of checking un-qualified enthusiasm for massive additional official aid, as required in the programme for an NIEO.

One extreme response to the discovery of such anomalies in the trade and aid proposals of the NIEO was to opt for complete *laissez-faire* in trade and the termination of all official aid. The counter-revolution, in the shape of Bauer, certainly sees these drastic policy changes as desirable. But other advocates of the counter-revolution fortunately make a more measured and thoughtful response. Before rushing to extreme conclusions, it is worth exploring how and why the observed anomalies arise. In fact, they arise for a very interesting reason, namely, that our notion of what constitutes 'justice' on a worldwide scale has still not been fully and satisfactorily specified.

Not surprisingly, this acts as handicap to the efforts of, for example, the Brandt Commission which, since 1980, has produced several reports broadly advocating the kind of fundamental restructuring of the in-ternational economic order sought by the South during the NIEO negotiations. There are parallels between the Brandtian idea of global justice and that contained in the political philosophy of Immanuel Kant (Toye 1983a: 51–4). Kant argued in 1784 that political justice could not finally be established within states until the problem of the lawful external relationship of states was also solved. Furthermore, conflict and destitution, which had led to the adoption of just constitutions within states, would act as an incentive to form a union of nations capable of protecting the security and rights of even the smallest state. It is global justice viewed as the product of a union of nations that is problematic for the NIEO proposals. Most of the anomalies observed by the counter-revolution in the NIEO proposals can be traced to this problem.

Kant's conception of justice between states never considered the issue of transfer of resources from one state to another in order to eradicate poverty in the receiving state. The Brandt Report (1980) does not notice that reliance on the Kantian conception of global justice runs into difficulties once international redistribution is placed on the agenda for action. It also fails to distinguish between the Kantian idea of global justice and another idea often confused with it – that of justice within a single worldwide state (Sen 1984: 292–3).[1] None of the anomalies highlighted by the counter-revolution would arise for income redistribution carried out within a single world state. They arise when global justice involves redistribution between states, rather than between rich and poor individuals worldwide.

The more judicious supporters of the development counter-revolution have usefully contributed to the elucidation of this essential distinction. Little, for example, called attention to the confusion of 'two different concepts, a universal humanistic morality and an inter-state morality', pointing out that the redistributive aspects of the NIEO were justified by the latter, rather than the former (1978: 47–8). Although the former basis would provide an adequate justification if a world moral community existed, Little further doubts that human beings at large could 'be regarded as forming enough of a society' to provide the framework of that particular theory of global justice. It is not clear what social bonds, apart from shared humanity itself, create a 'moral community', and this remains a very important unresolved question for the future.[2]

Thus one of the effects of the demand for an NIEO has been to lead its more sophisticated opponents in the developed countries to look more closely than they had done in the past at issues of international justice. Their efforts have not been as dismissive of the suggestion that justice requires further international redistribution as Bauer's have been. They have, however, served to remind zealous supporters of an NIEO that the appeal to international justice is a complex and sometimes treacherous one to make.

At the least, it is necessary to distinguish commutative from distributive justice. The latter may be of dubious force in a world of nation-states, but the former – the obligation to treat equals equally – has more force between states. The proposals of the NIEO concerning technology transfer, the malpractices of multinational corporations and the working of the international monetary system rest on the commutative criterion of justice, rather than the distributive criterion.

What a careful look at arguments about justice demonstrates is that, although moral philosophers may not be able to give an indisputably correct account of the nature of justice, that does not *ipso facto* render the concept redundant. The counter-revolution very clearly needs and wants to rest its development policies on some moral foundation. In order to do that, it must continue to seek its own accommodation with the complexities of moral philosophy. To fail to do so adequately can lead it into some self-evidently false extreme positions.

To underline this point, one only has to ask an obvious question. Why are the detected 'anomalies' of NIEO proposals for aid and trade indeed anomalies? They are so precisely because they offend standard moral intuitions, such as that the poor should not be taxed to benefit the rich, or that no person can be obliged to endanger their own survival. Such moral intuitions can only be defended as part of a larger system of ethical beliefs and as part of a comparative discussion of the merits of different ethical systems. The inconsistency between condemning official aid as regressive, and claiming that the existing distribution of income and wealth is 'natural', and a matter of indifference, is one that some counter-revolutionaries conspicuously fail to avoid.

As Sen has pointed out, some of the counter-revolution's opposition to the redistributive proposals of an NIEO rests on 'a conservative belief that the population of each country is entitled to what it happens to have currently, and while a change needs justification, the status quo does not . . . this approach [can be called] that of "entitlement valid for all substance I own now" – "evasion" for short' (1984: 293). The 'evasion' belief is an ethical evasion because it is inconsistent with the very moral intuition according to which anomalies in the NIEO redistribution proposals are themselves selected. On the basis of 'evasion', not only would regressive aid have to be ruled out; not only would all forms of aid have to be ruled out; all other forms of government expenditure financed by taxation would have to be ruled out also. The argument from regressiveness would be quite redundant.

The ethical evasion of the more extreme counter-revolutionaries does not, needless to say, validate the ethical position taken by the supporters of massive intergovernmental redistribution. Their approach, by contrast, relies on the 'fiction of all nations throbbing as symbolic individuals in existence', as Sen has put it, or 'fantasie' for short (1984: 292). Thus the search for a just international economic order has been, at worst, a debate between a morally 'fantastic' doctrine on the pro-NIEO side, and a morally 'evasive' response by the more extreme counter-revolutionaries. At best, it has heightened awareness of the relevance of ethical argument to the making of the international economic order and produced a more refined set of ethical problems to be explored.

Some pro-NIEO opinion distances itself from the moral debate by placing it in a long historical perspective. For example, it has recently been argued that 'intermittent attempts of liberal thinkers from the mid-nineteenth century to the present to revive the concept of economic justice have been unable to establish a theoretical foothold for it, because they have still relied on the allocative market whose supremacy the concept was designed to prevent' (Macpherson 1985: 2). In other words, theories of economic justice have been no more than a defensive tactic in the long, and ultimately unwinnable battle against the encroachment of market forces on the social life of capitalist societies.

This distanced, historical approach to justice has the effect of undermining the moral case for more global redistribution. It manages at the same time to endorse it and deprive it of force, by representing it as no more than a tactical or instrumental move. Will 'Third World' countries still find the concept of economic justice a useful offensive or defensive weapon against their subjugation by the 'advanced countries'? In a world of very unequal state power, Third World claims are only ever likely to be met when they are recognized as genuine moral claims. They will not be so recognized if they are made, and are seen to be made, as one more device of *realpolitik*.

Thus, there is a contradiction at the heart of Sartre's paraphrase of Fanon: 'let [the Third World] burst into history, forcing it by our invasion into universality for the first time'. Universality of obligation and respect are not created by force and invasion, although military power may be. Would it not indeed be miraculous if the moral unification of the world required only violence and boldness?

The unavoidable route is back into all the dilemmas of moral discourse. What is justice? Are the utilitarians – and, according to Little (1978: 42), 'most economists are rather unthinking utilitarians' – right to be ready to sacrifice part of the utility enjoyed by the poor for a larger gain in 'aggregate welfare'?[3] Or are those right who believe that 'the general conception of justice as fairness requires that all primary social goods be distributed equally, unless an unequal distribution would be to everyone's advantage' (Rawls 1972: 150)? Is justice what rational people would choose if they were ignorant of their own social position? If so, can we be very sure of what it would be rational to choose in that situation (Williams 1985: 103)? Can people choose anything in ignorance of their personal circumstances (Sandel 1984: 170–1)? And, if justice is the terms of a contract between rational people, how are obligations to the less than fully rational people in the world determined?[4]

Although competence in exploring such questions lies mainly with professional moral philosophers, the results of their labour – partial and perplexing as they often are – cannot be simply ignored. Citizens with what they believe to be moral claims to make on others need some insight into the differences between moral claims, special pleading, emotional appeals and the usages of custom, all of which can lurk under the banner of 'justice'. But more importantly for the subject of development policy, development economists need to discipline their tendency to disguise the values on which their particular policy recommendations rely. The false impression of being able to conjure scientific advice from a realm of knowledge far removed from the difficult conflicts of value with which ordinary people wrestle has conferred on economists more power and less responsibility than they should have had to bear (for example, Lal 1983: 11).[5]

Development economists particularly, given the comprehensive spread of values found in their worldwide field of operation, should adopt a self-denying ordinance, long ago proposed by Myrdal, to make explicit their value premises. That involves some minimal monitoring of the progress of moral philosophy, so that values can be expressed in a coherent and accessible way. In obedience to this rule of disclosure, what follows will be cast in the broad framework of justice espoused by Rawls (1972).

The Opposition to International Commodity Agreements

At the level of national economic management, the counter-revolution has always opposed controls over foreign trade, apart from a low uniform tariff which is sometimes regarded as permissible. At the international level, its opposition to 'managed trade' has been expressed through its critique of international commodity agreements (ICAs). ICAs are internationally negotiated schemes of intervention in the markets for exports of primary products (or 'hard' and 'soft' commodities). The counter-revolution's opposition to these schemes is based on various grounds, but a major one has already been mentioned in the previous section – their failure to alleviate the poverty to be found in developing countries.

One of the difficulties of appraising ICAs is that no two ICAs are exactly alike. It is worth distinguishing between schemes with different aims, and schemes with different mechanisms. ICAs may either aim to stabilize primary commodity prices around a medium-term market-clearing price, or may aim to stabilize the price at a level higher than the market-clearing level. For both of these purposes, they may use the mechanism of a managed buffer stock, with instructions to buy the commodity when its price is low enough and to sell it when the price is high enough. They may also use a system of production quotas limiting the supply of each producing nation, policed by the customs authorities of the consuming nations. Or they may adopt some combination of buffer stock and production quotas. The most long-lived ICAs have regulated the market for tin (1956) and for coffee (1962). More recently, a cocoa ICA has been operational. The OPEC nations do not constitute an ICA because only producer nations are members: they form an oil producers' association, with ambitions to act as a cartel.

The formation of ICAs for between ten and eighteen primary commodities became the principal practical objective for the NIEO in the mid-1970s. Although commodities and trade formed only one of the NIEO's six programmes of action approved by the UN in 1974, this programme came to fruition faster than the other five because considerable preparatory work had been done on ICAs at the Third

UNCTAD Conference of the 'Group of 77' developing countries in 1972. Thus the Fourth UNCTAD Conference held in Nairobi in 1976 approved the idea of an Integrated Programme for Commodities, including a Common Fund to finance the holding of buffer stocks for the intended new ICAs. The mode of operation of the Common Fund was finally settled at UNCTAD V in Manila in 1979, but its details need not be spelt out here.[6]

One of the reasons for the counter-revolution's opposition to the proliferation of ICAs, as envisaged by the NIEO, is that 'the increasing political management and cartelisation of trade . . . is unlikely to help the poor or the poorest states' (Little 1978: 52). From a Rawlsian point of view, this is a highly pertinent objection, because it holds that economic inequalities can be justified only if they are to the benefit of the least advantaged in society. It would certainly, according to Rawls's theory of justice, be unjust to create special marketing arrangements which not only did not improve the lot of the poorest, but actually worsened it.

The negligible impact of ICAs on the poor in the Third World has been argued to derive from the fact that 'the poorest countries in the Third World rarely produce for export' (Bauer 1981: 160). If one takes the group of least developed developing countries (LLDCs) as being the poorest, this proposition does not entirely hold up. In 1982, no less than one-third of the LLDCs for whom figures were available had exports that accounted for 20 per cent or more of their own domestic product. Further, on average, 60 per cent of the exports of the LLDCs were of fuels, minerals or other primary commodities (World Bank 1984: 226, 236).

The counter-revolution is on somewhat firmer ground in saying that the poorest groups within developing countries are minimally involved with production for export. It is generally well appreciated that the poorest of the poor tend to be remote, isolated and lacking the skills and confidence to forge effective links with their surrounding society. Anyone who is not part of a large trading network cannot be affected directly by an ICA. They could, however, be affected indirectly, if the ICA augments government revenues, which are then spent on special projects for the poorest of the poor. A reasonable assumption is that the effect on them will be neutral.

The strongest objection to ICAs on distributional grounds is that the poorest producers for export are affected most harshly by the working of a quota-based ICA, because they will be treated as the marginal producers whose output will be prohibited in lean times and grudgingly permitted in a boom. There does seem to be evidence that this happens in the tin industry, for example, to the gravel-pump miners of Thailand and Malaysia. However, they are not totally deprived of income for production by being excluded from an official quota. They are forced into the illegal channels of smuggling and black-market sales in Singapore, with its attendant hazards of harassment and loss through confiscation by national customs officials.

To establish whether this regressive feature characterizes ICAs other than tin, and would also appear in ICAs for other primary commodities if they were to be established, would require more detailed research than is available. One very thorough study of the microeconomic theory of ICAs shows that ICAs designed only to stabilize prices at a level that clears existing supply will depress consumers' expenditure on the product concerned and thus also lower the revenue of producers. This effect arises because typically the income elasticity of demand for primary products is less than unity. Just to prevent this happening, some quota restrictions on supply would have to be operated alongside a managed buffer stock (Newbery and Stiglitz 1981). At the same time, the precise consequences for distribution of income between producers and consumers cannot be easily derived from economic theory. They are sensitive to the numerical estimates that are made of demand and supply elasticities for the different primary commodities (Newbery and Stiglitz 1981: 271).

To some extent, the counter-revolution is in a position to cut through the debate on the exact distributional impact of ICAs. It could do this by comparing stabilization achieved by ICAs to stabilization achieved by the use of forward markets. In principle, Third World producers can protect themselves against price fluctuations by 'hedging' their sales on forward markets. 'Hedging' is the purchase of a contract for delivery of the same amount of the same commodity as the producer himself intends to supply, both contracts maturing at the same date: if the price has changed, the gain on one transaction will offset the loss on the other. In these forward markets, the risks of price change are borne by speculators. In order for producers to be able to hedge themselves against loss or gain, there must be other participants who are willing to gamble on price changes. These speculators are normally wealthy people who volunteer to bear risk in the hope of gain and in the knowledge that losses on particular transactions will not plunge them into personal disaster. A system which deals with risk by having such people bear it is superior from a Rawlsian perspective than one which, like an ICA, distributes risk around within the Third World regardless of the exact allocation between different classes of producer and consumer.

The problem is that, in practice, it is only the larger Third World commodity producers who have so far begun to use the forward markets. At present, the small operator loses out both in terms of government intervention and in terms of poor access to markets. But there is every reason to 'encourage the use of forward contracts by small producers and traders and the development of organised commodity markets in local centres' (Bauer 1981: 159). It is likely to be a lengthy and complicated task, given the current state of communications and financial expertise. But it is hardly a part of a structuralist approach to argue against the making of new markets where none exist now.

Where Keynesians might wish to enter a caveat is at any attempt to conclude an assessment of ICAs after scrutinizing only their microeconomic effects. The counter-revolution, as suggested in chapter 4, seems to believe rather too easily that microeconomic analyses are all that is necessary and that no separate macroeconomic work is called for. This can be misleading. It is certainly possible that ICAs could have, on certain assumptions about aggregate supply response for the product concerned and for the country's other export industries, the result of increasing the developing country's national income. It could also have, again on special assumptions, beneficial effects in dampening inflation in developed countries which are large consumers of the commodity whose price the ICA stabilizes. These aggregate effects of ICAs, while not entirely neglected, have received much less sustained attention, although certain analysts have suggested that they might be quantitatively significant (Kanbur 1983: 19–25).

Although, therefore, a number of questions about the distribution of the benefits and costs (micro and macro) of ICAs remain to be explored, the counter-revolution's prima-facie case that their impact is unjust still has not been decisively refuted. But, for all the intrinsic interest of the debate about justice – especially in the context of the demand for an NIEO – it is not the key to the future of managed commodity trade.

What more than anything else has produced the débâcle of UNCTAD's Integrated Programme for Commodities is the sheer practical difficulties of starting ICAs and keeping them going. The inhibitions on starting an ICA are well illustrated by the recent international negotiations for an ICA for tea (1977–83). The vulnerability of even well-established ICAs to sudden death is evident from the dramatic collapse of the tin buffer stock in October 1985.

The abortive attempt to create an ICA for black tea failed partly because, although a target price level for stabilization (95 pence per kilo) and a global export quota (825–875 thousand metric tonnes per annum) were both agreed at an early stage, the conflict between old and new producers over country quotas was never really resolved. The old, high-cost producers, while prepared to accommodate the output from current new producer investment in expansion, were not prepared to concede an indefinitely continuing erosion of their market share. As Keynes stated clearly in his original wartime memorandum on commodity control, any scheme for an ICA has to reconcile short-period stabilization of prices with 'a long-period price policy which balances supply and demand and allows a steady rate of expansion to the cheaper-cost producer' (CW XXVII: 140). Conflicts of economic interest between developing countries with markedly different long-run marginal cost curves may well prevent such a reconciliation taking place. In the example of tea, the opposed interests of India and Sri Lanka, on the one hand, and the East African tea producers such as Kenya and Tanzania, on the other, were never able to be reconciled within a single quota system. Why should the rapidly growing, lower-cost tea-producing countries agree to a limit on their exports? Particularly when, as it happened, the market price of tea was rising above the ICA target price?

The collapse of the International Tin Council's buffer stock operation in late 1985 occurred despite the fact that it was designed merely to stabilize the tin price around a market-clearing level and not to maintain a higher one. But even this more modest kind of intervention requires an accurate estimate of the future market-clearing price of the commodity. The making of such an estimate is a tricky business. Even when supply can be forecast correctly on the basis of the ICA's own quota system, plus supply of non-ICA-member producers and existing private stocks, demand factors may contain some nasty surprises. A prolonged industrial recession, as in the early 1980s, can undermine the most careful commodity price forecast for a metal.

In essence, that is what happened in the case of tin. But the ICA obliged the tin buffer stock manager to continue buying tin on credit to support an unrealistic target price, until eventually the ITC went bankrupt with bank debts of £340 million. This was followed by suspension of the tin market, wrangles over who should pay the debt and a massive drop in the tin price once trading resumed. At the time of the collapse, the ITC had undertaken to buy 62,000 tonnes of tin at £8,900 per tonne, in a hopeless attempt to stop the price falling below the floor of £8,500 per tonne specified in the ICA. The free-market price would have been less than £6,000 per tonne. Eventually the banks realized that accepting the tin as collateral for further credit was not exactly sound banking practice and no more credit was forthcoming.

In an uncertain world, it appears that ICAs can even out price fluctuations for some time, but only at the cost of very severe adjustments when adjustments finally come. In this, they are comparable with fixed exchange rates, which produce small variations followed by a speculative crisis and revaluation or devaluation. When the crisis of an ICA arrives - and, incidentally, it is hastened when the target price is set in one currency and exchange rates are fluctuating – the developed country producers are better able to shield themselves than the developing country producers. RTZ, the UK mining multinational which invested

in Cornish tin mining when the ICA-maintained price was high, succeeded in extracting £25 million in interest-free loans and loan guarantees from a notoriously anti-interventionist UK government, for the
official purpose of reducing its costs to make its operation profitable at
the post-ICA market price of tin.[7]

The tin crisis was especially dramatic, but it should not been seen as
typical of ICAs. The typical ICA is one that never gets born, rather
than one that dies violently. Apart from the conflict of interest among
producers, the conflict of interest between producers and consumers is
a major obstacle, as are such awkward features of commodities as their
perishability and their occurrence in multiple grades and qualities. One
other inhibition, which has been less commented on, is that the existence of the ICA actually deters the formation of another, if the products
are substitutes in consumption. For example, the existence of an ICA
for coffee, which keeps the coffee price above free-market levels, keeps
the demand for tea artificially high. If the tea producers were to follow
the example of the coffee producers, the latter would be able to relax
their quota restrictions without reducing the price of coffee and so
would be better off. In the case of tea and coffee, for the East Africans
to join a tea ICA would be a concealed benefit for Brazil's coffee
industry, which already enjoys a favoured position in the coffee ICA
relative to the East African coffee producers. Similar considerations
apply to other commodities which are partial substitutes – copper
concentrates and alumina, for example.

Thus it is a combination of technical, economic and political inhibitions which has frustrated the NIEO's Integrated Programme for
Commodities. It is not lack of finance, which the Common Fund has
provided beyond the amounts likely to be needed. Nor is it the
questionable justice of ICAs' impact on income distribution which the
counter-revolution has emphasized, even while declaring its indifference to distributional issues. It follows from this that preaching about
the dangers and difficulties of administered trade in primary products,
wholesome as much of it is, will have a very limited impact. It may even
be misunderstood by developing countries who can observe the grain
mountains of the USA and wine and milk lakes of Europe.

Steering Aid to the Private Sector

The counter-revolution's hostility to the 'over-extension' of the public
sector in developing countries, discussed in chapter 3, carried implications for aid policy. Specifically, is aid, which by definition is a financial transfer from one government to another, one of the causes of the
alleged undesirable over-extension? Are developing-country governments

just using the aid money that comes their way to extend a grand bureaucratic empire, without regard to economic considerations such as the productivity of investment?

Some critics of aid, at both ends of the political spectrum, deploy a sceptical argument against aid-giving, based on the problem of fungibility. Fungibility arises when gifts or borrowed money, although nominally used for project X actually make possible project Y, because project X would have been undertaken whether the gift or loan was forthcoming or not. Since it is hard for an external observer to know whether it was project Y that was financed, rather than projects A, B, C or Z, the fungibility argument implies that the true use of aid is known only to developing country economic planners. They will be unwilling to disclose their knowledge, particularly if project Y was the purchase of additional military aircraft.

Aid and the Public Sector

To the extent that the counter-revolution holds that aid has fed bloated public sectors in developing countries, it has to abandon the fungibility argument to insist that the true uses of aid are known. Aid's impact is claimed to be the increase in the size of an unproductive public sector beyond what it would have been in the absence of aid. Moreover, this is claimed to have an opportunity cost to the private sector, because potential private sector investors are 'crowded out' by aid-fuelled expansion of the public sector.[8]

Just because all official aid is a government-to-government transaction, it does not follow that the final users of aid are in the public sector. Some 20 per cent of all World Bank aid, for example, is currently passed on to the private sectors of developing countries. Using various financial intermediaries, much of this goes as credit for small and medium private enterprises and cultivators in the rural sector. Of the remainder, about half (another 40 per cent) is spent on general infrastructure such as energy, communications, water, roads, other transport, urban services and so on. Although these services are provided by the public sector organizations – not always very efficiently – they are necessary for productive private enterprise, and there is little evidence in developing countries that private enterprise is either willing or able to provide infrastructure for itself. A further 25 per cent is spent on infrastructure specific to agriculture – such as public sector irrigation projects and area development projects. Thus the upper limit of World Bank aid which could plausibly be said to compete with private capital is 15 per cent.

In bilateral aid programmes, that is, those where the money passes directly from one country to another instead of indirectly through an international agency such as the World Bank, there may have been more scope for 'crowding out' to take place. It was the bilateral, national aid agencies which, for example, competed vigorously with each other to be allowed to finance steel mills in the Indian public sector in the early 1960s. However, since 1980, many of these (excluding the Dutch and Scandinavian agencies) have swung in a diametrically opposite direction and are now keenly competitive in seeking private sector projects to finance with bilateral aid. Bilateral aid tends to be much more responsive to swings in political opinion than does multilateral aid.[9]

As was pointed out in chapter 3, much confusion over the counter-revolution's claim that developing countries have 'over-extended' public sectors springs from the simple fact that there is no agreement on what constitutes the 'correct' division of functions between the private and public sectors of a mixed economy. It is reasonable to assume that the United States would be seen by most supporters of the development counter-revolution as having a division of functions as close to ideal as is possible in an imperfect world. Just for the sake of argument, let us accept that view. The following question can then be put. How much World Bank money has been channelled, over the years, to institutions in developing countries in the public sector which would have been in the private sector if the developing countries had all adopted the US line of division of functions? The answer is that only between 6 and 8 per cent of total World Bank aid has been directed to such institutions (Cassen and Associates 1986: 244–5). Such a modest percentage, when such a favourable assumption is made, suggests that the counter-revolutionary view of aid bloating the public sector is itself considerably overblown.

Their policy conclusion that aid, if it is to continue, must be steered to the private sector in developing countries, seems in the light of that estimate much ado about very little. If the justification for the present position is that local entrepreneurship is hard to find and then difficult to support sensibly, one can have no qualms about agreeing that everyone should look harder and try to develop types of support that do not perpetuate dependency. But there is no need to change greatly one's expectations about the likely outcome of the new policy emphasis. The main reservation that is appropriate concerns the nature of the private sector. The counter-revolution tends to see the private sector as composed exclusively of profit-making or profit-orientated enterprises. This is an unnecessarily restrictive view. There are many cooperatives, charities and other forms of voluntary society at work in the Third World at various tasks which contribute to economic and social development. The non-profit organizations have many of the qualities of profit-seeking non-government organizations – the ability to take initiatives, to find low-cost strategies and generally not to be bureaucratic in the perjorative sense. Channelling aid to such bodies may be just as valuable, or more valuable, than channelling it to firms.

The development counter-revolution has made much of the question of the so-called politicization of life, which is said to be the bad political effect of aid. One can look at a number of case studies which show that the causal link between aid and *dirigisme* is very difficult to establish. Where one has countries which rely very heavily on the public sector and which control to a considerable extent their private sector, the advent of economic *dirigisme* predated the arrival of large-scale aid. In the case of India, it is clear that the whole apparatus of direct controls was already there, more or less, before the World Bank set up the Aid-India Consortium in 1958. What has happened since then is that under Bank leadership, there has been a very slow process of dismantling direct controls, a gradual process of economic liberalization, which has increasingly gathered momentum in the 1980s.

There is a similar story in Bangladesh, where the social and political deformations complained of by critics of aid also essentially predated the arrival of aid. So it seems to be a mistake to suggest that aid has created them. Aid agencies, at times, having decided to enter a country which has such conditions, do bolster and prop them up for a while. But it is usually the case that there is a transition, perhaps a slow transition, and generally the apparatus of control is eroded in some way or another. Sometimes, it was precisely in order to acquire multilateral aid that the apparatus of *dirigisme* was dismantled. South Korea is a very good example of that. The period of heavy US bilateral aid in the 1950s underwent a transition in the early 1960s precisely because the US aid agency wanted Korea to switch to multilateral lending and knew that they would not be able to do that if they did not get rid of some of the economic controls that then existed. That was the conjuncture at which the exchange rate was reformed in South Korea, and policies of substantial currency overvaluation ended. The cases of India, Bangladesh and South Korea show, in different ways, that aid rarely creates what the counter-revolution sees as a *dirigiste* syndrome and, in time, can have a weakening effect on it.[10]

Mixed Credits: Aiding the Donor's Private Sector

The development counter-revolution's wish to see official aid increasingly directed towards the private sector in developing countries must be considered in the context of pressure simultaneously to extract more benefits from bilateral aid for the private sector in the developed donor countries. Since the middle 1970s, and especially as the recession has deepened and persisted with only mild recovery, new ways of using bilateral aid have been developed, by France, the UK, Canada and others. They link aid more visibly with export orders than normal tied aid and raise the quantum of export orders secured per unit of aid given. One device of this kind is the mixed credit package.

Mixed credit differs from traditional types of capital aid in two interesting ways. Instead of being merely conditional on procurement of equipment from the donor, mixed credit is given to secure the purchase of a specific piece of equipment from an identified supplying firm. Secondly, mixed credit – the use of one part official aid with two or three parts normal export credit – achieves what is called 'aid gearing', raising the value of identifiable export orders for every unit of aid money spent.[11]

Although originally mixed credit was used to benefit public sector corporations or public companies in the UK, it has increasingly become a thinly disguised form of export subsidy for UK private sector firms, notably in the electrical and mechanical engineering industries. The consequence of mixed credit for the developmental aims of aid have not been very happy. It involves a move backwards to former mistakes with capital aid. Once again, the old fallacy is trotted out: 'these countries need buses/trains/telecommunications/mining gear, so any use of aid that gets them there must be a good thing'. Since capital equipment never runs, maintains or repairs itself, merely putting more of it in a developing country achieves nothing by itself. And whether it is destined for the private or the public sector makes precious little difference to that.

Thus, at the same time as concern for steering aid to developing countries' private firms has become an objective of policy, a less publicized concern for capturing more benefits of aid for donor countries' private firms has begun to undermine the developmental effectiveness of many bilateral aid programmes. Because mixed credit is a form of disguised export subsidy, the development counter-revolution could not endorse its use by developed countries as an instrument of aid and trade policy. What the development counter-revolution consistently overlooks is that its programme of economic liberalization on developing countries is actually taking place while protectionism is increasing in international trade and bilateral aid programmes are being increasingly refashioned to supplement the existing armoury of protection (Toye and Clark 1986).

Although the theory of the development counter-revolution does not justify the injunction to developing countries of 'you must liberalize, while we in the developed countries must increase our protection', the real impact of the development counter-revolution is undoubtedly highly selective. Whatever the theory, a hail of books and pamphlets about liberalization of economic life in the Third World, some containing a statutory line or paragraph deploring rising protection in the First World, demonstrates a very one-eyed view of the problems of realizing economic liberalism.

Exchanging Aid for Policy Reforms

The call for a new international economic order foundered partly on the rocks of moral confusion – between a humanistic morality focused on the well-being of the most disadvantaged individuals worldwide and an inter-state morality focused on the equality of rights and power of national states. These two different moralities may, in some situations, point to diametrically opposed courses of action. When this happens, those who do not recognize that the moralities are different will recommend actions that are anomalous.

Aid and Policy Reform

One of the anomalies most emphasized by the counter-revolution is the giving of aid to developing countries which either do not alleviate the poverty of their citizens, or which take measures which might have the effect of worsening it. Humanism tells us that this is not justified. The morality of inter-state relations asks why the recipient's sovereignty should be infringed by inquisitions into the socioeconomic effects of its internal policies when no inquisition is thought necessary into the internal policies of the donor or its motives in offering the aid, which may not invariably be altruistic.

The device of making the giving of aid conditional on the recipient agreeing to follow certain kinds of internal policies appears to be an ingenious way of dealing with this anomaly. The developing country is essentially presented with a choice: whether or not it is prepared to offer to change certain internal policies at the time when it accepts the aid. It can make up its mind whether the changes required are substantial or symbolic enough to constitute an infringement of sovereignty and, if so, it can refuse the aid. Alternatively, if changes are volunteered before the aid is given, no infringement of sovereignty has occurred. This device is assisted by the fact that, although the legal meaning of the word 'sovereignty' is well known, few people can define 'sovereignty' in the sense of 'fullness of state power' being used here. It is a very subtle political judgement whether this kind of sovereignty is or is not being infringed in any particular situation.

A precedent for attaching policy conditions to financial flows to developing countries was available from the lending activities of the International Monetary Fund (IMF). Since IMF lending was for the purpose of eliminating short-run disequilibria in the country's balance of payments, it was given on condition that the borrowing country would take the measures necessary to enable it to repay the loan within the specified period for which the IMF was allowed to lend. Conditionality flowed very obviously from the purpose of the loans themselves and the off-setting character of the balance of payments deficits and surpluses worldwide.

In 1980, the World Bank introduced a new form of aid called 'structural adjustment lending' (or SAL) aimed at dealing with medium-term balance of payments adjustment without unduly cramping the economic growth of the developing country concerned. SAL measures 'modify the pattern of supply of domestic goods and services, specifically so that exports are increased and the rate of growth of imports is decreased while maintaining a reasonably high rate of overall economic activity and achieving other development objectives' (Please 1984: 18–20). To achieve the necessary modifications, 'phased programmes for the implementation of policy changes require to be worked out, agreed [with the developing country's government] and monitored' (p. 23). The policy changes which are part of SAL adjustment are changes towards policies favoured by the development counter-revolution: the avoidance of overvalued exchange rates; rates of interest which reflect the market forces of supply and demand; shrinkage of the public sector; deregulation of markets; the setting of agricultural prices which are 'properly remunerative' to cultivators; the dismantling of direct controls over trade and investment; the equalization of domestic and imported energy prices and the reform of energy taxation. In short, the entire policy programme of the counter-revolution appears to be required to achieve 'structural adjustment' in developing countries and aid is being used as the *quid pro quo* for adopting the counter-revolutionary programme.[12]

Is there anything much the matter with this, one may ask? After all, if developing countries had got themselves into economic difficulties, or were not attending properly to the needs of their own poor, why should it be wrong to give them a financial incentive to reorganize themselves for the better? In the first place, it does very much assume that the impact of the counter-revolution's policy changes on the balance of payments and economic growth will be as beneficial as is intended. Is this confidence justified? It ought to be clear that a single package of policies derived from applied welfare economics is very unlikely to be suitable as it stands for implementation in a wide variety of developing countries. The fact that the Third World has always been heterogeneous and is becoming more so; the fact that some key markets do not exist or do not work normally for reasons entirely unconnected with government intervention, so that perverse results occur from deregulation; the fact that certain of the counter-revolution's policies rely on implicit norms which may or may not be appropriate; the fact that welfare economics itself is not a sufficiently robust intellectual apparatus to sustain all the policy conclusions that are attributed to it – all of these things indicate that any single policy programme, cannot, and indeed should not, be applied as a universal economic remedy in the Third World.

This point is often taken by Bank staff. The response is that, for any particular developing country, the package is implemented pragmatically. But such admirable pragmatism is feasible only once the lessons of structural adjustment experience have been thoroughly internalized. The key to successful pragmatism is the proper evaluation of previous adjustment programmes. But the evaluation of structural adjustment policies comes up against considerable methodological problems. The objective is to measure the effect of adopting a package of policies on a set of policy objectives, like the growth of output, exports and investment. In order to do this, it is necessary to disentangle the effects of the new policy package from the effects of other powerful influences which may be operating simultaneously with the introduction of the reforms – such as the weather, changes in world prices of traded goods, changes in international interest rates, and the increased inflow of aid which is the counterpart of a structural adjustment effort. Simple comparisons of the economic performance of adjusting and non-adjusting countries fail to address these complications. Judicious selection of the countries included in both groups can easily produce 'results' which show the group of adjusting countries as the superior performers. The World Bank has not hesitated to use such misleading comparisons in some of its published commentaries on structural adjustment.

Critics of structural adjustment have also been unwilling to tackle the problem of separating out the effects of the policy package from the effect of other simultaneous influences. The fact that many adjusting countries had lower per capita incomes and consumption levels during the reform period compared with the pre-adjustment period is taken to be the significant comparison, on the ground that 'macro-policies will only be satisfactory when they lead to sustained growth and rising levels of investment' (Stewart 1992: 179–82). Again, this argument rejects the view that the effects of a set of policies have to be measured against a scenario of what would have otherwise occurred, rather than what happened beforehand or what happened to other countries which lack such policies. However, the scenario of 'what would have otherwise occurred', which is referred to as 'the counter-factual', is the basis of the evaluations which are discussed further here.

It is undeniable that there is no single foolproof method of constructing the counter-factual. Some countries conveniently present the researcher with a worked-out alternative programme of policies to Bank and Fund-style structural adjustment, but others do not. So, in the latter case, although it is possible to suppose that the appropriate counter-factual would be no change at all in the existing economic policies, that remains only a speculation. At least three says of approximating a counter-factual are possible. The most sophisticated is to build a country economic model, and use its base run as the counter-factual. But this is also the most laborious and costly. Less sophisticated, but still useful to a degree are multiple regression estimates, taking the objective as the dependent variable and the policy package as one among a variety of independent variables, and cross-section comparisons in which adjusting and non-adjusting countries are strictly paired with each other to eliminate the effect of irrelevant differences.

These three approaches have been applied to the evaluation of the adjustment experiences of many developing countries during the period 1979–88 (Mosley, Harrigan and Toye 1991: I, 181–295). Although none of the three methods used is flawless, it is significant that all give quite similar results, and that these results are broadly in agreement with the findings of the first two of the Bank's own evaluations of structural adjustment lending, which cover the same period. The main findings suggest that the impact of adjustment policies are as follows:

1   The policies produce an increase in exports and an improvement in the external account.
2   They also result in a decline in the share of national income that is devoted to investment.
3   Their impact on national income growth was mildly beneficial at best and neutral at worst.

Taken together, these results do not suggest that the package of reform policies was deleterious to developing countries, or should not have been undertaken – although there is still room for argument about exactly how they should be interpreted. What comes out most clearly is that the outcome is quite disappointing compared with the advance claims and expectations raised by the development counter-revolutionaries. In particular, the claim that all the economic troubles of developing countries stemmed from bad internal policies looks hollow when one sees how small are the benefits to be derived by the wholesale reversal of these policies. The development counter-revolution clearly over-sold its policy proposals.

One can take an even gloomier view by pointing to some of the ambiguities and unresolved questions which flow from this evaluation. The real value of exports has grown for the countries which have adjusted, but how was that achieved? Did the export drives of so many adjusting countries help to worsen their terms of trade? Was some of the fall in primary commodity prices which characterized the 1980s caused by the adjustment process itself, making the export success more costly in terms of domestic resources than it would otherwise have been? At least for the beverage crops (coffee, tea, cocoa), that seems to have been the case (De Rosa and Greene 1991: 32–4). Those who argued that the strategy of adjustment was based on a 'fallacy of composition' seem to have been at least partially vindicated.

What does the falling ratio of investment to GNP, as a result of adopting the reform package, imply? The optimistic view is that the fall will be temporary, caused by the elimination of misdirected or unsustainable public investment, plus caution on the part of private investors waiting to see whether the reformed pattern of incentives can be made to stick politically. The more pessimistic view is, far from public investment 'crowding out' private, it crowds it in because the two are highly complementary. If this view is right, the squeeze on public investment in pursuit of minimalist government and balanced budgets will inhibit the private sector investment response rather than stimulate it (Taylor 1988: 36). In such circumstances, the prospects for the recovery of economic growth will be bleak.

In assessing the success of adjustment lending, the third Bank evaluation study distinguished between middle-income countries and poorer countries. It finds a much better growth response in the former, but admits that 'the low-income group barely grew in per capita terms' as a result of undertaking adjustment (World Bank 1992: 68–9). The reasons given for this difference were the latter countries' 'relatively weak base in infrastructure and human, small private involvement in the formal sector, and weak public institutions'. Put into other words, there are structural differences between the poorest developing countries and middle-income countries which mean that, although getting the prices right may be both necessary and desirable, it is far from sufficient to promote a transition to sustainable growth. The old-fashioned structuralists might perhaps now be forgiven for saying: 'we told you so'.

Thus far, we have considered only aggregate economic objectives: exports, investment and growth. What about the distributional results of structural adjustment? The willingness of the Bank and Fund in the early 1980s to dismiss this entire question as irrelevant was gradually eroded, as it became clear that adjustment could not be a one-for-all quick fix lasting two or three years, but on the contrary was a long, long haul. UNICEF's campaign for 'adjustment with a human face' in the mid-1980s was crucial in putting poverty and inequality back on to the international financial institutions' agenda (Cornia, Jolly and Stewart 1987). Although the standard socioeconomic indicators gave mixed signals, some of these – like falling primary school enrolment ratios – raise real anxieties about the welfare of the poor during the adjustment process. Some lower-income groups were adversely affected, such as the newly unemployed in the towns and the growers of domestic food crops. Added to this were other groups of newly poor who were not the victims of the adjustment process but of the external influences that were adversely affecting so many developing countries, despite adjustment. Renewed efforts to alleviate poverty were called for on behalf of both groups. In policy terms, it makes sense to address their needs together rather than separately.

If the economic impact of the reform packages was disappointingly small, as has been argued, it is implausible to suggest that the social damage that can be attributed to them is huge. In any case, the question of how the costs of adjustment (where they do exist) are to be distributed is one which is, at least partly, within the area of the domestic government's policy discretion. If total government expenditures have to decline as a result of adjustment, a choice remains about how far social welfare expenditures are protected. Increasingly, the protection of social welfare spending has become one of the conditions incorporated into the entire reform package. But the expansion of policy conditionality in the interests of the human face of adjustment, while addressing one problem, merely draws attention to another – the gradual move by donors beyond technical economic conditions into much broader areas of social policy and 'governance'.

This move has been greatly accelerated by the liberal revolutions of 1989 in Eastern Europe and the subsequent disappearance of the Soviet Union. Some Western aid to these areas carries with it quite explicit political conditionality – the requirement not to return to the old communist and state socialist political structures. The World Bank is prevented by its charter from strong conditionality of this kind. But it has been emboldened to make conditions for its developing country aid which gets quite close to it– such as limits to defence spending, respect for human rights and an improvement in the accountability of governments to civil society at large. This is a most welcome shift away from the covert preference for authoritarian regimes which affected some influential figures in the Bank in the early 1980s. It represents a swing back to the attempt in the late 1970s, under the influence of the Carter administration and the Labour government of Callaghan, to soften the *realpolitik* of aid-giving with some humanitarian principles. Nevertheless, this approach is not free of its own moral dilemmas.

One important question is the extent to which aid conditionality constitutes an infringement of the national sovereignty of the recipient country. Most of the adjusting countries have had a period of formal independence which is brief relative to their history as colonies. The substantial increase in external policy guidance which conditionality involves, not to mention the large accompanying increase in the presence of expatriate technical assistance personnel, must raise the issue of neo-colonialism. The salience of that issue will become greater the more that conditionality is extended from economic policy to the broader and more politically sensitive area of 'governance'. To some extent, this potential conflict has been defused by efforts to ensure that the recipient government 'owns' the adjustment programme. Promoting ownership means ensuring understanding of the purposes of the reform, informed commitment to them, and, to the extent possible, participation in its design. But it is much easier to envisage meaningful ownership of an economic reform programme than of a much wider programme of constitutional change which may lead to the government's own demise, or at least important new constraints on its freedom of action. The hard-nosed among the donors may reply: 'Neo-colonialism? So what, provided it is used to install a political economy which is truly liberal?' But ends and means cannot usually be so neatly separated. That is why the end usually does not justify the means.

Another form of justification is to argue that, since the plight of developing countries has been caused by the policy mistakes of their own governments, any improvement in their situation must come from external leverage on policy. By now, the doubtful of the premise of this argument ought to be clear enough. There is plenty of evidence to suggest that their plight has also been caused in part by the shortcomings of the internal policies of the developed countries. In the following chapter, the effects of neo-conservative economic policies in the US and the UK are explored in detail, with special reference to the causes of the world debt crisis. Apart from the debt crisis, the rising tide of trade protection in both the US and Europe, impinging on both industry and agriculture, restricted the developing countries' opportunities to exploit their comparative advantage. Against this background, the project for installing liberal political economies in the developing countries has to be seen in a distinctly different light. The Bank, to its credit, now regularly draws attention to the policy deficiencies of the developed countries. But the fact remains that the development counter-revolution is involved in a world situation where liberalism is asymmetric in its impact. Developing countries are being pressed to do as we (the Western world) say, and not as we do. The developed countries are strong enough to limit their own commitment to a liberal world economic system at the same time as they press developing countries to make an unlimited commitment to it – despite the greater risks that they will run in doing so.

Late in 1992, this situation was given a new twist when the chief economist of the World Bank made a public call for the developed countries to retreat from the tight money, non-interventionist policies which the counter-revolution tried to pursue through the 1980s. This seemed to signal that the stance of 'do what we say, not what we do' was about to be modified by reversing what we say (*Financial Times*, 22 October 1992). Should such a reversal occur, as a result of a new electoral mood in the US, the whole question of appropriate adjustment policies in developing countries would be thrown wide open, and the development counter-revolution's life expectancy would be put in serious doubt.

No doubt if developing countries were to ask for reciprocal measures to monitor and discipline the use to which resources are put in the developed countries, they would get the kind of answer which would underline their place in the international power hierarchy – at the bottom. The weak are being made to understand that they alone are to blame for their own poverty. Whether this provides the political basis for a serious partnership between North and South to promote sustained development remains to be seen. If the developed countries want to see the fruit of co-operation, rather than of sheer power, they will have to adopt very different attitudes to structural adjustment in their own backyards.[13]

Conclusion

The counter-revolution in development policy has energetically defended the existing international economic order against the demands of developing countries in the 1970s for radical structural change. The proposal to narrow inter-country differentials in assets and income by massive transfers in the form of official aid was resisted particularly strongly. There were many different arguments deployed to do this, including those of administrative infeasibility and inflationary economic consequences. But the moral argument was perhaps the most persuasive – that carrying out the proposal could create injustice between individuals in different countries, as well as alleviate it.

But the price of this victory has been to focus attention much more sharply and clearly on the issue of what the morality of an international order might mean. If it does not require what the NIEO enthusiast said that it required, it certainly requires something other than the manipulation of the weak by the strong. Even when intergovernmental redistribution is ruled out, it seems to entail an obligation to outlaw all forms of oppression and domination of one state by another, all forms of unfair exploitation of one state's resources and people by another and all forms of arbitrary discrimination against particular states in international dealings. This applies even when the weaker party is coerced into approving the injustice. Any serious reduction of inter-state domination, exploitation and discrimination would produce dramatic enough results to satisfy for a long while those with a taste for radical change.

The resort to moral argument can be sincere, or it can be cynical. Scruples can be paraded merely to safeguard vested interests. Morality can become one more method of manipulating public opinion and virtue can be paid the doubtful tribute of hypocrisy. Cynicism and sincerity are no doubt mixed in the advocacy of the development counter-revolution, as they were in that of the NIEO before it. It would be a bold person who claimed to be able to tell in what measures they are mixed.

What is important is something different. Since the development counter-revolution has so publicly committed itself to the need for moral standards in international affairs, there is now no going back. They apply when it is convenient to lecture poor countries about their follies and failures. They apply no less, and no more, to the postures and policies of the rich developed countries of the world, as they impinge powerfully on poor neighbours. That, as we approach the genuine dilemmas of world development at the end of the twentieth century, should be both a heartening and a sobering thought.[14]

Notes

1   That the Brandt Report relies on the Kantian idea of a 'union of nations' is made clear in the following passage: 'One ambition of this Report is to propose steps along the path to what could genuinely be called a society of nations, a new world order based on greater international justice and on rules which *participating countries* observe. This requires nation states . . . to be concerned about the *less fortunate members of such a society*' (p. 75 with emphasis added). In this context, 'the less fortunate members' is obviously synonymous with 'poor countries'. The confusion between inter-state and inter-personal morality is shown clearly in an extract which closely follows that previously quoted. 'All the lessons of reform within national societies confirm the gains for all in a process of change that makes the world a less unequal and more just and habitable place. *The great moral imperatives that underpinned such reforms are as valid internationally as they were and are nationally*' (p. 77, with emphasis added).

2   One particulaly pertinent question in this connection is the following. If the entire world does *not*, as Little believes, constitute enough of a society to qualify as a 'moral community', what is it about diplomacy, trade, investment abroad, international sport, international labour migration, international cooperation on aviation, maritime links, postal services and so on which allows them to be carried on in the absence of a moral community?

3   Little seems to be a thinking rather than an unthinking utilitarian. He asks rhetorically: 'Who would not want to benefit 99 per cent of Indians by 100 Rs a year per head at the cost of further impoverishing the poorest 1 per cent by 1 rupee?' (1978: 43). The answer to this question is, surely, 'anyone who is opposed to increasing absolute or relative poverty'. It is the

persistent neglect of these issues which lies at the heart of objections to utilitarianism.

4   This list of debating points which arise out of the Rawlsian approach to justice could be greatly extended. One other question which it is always well worth putting to any moral philosopher is 'who is to count as a person'. Locke and Kant, for example, took 'person' to mean a male head of household, with wife, children, other dependents and household servants subsumed within the personality of the patriarch. Today, this definition of 'person' seems debatable, if not downright daft. So what definition of 'person' are today's moral philosophers using?

5   The position of Lal, relying on earlier work of Little, is that 'the most useful results of modern applied welfare economics . . . are "the logical conclusions of a set of consistent value axioms laid down for the welfare economist, by some priest, parliament or dictator" '. This account of what economists do is quite misleading, for the following reasons:

> In fact, it is highly unusual to find any axioms . . . laid down by priest, parliament or dictator. Nor do we find any careful empirical investigation of consistent axioms presented by developing country governments in the work of the World Bank group, before they come to policy prescriptions . . . That being so, then it is clear that these economists are not simply deriving the logical conclusions from axioms laid down by the government, but taking a view themselves or the desirability (or otherwise) of certain outcomes.
>
> (Stewart 1985: 287).

6   The details agreed at Manila were that the Common Fund should have two separate 'windows'. The first, with $450 million, was available to finance ICA buffer stocks and national stocks placed under some form of international control. The second window, with $70 million, was made available to finance research and development and marketing schemes aimed at commodity diversification.

7   As the late David Penhaligon, MP for Truro, commented, when the government financial assistance to the Wheal Jane and South Crofty tin mines was announced: 'This is a remarkable moment. It is the first time this Government has given a farthing to anything but a bank since 1979' (*The Times* July 1986).

8   It is odd that, although the counter-revolution is generally unwilling to see economic activity as a 'zero-sum game' (i.e. a game where one player's gain is exactly balanced by another player's loss), investment opportunities in developing countries are treated in exactly that manner in the discussion of crowding out of private investment by public investment.

9   See, for example, US Agency for International Development (1982) *Private Enterprise Development*, Washington DC May. This USAID Policy Paper, on page 2, singles out Bauer as the development economist with whose opinions it most closely agrees.

10   For an expanded treatment of the themes in the preceding three paragraphs, see Cassen and Associates (1986: chapter 8).

11   Aid gearing works like this. £10 million of aid given to a developing country as a grant will buy it £7.5 million worth of 'free' imports, if the tying of the purchases to the donor country results in a $33\frac{1}{3}$ per cent

inflation of the price of the imports. £10 million of aid given as part of a £40 million mixed credit package will lead to the 'recipient' country paying £30 million for £30 million worth of imports, again assuming a 33⅓ per cent price inflation as a result of procurement tying. Thus aid gearing allows, in this not unrealistic example, all the 'aid' to be passed on to the donor country's supplier via price inflation.

12 It should be emphasized that SALs are not the only type of World Bank loan with policy conditions attached. Some project loans in the past have had sectoral policy conditions attached, e.g. an electricity generation project carrying conditions about the reform of electricity and other energy tariffs. In the 1980s, 'sector adjustment loans', 'economic recovery loans' and 'trade adjustment loans' are similar to SALs in that they are conditional on promises of widespread policy reform in the borrowing country.

13 It is interesting that the same *Times* correspondent who hailed the 'development counter-revolution' in 1983 when Lal's pamphlet was published, was by 1985 penning the following thoughts:

> The point here is that poor countries, often short of skilled administrators and hampered by weak institutions, cannot be expected to plunge into policy reform at the behest of richer and better equipped countries if the latter do not put their own houses in order. It is therefore an over-simplification to regard the fate of developing countries as being chiefly in their own hands. The high public sector deficits, rigid labour markets and the erosion of free trade which have characterised industrial economies in recent years have been as inimical to developing countries as their own often incompetent and corrupt governments.
>
> (*The Times* 4 July 1985)

Perhaps the policies of the development counter-revolution are gradually coming full circle, at the same time as the structuralist insights of the old-style development economics start to be applied to the developed economies themselves.

14 Only once in *The Wealth of Nations* does Adam Smith qualify his principle of individual pursuit of self-interest by the phrase 'as long as one does not violate the laws of justice' (Hirschman 1981: 302, n. 9). But that does not indicate Smith's lack of concern for justice. On the contrary, it indicates his assumption that '[men] could safely be trusted to pursue their own self-interest without undue harm to the community not only because of the restrictions imposed by law, but also because they were subject to built-in restraint derived from morals, religion, custom and education' (quoted in Hirsch 1977: 137). In the modern world, with its diverse moral codes, religions, customs and forms of education, this assumption is clearly more difficult to make. For neo-classical economics, the question of justice tends simply to disappear from sight, however. Once Jevons attempted to prove the superiority of results achieved by Smith's 'invisible hand' in terms of Bentham's felicific calculus or 'moral arithmetic', economists tended to lose sight of whether the social restraints of justice are present in the actual situations for which they prescribe. When economists operate at a global level, that constitutes a serious abdication of responsibility.

CHAPTER EIGHT

The Counter-Revolution and the World Debt Crisis

The Anglo-American Special Relationship and the Counter-revolution

The world debt crisis of the 1980s and beyond provides a detailed case study of the deleterious impact that the economic policies of industrial countries can have on the welfare of developing countries. The damage may arise in two different ways, and as is argued in this chapter, both have been involved in the effect of counter-revolutionary economic policies of monetarism and supply-side economics on the indebtedness of poor nations. The first source of negative impact arises from the pursuit of such policies in themselves. Regardless of whether they benefited the industrial countries, they had bad spill-over effects on the non-industrial, which were not taken into account at the point of decision making. The second source of negative impact is not intrinsic to the policies, but arises because they are implemented incompletely and inappropriately. A gap existed between the ideal version of the policy and the actual version which came to pass, because of errors in its execution. Sometimes such a gap arises because of excessive bureaucratic departmentalism. When one official tells another that a proposed policy is unworkable, the other official calmly replies: 'That is nothing to do with me: I am only in charge of policy-making, you are in charge of execution.' But in the case which we are about to consider, the cause of the gap arose because of confusion and conflicting objectives at the highest levels of policy-making. Blaming the bureaucrats will not wash.

In 1982, it was finally recognized that much of the lending to developing countries that US and British banks had undertaken since the

1973 oil shock could not be serviced or repaid on the terms that had been agreed. The realization came in August 1982, when Mexico suspended payment on its debt. The international economic crisis, which soon changed the long-standing positive net flow of financial resources from the developed to the developing countries into a negative net flow, still in the early 1990s blights the economic prospects of many developing countries, and thus the prospects for world economic development in general (Muscatelli and Vines 1991). In the US, the debt crisis coincided with the Republican administrations of Ronald Reagan (1981–89) and George Bush (1989–93). In the United Kingdom, it coincided with the administrations of Margaret Thatcher (1979–90) and John Major (1990–). This coincidence poses two questions for economic historians of the recent past. How far were US and British policies responsible for the state of affairs revealed by Mexico's suspension of debt service in mid-1982? Secondly, how far were US and British policies during the years after 1982 helpful in alleviating the economic problems of indebted developing countries? This chapter attempts to answer these two questions. Before doing so, however, it is necessary to establish the general background of policy against which the world debt crisis unfolded. It is important to highlight the interactions between the conduct of economic and of foreign policy in both countries, and to examine with this in mind, the crucial issue of the Anglo-American 'special relationship'. This is a complex matter, consisting not merely of personal and ideological affinities, but also of structural features and partially divergent interests. It is necessary to understand these complexities in order to avoid an over-simple presentation of Reagan and Thatcher as merely conservative counter-revolutionaries in action.

We begin with the British side of this relationship because Mrs Thatcher preceded Ronald Reagan on to the world stage and was, therefore, the key pioneer of the transfer of the counter-revolution from think-tanks and media discussion to real practical politics. She had been a thoroughly insular politician in 1975, when, almost by happenstance, she was elected as Leader of the Conservative Party. She knew little about foreign affairs and had rarely travelled abroad on official business (Young 1990: 119). In the next four years before she became Prime Minister, she started to travel widely to Europe, and also visited the Middle East and China. She also established her strong anti-communist credentials with the speech which brought her the Soviet soubriquet of 'the Iron Lady'. Despite these preparations, however, her political trajectory remained largely a domestic one, and foreign affairs provided an unwelcome distraction from her self-imposed mission of economic and institutional reform within Britain.

Apart from her 1979 visit to Zambia to negotiate independence for Zimbabwe, her early trips to developing countries were either ceremonial or commercial, or a combination of the two. Her presence at the North-South summit at Cancun produced nothing but some British aid for an ill-conceived Mexican steel project. Her Middle East visit in the same year (1981) produced more British arms contracts with Saudi Arabia and the Gulf states, and much personal publicity. The raising of overseas students' fees in 1981 caused great dismay in Malaysia and Singapore, from where many overseas students came to Britain. Nothing was done to soften the blow for these countries until Malaysia had run a 'Buy British Last' campaign. Subsequent improvement in relations centred around an abortive attempt to sell Malaysia a £1.5 billion package of British armaments (Byrd 1991: 65–6).

Ronald Reagan had also remained primarily a domestic politician until 1979. He was a long-established anti-communist, in reaction to his period as a trade union leader. As Governor of California, he had prospered by attacking the University of California, site of the student rebellions of the 1960s. He had built up his national standing by support for the 'moral majority' on issues like school prayers, opposition to abortion and various other obscurantist demands. It was by cultivating the far-right conservative supporters of this social agenda, particularly in the West and South of the US, that Reagan constructed his political base. Not until early 1980 was Reagan converted to the economic agenda of the supply-side Republican intellectuals who worked with Jack Kemp, and the conversion – despite helping him to defeat Carter for the Presidency later in the year – remained superficial.

Reagan appreciated that Carter had been fatally weakened in his second presidential bid by his failures, both military and diplomatic, to rescue the US hostages being held by Islamic revolutionaries in Iran. His domestic credibility had been further eroded by his plan for increased gasoline taxes to save energy. Reagan was persuaded by Kemp, who became his chief policy adviser, to advocate a dramatic cut in tax rates. But when it came to cutting government expenditure to achieve a balanced budget, Reagan was more influenced by the populist clamour for a 'strong America' than by the logic of supply-side economics. Early efforts to reduce the size of the State Department failed. Far from cutting the budget of the Department of Defense, a massive armament build-up was begun early on in the first Reagan presidency. Reagan never absorbed in full the economic doctrines of the counter-revolution. He remained a pragmatic politician who gave priority to national security, as defined for him by the US military–industrial complex. His support for the supply-siders in his own administration was partial and inter-mittent. Of all the budgets which affected the fate of developing countries, only that of USAID was seriously squeezed.

A significant change in both American and British relations with developing countries occurred after Britain recaptured the Falkland

Islands from Argentina, with US logistic support, in mid-1982. The impact of the 'Falklands factor' in securing Mrs Thatcher's overwhelming re-election in 1983 was quickly appreciated in the US. This led to a revival of US gunboat diplomacy with British acquiescence and/or assistance. Shortly after 241 US marines were massacred in Lebanon, the US invaded Grenada (October 1983) and Britain acquiesced in this violation of international law. Britain also permitted the US to use its air bases in the UK to bomb Tripoli in Libya (April 1986). Britain later supported the US invasion of Panama to destabilize General Noriega (December 1989). These incidents yielded a regular supply of easy victories against some of the more obnoxious of Third World leaders, while little was achieved towards stabilizing the major sources of international turbulence, the Arab–Israel problem and its interconnections with Islamic fundamentalism.

Reagan and Thatcher's dismissive attitudes and punitive actions towards many developing countries were underpinned by the US-UK 'special relationship'. Mrs Thatcher was an Atlanticist by conviction, in sharp contrast with those she placed in charge of her Treasury and Foreign Office – Geoffrey Howe and Nigel Lawson, who remained convinced Europeans. She was fortunate in the fact that the US President for most of her time in office was someone who sincerely shared her simple conservative beliefs and her populist style of politics. She created assiduously out of these affinities a strong personal alliance that withstood several sharp disputes about policy. She was much more doubtful about US military action in Grenada and Libya than she ever admitted in public, for example. In short, these *was* something special in her political and personal relations with President Reagan.

But although Mrs Thatcher undoubtedly personalized the 'special relationship' and made it live for the 1980s, she was also recognizing and making obeisance to one of the most robust (if not one of the most obvious) features of Britain's position in the mid-twentieth-century world – fundamental military dependence on the United States. Every British government (except one) since 1945 co-operated extremely closely indeed with the US administrations of the time. Eden's government of 1955–7 did not, coming to grief when Eisenhower aborted the Anglo-French Suez invasion of 1956. Some, like Wilson's government of 1964–70, preferred to keep their over-arching strategic and financial understandings with the US hidden from public view (Ponting 1989). Others, like Macmillan's, preferred to flaunt and dramatize them. Thatcher followed the Macmillan route, making a spectacular virtue of this basic cold war necessity. Both Macmillan and Thatcher had a similar technique for presenting the closeness of the US–UK link. Macmillan patronized the youthful President Kennedy in mock-patrician style. Thatcher, despite the reversal in age differences, 'matronized' Reagan, her self-appointed mission being to ensure 'that Ronnie never gets isolated' (quoted by Young 1989: 254).[1]

Insular Monetarism and Supply-side Economics

The economic significance of Mrs Thatcher was as a pioneer of the application of monetarist economic doctrines to economic policy. The first of the Western conservative leaders to secure power in mid-1979, her government's initial decisions in the field of economic management were widely viewed as a crucial experiment to test the validity of monetarist doctrines in practice. Here 'monetarism' is defined simply as the three propositions that control of inflation is the supreme economic objective; that control of the money supply is both a necessary and sufficient condition for the control of inflation; and that governments can indeed control the money supply exogenously (Milner 1987: 259). Monetarism in this sense had been very much a minority opinion among academic macroeconomists until the mid-1970s. Then a series of rapid 'conversions' ensued, among economists, journalists and lastly among politicians.[2] The beliefs of many monetarists were ideological in character, and the beliefs of many others were politically opportunistic. Mrs Thatcher herself was one of these recent converts to monetarism, while her Chancellor (Geoffrey Howe) and Financial Secretary (Nigel Lawson) were even more recent converts – in Lawson's case from Keynesian views extensively developed in the course of financial journalism (Keegan 1989: 1–57).

In the United States, the counter-revolution in economics took a distinctly different form. Like monetarism, it was fuelled by a revulsion from the interventionism practised by the otherwise conservative governments of the early 1970s, and its perceived failure to cure 'stagflation', the simultaneous occurrence of high inflation and low economic growth. Like monetarism, it was a radical, even idealistic doctrine, held with a deeply self-righteous conviction of its ability to break through the accumulated muddles and confusions of economic policy-making. The stagnation of economic growth was attributed to a mass of government interventions which destroyed the producers' incentive to produce, to innovate and to take risks in business. Economic regulations, protection of certain industries as well as excessive taxation were identified as depressants of the supply side of the economy. The remedy was a thorough-going liberalization of the economy, as well as a dramatic reduction in the burden of taxation. At the same time, the subsidies which swelled the public expenditure side of the budget needed to be eliminated. Finally, the distorting effect of inflation had to be conquered, and a way found of re-introducing the stability of the real value of the dollar (Stockman 1985: 41–5).

The main unresolved difficulty about this recipe arose from the now-famous diagram, drawn by its creator Arthur Laffer on a Washington restaurant table napkin. This Laffer Curve purported to show that a drastic reduction in tax rates would so dramatically revitalize the supply side of the economy that total tax revenue would actually *increase* as a consequence. To say the least, the Laffer Curve created uncertainty about the role that spending cuts would have to play in the supply siders' strategy. Was the increase in revenue conditional on the continuation of existing high rates of inflation, with attendant high levels of fiscal drag (bracket creep)? Or was it an effect that would dispense with the need for aggregate spending cuts once inflation began to be squeezed out of the system by deflationary monetary policies? No-one in the supply side camp was sure, nor even was it seen that this was the fundamental question about the feasibility of the supply-side policy programme. The basic appeal of supply-side economics, as of monetarism, was its apparent simplification of the task of economic management, through the downgrading of past policy objectives, such as full employment and the discarding of past policy instruments, such as fiscal fine-tuning for demand management, the official regulation of credit and incomes policies to control wage inflation.

The new Thatcher government in Britain committed itself to what has been called 'insular monetarism' (Keegan 1989: 173). The one overriding objective of policy was defined as the reduction of inflation, and the sole instrument to achieve this was the control of the money supply, 'money' for this purpose being 'broad money' or M3. It was believed that the government could control the money supply by reducing the public sector's borrowing requirement (PSBR). This would be done by reducing public expenditure until it equalled tax revenue. Sound money and lower direct tax rates were seen as the right incentives to create growth in output and employment. The foreign exchange rate would continue to float according to market pressures, all attention and effort being focused on the domestic monetary front. This was the basic programme of insular monetarism.

Many professional economists at the time were sceptical, not to say incredulous, of this programme. Some scepticism was fuelled no doubt by dislike of the social implications of the retreat from consensus objectives which had dominated post-war British politics. But it was also firmly based on a professional judgment that so many simplicities were not likely all to come right at once. Can governments really control the money supply, especially when central banks function as the lender of last resort? Or when the government is deregulating the supply of credit, and as usual new monetary technologies (e.g. credit cards, cash dispensers) are developing rapidly? Are changes in the PSBR well correlated with changes in the money supply? Does an excess supply of money necessarily generate excess demand for a given supply of goods and services – and thus cause inflation? What about rising import prices and labour costs? Do these not cause inflation, to which the money supply has to accommodate itself? What about Goodhart's law, that any stable monetary function collapses as soon as the dependent variable in it is made into a policy target? One could easily extend this catalogue of doubts.[3]

In the intellectual confusion which the new monetarism generated, it was possible to think the unthinkable, but also to believe the unbelievable. This made it easier to defend apparently ill-designed policies, and to rationalise what appeared to be policy failures. Keynesian thinking would have suggested that the pre-1979 election Clegg pay awards to the public sector would have been inflationary, and should have been repudiated by an incoming Thatcher government. But they were not.[4] Keynesian thinking would have suggested that the doubling of value added tax would also have been inflationary, in view of its effect on the next round of wage bargaining. Nevertheless, the Clegg awards were validated by Mrs Thatcher, and VAT subsequently doubled to pay for them and the modest reduction in income tax rates in the June 1979 budget. Inflation quickly rose from an annual rate of 14.5 per cent in 1979 to 19.9 in 1980 (GNP deflator). This catastrophic start to the British anti-inflation crusade was a key event, because of the way in which it subsequently influenced the thinking of the 'supply-siders' in the Reagan administration. They came to believe in 1981 that Thatcherite monetarism had 'failed', and failed because taxes had been increased.

The Medium Term Financial Strategy was introduced in March 1980 in order to change inflationary expectations. The means was the commitment to a four-year plan for the reduction in the rate of expansion of the money stock. Starting from 1980–1, the target for M3 was to be within the ranges 7 to 11 per cent, then 6–10 per cent (1981–2), 5–9 per cent (1982–3) and 4–8 per cent (1983–4) (Keegan 1989: 66). It is indisputable that these ranges were always overshot, at times substantially. The annual growth of broad money in the UK followed a path between 1979 and 1983 as follows – 12.6, 15.2, 17.3, 11.7 and 10.5 per cent (IMF 1987: 131, Table A.14). Despite the outright failure to get within the target M3 ranges, UK inflation did gradually fall from its 1980 peak, reaching 4.6 per cent by 1983. Fiscal contraction throughout 1980–2, including the strongly deflationary budget of 1981, was assisted by the dramatic over-valuation of the pound, which peaked in early 1981 and was gradually corrected, by the rise in oil prices and by the fall in commodity prices induced by recession in the OECD world. Thus success in lowering inflation came about 'as much by accident as by design' (Johnson 1991: 253). Falling inflation allowed

TABLE 8.1 UK MACROECONOMIC INDICATORS 1979–1990 (PERCENTAGE)

	Real GNP	*Employment*	*Consumer prices*	*Broad money M3 (M4)*	*Interest rate: long 20 (10) yr*	*Fiscal impulse*[a]
1969–78	2.2	0.1	11.7			
1979	2.7	1.1	13.4	12.6	13.0	−0.8
1980	−2.5	−1.0	18.0	15.2	13.8	−1.7
1981	−1.3	−3.4	11.9	17.3	14.9	−1.6
1982	1.7	−1.9	8.6	12.0	13.1	−0.8
1983	3.7	−0.2	4.6	10.5	10.8(11.3)	0.5
1984	2.1	2.2	5.0	9.2(13.8)	10.7(11.3)	0.3
1985	3.6	1.1	6.1	15.0(13.0)	10.6(11.1)	−0.3
1986	3.8	0.3	3.4	18.1(15.7)	9.9(10.1)	0.2
1987	4.5	2.3	4.1	(16.1)	(9.6)	−0.1
1988	4.3	3.4	4.9	(17.5)	(9.7)	−1.3
1989	1.8	3.1	7.8	(19.1)	(10.2)	−0.3
1990	0.6	1.3	9.5	(12.0)	(11.7)	0.7

[a] In per cent of GNP, + expansionary, − contractionary.
Source: IMF World Economic Outlook (1987, 1991)

the gradual decline in nominal interest rates between 1981 and 1985. But the real rate of interest was rising rapidly, moving from negative in 1980 to 3 per cent in 1981 and to 4 per cent by 1982. The main UK financial indicators are presented in table 8.1. The table also shows the losses of output and employment of the period 1979–85, during the severest recession the UK had experienced since the 1930s. This seems to validate the judgment that forcing of nominal interest rates still higher in 1981 caused matters to get worse and not better for the British economy itself, never mind the indirect effects on the developing countries which were heavily in debt (ibid.).

The Origins of the Debt Crisis

The first seeds of the world debt crisis were sown after the first oil shock in 1973. The sudden, huge redistribution of income to OPEC oil exporters brought about by the oil price rise was not matched by an equally rapid increase in OPEC consumption. OPEC's huge new surpluses were, to a large extent, placed as bank deposits, and then on-lent by the commercial banks to other borrowers. The industrial countries adjusted their economies to the first oil shock surprisingly well, and thus generated rather little demand for OPEC savings. This put downward pressure on world interest rates. Many developing countries, particularly in Latin America did not adjust their economies to the oil price shock, but instead borrowed at what seemed (and indeed were at the time) favourable rates of interest – and without any accompanying policy conditionality.

The increased instability of interest rates and exchange rates which followed the collapse of the Bretton Woods framework of international finance was, during the 1970s, maturing new departures in the methods of international finance. Depositors sought protection against adverse interest and exchange rate changes, and the commercial banks increasingly switched their terms from fixed-rate interest to variable-rate interest, usually denominated in US dollars. Neither developing country borrowers, nor the banks themselves seemed to understand the implications of this change. The commercial banks appeared to believe that sovereign debt would, by definition, necessarily be repaid. The developing country governments did not anticipate the financial upsets which would later be caused by Western governments dedicated to disinflation. Even without variable interest rates, severe disinflation would have squeezed borrowers who had borrowed at nominal rates of say, 10 per cent, in the mid-1970s. Disinflation plus variable interest rates, however, made the squeeze quite insupportable.

By the time of Reagan's inauguration, Thatcherite economics seemed discredited. UK long-term interest rates had risen to 15 per cent, while inflation had risen rather than fallen. The real squeeze in Britain was still to come. President Reagan and his new economic team began to try to apply supply-side doctrines to what was still the largest economy in the world. Supply-side economics in any case differed from monetarism in its focus, because US monetary policy is in the hands of the Federal Reserve Board, rather than the US government. The Reagan team determined that fiscal policy should be geared around the incentive effects of taxation, rather than around tax revenue as a regulator of aggregate demand. As has been explained, they had been convinced by the supply-siders that cutting tax rates can have such strong incentive effects that tax revenues rise rather than fall when tax rates are cut. This effect was alleged to provide inflationless growth.[5]

Two tax cut proposals based on supply-side logic had been part of Reagan's election platform. One was the Kemp–Roth reduction of 30 per cent in personal income tax rates. The other was Barber Conable's plan to liberalize corporate depreciation allowances, allow faster capital asset write-downs and thereby reduce corporate taxes (the so-called '10–5–3' tax cut).[6] In order to legislate these proposals into law in the US Tax Reduction Act of 1981, the Reagan administration agreed to a *further* set of tax reductions, to cater for the sectional interests of both Republican and Democratic Congressmen whose votes were needed to

TABLE 8.2   REVENUE COST OF US TAX REDUCTION BILL, 1981
(US $, BILLIONS)

Year	Kemp-Roth	Coalition Bill (10–5–3)	Politicians' tax ornaments	Total cost	% of GNP
1982	25	10	6	41	1.3
1983	58	18	17	93	2.9
1984	87	26	24	137	3.8
1985	100	36	33	169	4.4
1986	113	50	48	211	5.0
1987	127	61	63	251	5.5
1988	142	65	76	283	5.8
1989	158	66	92	316	6.0
1990	173	70	109	352	6.2
Total	983	402	468	1,853	—

Source: Stockman (1985: 287)

pass Kemp-Roth in the modified form of 5 per cent–10 per cent–10 per cent cuts over three years. These further cuts are those under the heading 'politicians' tax ornaments' in table 8.2, which shows the huge losses of revenue which the Act would produce over the 1980s.

Because of the doctrine that tax rate cuts produce tax revenue increases, the expenditure implications of the Republican tax plans for the US budget deficit were never properly explored in advance. Such calculations as were attempted were vitiated by inconsistent assumptions about future growth and inflation, initially making the required spending cuts seem manageable. As it gradually became clearer in early 1981 that massive expenditure savings would be required if the budget was to be balanced, it became equally clear that they simply could not be found. This was largely because of the huge planned build-up of defence expenditure that was gathering momentum, and partly because Reagan decided, also for political reasons, to ring-fence social security spending.

There were two reasons why the Reagan economic team did not abandon its tax plan, or raise taxes other than those specified in the plan, to neutralize the expected loss of revenue. Politically, Reagan decided it was better to 'win' on the tax cuts, even if he were defeated on spending cuts, because in political terms half a loaf was better than no loaf at all. But, in addition, Mrs Thatcher's experiences of 1979–80 were taken as an awful warning. Her 1979 decision to double VAT was

TABLE 8.3   USA MACROECONOMIC INDICATORS, 1979–1990
(PERCENTAGE)

	Real GNP	Employment	Consumer prices	Broad money M3	Interest rate: long 20yr	Fiscal impulse[a]
1969–78	2.8	2.4	6.5			
1979	2.5	2.9	11.3	8.3	9.4	−0.8
1980	−0.2	0.5	13.5	8.0	11.5	−0.4
1981	1.9	1.1	10.4	9.4	13.9	0.0
1982	−2.5	−0.9	6.1	9.1	13.0	0.3
1983	3.6	1.3	3.2	12.0	11.1	0.8
1984	6.8	4.1	4.4	8.6	12.5	0.5
1985	3.4	2.0	3.5	8.2	10.6	0.6
1986	2.7	2.3	2.0	9.2	7.7	0.0
1987	3.4	2.6	3.6	3.5	8.4	−1.2
1988	4.5	2.3	4.1	5.5	8.8	−0.2
1989	2.5	2.0	4.8	5.0	8.5	−0.4
1990	1.0	0.6	5.3	3.3	8.6	0.0

[a]   In per cent of GNP, + expansionary, − contractionary.
Source: IMF World Economic Outlook (1987, 1991)

read as the cause of her subsequent failure (by 1981) to stop inflation and interest rates rising (Stockman 1985: 147). The Reagan team simply ruled out all tax increases of any kind, for whatever reason. It is hardly surprising, therefore, that the US quickly found itself with a structural budget deficit. Expenditures were 24 per cent of GNP by 1984, while revenues were only 19 per cent. The supply-side revolution had succeeded not only in putting the US government on the unhappy side of the Micawber theorem; it did this so comprehensively that the damage would take many years to reverse. If Howe and Lawson[7] were insular monetarists, Donald Regan and his team were supply-siders who, under the pressure of events, behaved like 'military Keynesians' (cf. Leys 1989: 106).[8]

But just as the former had, as we have seen, produced a sudden rise in real interest rates in 1981–2, so, by a different route, did the latter (see table 8.3). The Federal Reserve Board exercised a quite tight control over growth in monetary aggregates and this had the effect of pushing nominal interest rates higher. The tax cuts neutralized the effects of higher interest rates on the demand for investment, which was maintained despite the monetary squeeze. The need to finance the very large government budget deficit and the simultaneously emerging large current account deficit, plus strong investor demand for finance, implied a large call by the US on foreign savings. Indeed the World Bank calculated that the increase of $162 billion in the US government budget deficit represented some 8 per cent of total world saving in 1979 (World Bank 1985b: 37). There is little doubt that budgetary movements of this size would have had a significant effect in increasing real interest rates, and given the structural nature of the deficit, keeping them high throughout the 1980s. The sheer size of the US government's need for finance would have forced governments borrowing less to offer similar high interest rates to those of the US in order to sell their bonds.[9]

The disastrous impact on heavily indebted developing countries was soon felt. The dramatic rise in nominal interest rates in the strongly inflationary conditions at the end of the 1970s, and the failure of these historically high nominal rates to fall back very much once recession took hold of the developed economies in 1981–2, not only raised the cost of new borrowing by developing countries, but also raised the cost of servicing all old debt with variable interest-rate terms. Since none of the developing-country borrowers had ever imagined that real interest rates could move to the then prevailing levels, and since none of the responsible international financial institutions had ever warned them of such a development, they were caught in a classic debt trap.

The world debt crisis which erupted in mid-1982 was something over which the developing countries had precious little control. They might have foreseen that favourable terms of borrowing would not last. They might have resisted the lenders' transfer to them of the risks of interest rate variation. But they lacked the vision for the former – along with everybody else[10] – and they lacked the bargaining strength for the latter. It is also true that much of what was borrowed was invested unwisely by developing countries. But what turned a drama into a crisis was the sudden leap in real interest rates and the effect that this had in leading to a rapid accumulation of indebtedness which was no longer within the borrower's control.

The other major consequence of the deflationary macroeconomic policies pursued by the US, the UK and other Western governments was the dramatic collapse of world commodity prices – including that of oil after 1981. The explanation for the failure of the international financial institutions to anticipate the debt crisis lies, at least in part, in their consistent forecasts of strong commodity prices, and hence of the manageability of the rapid accumulation of commercial debt in government hands. But the heavily indebted developing countries experienced a strong terms-of-trade shock in 1981–3, and (after a brief reversal in 1984), deterioration in their terms of trade continued from 1985 to 1988 (see table 8.4). These unfavourable movements were associated with the slackening of demand for industrial raw materials during the 1981–3 recession in OECD countries, with the slow recovery thereafter,

TABLE 8.4 TERMS OF TRADE (ANNUAL CHARGES, PERCENTAGE)

	1979	1980	1981	1982	1983	1984	1985	1986	1987	1988	1989	1990
DEVELOPING COUNTRIES	9.5	16.6	2.9	-1.5	-3.6	1.4	-2.0	-16.3	1.5	-3.4	1.9	0.2
Africa	8.1	17.0	0.1	-8.0	-2.0	0.3	-0.8	-25.2	0.7	-5.2	0.2	-1.8
Asia	1.8	-1.4	-0.8	0.6	0.8	1.8	-0.5	-3.6	1.2	0.8	0.8	-1.0
Europe	-3.8	-5.6	0.4	1.1	-1.7	-0.9	-0.6	2.2	0.0	1.7	0.4	-2.1
Middle East	23.9	41.5	11.7	2.1	-8.4	0.3	-3.7	-44.3	8.6	-19.0	9.6	8.6
Western Hemisphere	5.6	7.4	-5.7	-7.8	-4.7	5.1	-5.2	-10.5	-3.2	-2.5	0.4	-1.5
Memo:												
Heavily indebted countries[a]	9.3	13.7	-3.9	-6.8	-4.3	4.6	-5.5	-14.5	-1.6	-3.0	1.1	-1.7
INDUSTRIAL COUNTRIES	-2.9	-7.3	-1.6	1.6	1.8	0.3	0.6	9.0	0.8	1.2	-0.2	-0.5
Memo:												
United States	-3.9	-13.4	1.9	3.0	3.3	1.9	-2.2	-0.3	-6.9	2.0	1.0	-1.9
United Kingdom	4.3	4.7	0.8	-0.5	0.4	-0.3	0.9	-5.1	2.0	1.1	3.1	2.5

[a] Argentina, Bolivia, Brazil, Chile, Colombia, Cote d'Ivoire, Ecuador, Mexico, Morocco, Nigeria, Peru, Philippines, Uruguay, Venezuela, Yugoslavia.

Source: IMF World Economic Outlook (1987–91)

with the reduced demand for commodity stockholding at higher interest rates and with adjustment policies which neglected the cumulative effect of export supply increases on the world market price.

A country that is caught in a debt trap – accumulating liabilities and diminishing ability to pay, soon begins to experience other strong destabilising forces. There is nothing novel in this. The process was lucidly described by Ricardo:

> A country which has accumulated a large debt, is placed in a most artificial situation; and although the amount of taxes, and the increased price of labour may not, and I believe does not, place it under any other disadvantage with respect to foreign countries, except the unavoidable one of paying those taxes, yet it becomes the interest of every contributor to withdraw his shoulder from the burthen, and to shift this payment from himself to another; and the temptation to remove himself and his capital to another country, where he will be exempted from such burthens, becomes at last irresistable.
>
> (Ricardo, *Principles of Political Economy and Taxation*, quoted by Fry 1991: 7)

Capital flight from heavily indebted countries, despite exchange controls, usually grows very rapidly, once a repayments crisis is acknowledged, both for Ricardo's reason of escaping additional taxes, and because it becomes attractive to speculate on the depreciation of the country's real exchange rate. Capital flight can quickly exceed the inflow of new foreign borrowing, both the quantity and the quality of investment can decline, and it becomes impossible to grow out of the debt crisis.

Even conservative-minded commentators now admit that 'the work of "a small band of ideologues" can have a profound effect on living standards in São Paulo, Buenos Aires and Lima' (Congdon 1988: 48). What seems more difficult to acknowledge is that the ideologues concerned were ultra-right ideologues operating within profoundly right-wing governments. Incredibly, responsibility for the debt crisis is now shuffled off on to Maynard Keynes! Congdon, for example, audaciously claims that Reagan's economic policy-makers were victims of the 'corrosive influence' of Keynesian ideas (ibid.: 43). This imaginative obfuscation calls for three comments. The first is that everything which the people in question said, or wrote, about economic policy suggests a profound and irrational opposition to everything Keynesian. The second is that the fiscal expansion over which they presided was in the nature of farce rather than fine-tuning. Finally, as has been noted already, it was the absence of a Keynesian-style policy of international macroeconomic management which made the effects of US and UK policy on the developing countries as damaging as they were.

The economic policy of the Thatcher government undoubtedly pushed up UK nominal interest rates between 1979–81, and thereby contributed to the emerging debt crisis. But developments in the UK alone would not have been weighty enough to trigger a major crisis. The Federal Reserve Board in the US was allowing the US prime rate to rise to unprecedented heights from 1979 onwards, in the attempt to control inflation. What 'Reaganomics' achieved between 1981 and 1985 was the persistence of high nominal interest rates, once recession had brought inflation down, and severely weakened the demand for developing countries' exports. Although the policy content of Reaganomics somewhat differed from that of insular monetarism, it was incompetence as well as doctrine which produced the US government's structural deficit. The US–UK special relationship required a mutual blurring of differences on economic doctrine and a prolonged collusion with incompetence, at the expense of indebted developing countries. No one would deny that some developing countries spent unwisely what they borrowed. Many had indulged in lavish rearmament (Lever and Huhne 1985: 47). But in so doing, they had had strong encouragement both from the US State Department and from Mrs Thatcher, who used her visits to developing countries to ensure that British companies gained important arms contracts. Subsequent criticism of debt-distressed countries for unproductive spending of loans simply ignored the US and the UK role in the governmental promotion of arms exports.[11]

The Aftermath: British and American Policy on Debt Distress

British and American government policy towards the indebtedness of developing countries did not begin with the August 1982 Mexican suspension of debt repayment, which marks the start of the period of debt crisis. Already at the start of the 1980s, the relevant officials seemed to have had some apprehension that all was not entirely well with the process of recycling petro-dollars by means of commercial bank lending to the Third World. At the same time, too public acknowledgement of impending problems might have precipitated the crisis which they hoped to avoid. In retrospect, it is difficult to be sure how many of the emollient official statements on developing country indebtedness were genuinely complacent, and how many were merely tactically complacent. The underlying anxiety which showed through most strongly was that commercial lending might be inappropriate for supporting the balance of payments of indebted countries, in the absence of an IMF stabilization programme. By implication, the commercial banks might be willing to go on financing a balance of payments gap which was fast becoming unsustainable, whereas the IMF would be able to identify the point at which the macroeconomy had to be stabilized. Much confidence was publicly expressed that the Fund, its quotas recently increased, was adequate to this task, amidst the provision of a range of statistics which were interpreted to show that the LDC indebtedness problem was becoming less acute. No-one seems to have spotted the implications of falling oil prices for heavily indebted oil-exporting developing countries like Mexico. It was evidently difficult for the financial officials of two governments so ideologically committed to the beneficence of freely operating market forces to suggest, even in the face of real interest rates that were rapidly rising to unusual heights, that danger might be at hand. The only market imperfection that was conceded was that the banks may have lacked all the information that they needed to assess the creditworthiness of individual developing countries. Even this problem was said to be greatly improved. Apart from maintaining good information flows, nothing else needed to be done by the authorities – no contingency planning, no identification of a lender of last resort, no increase in the bank's had debt provisioning other than what they freely chose for themselves – which the British Treasury regarded as 'very satisfactory' (House of Commons 1983: 170).

Once Mexico's moratorium revealed the true seriousness of the indebtedness problem, a different tone was evident in governmental pronouncements. Early in 1983, the British Chancellor (then Geoffrey Howe) admitted that the scale of the problem 'at times threatened to overwhelm the international financial and banking system'. He also acknowledged the 'huge changes being made in the pattern of poverty [in Mexico] . . . because they have not got the institutions we have in the industrial countries which cushion us against the consequences' of massive macroeconomic stabilization programmes. Despite the sympathy for Mexico, it is clear that minimizing the self-inflicted damage to the international banking system was the government's primary objective of policy. That could be attained by a mixture of cautious debt rescheduling, to be accompanied by an IMF stabilization package and the encouragement to the commercial banks to continue lending to debt-distressed countries. The provision of so-called 'new lending' by banks was (and remained) the most problematic element in this survival recipe. Having lent well beyond the limit of creditworthiness, the banks were reluctant to re-cycle any of the debt repayments which they received back to the debtors in the form of 'new' loans. In a classic illustration of Sen's isolation paradox, each bank wanted to minimize its *own* exposure, without regard to the effects of all banks behaving in this way on every bank's exposure. But just as the authorities had steered clear of giving directions on maximum lending, so now they avoided giving formal directions on minimum levels of continued lending, even through the mediation of the IMF. Nevertheless, behind the scenes, considerable pressures to continue lending were put on creditor banks in 1982–3.

As for the plight of the debt-distressed developing countries, the time had come for grasping at straws. The role of the US federal government deficit in pushing up interest rates (and thereby precipitating the crisis) was acknowledged, as were the protectionist policies of the industrial countries themselves in prolonging it. But all of this was so much hand-wringing. Avoiding protectionism to help the payments' prospects of debtor countries was the ultimate counsel of perfection in the 1980s. The US relied on large Japanese and German payments surpluses to finance their own current account deficit. Such surpluses required ready access to the US goods market. This in turn spurred protectionist sentiment and action in the US. Calls to revive world economic growth to assist the debtors by pulling up commodity prices had somewhat more substance, but nothing like enough. Although growth did resume in developed countries after 1982 for seven years, it was never vigorous enough to stop the general deterioration in the terms of trade of developing countries (see table 8.4). In the highly indebted countries themselves, despite some growth between 1984 and 1987, real GDP growth before the 1990s was slight or negative. They were not enabled to grow out of debt.

Underlying this first phase of the Anglo-American policy response was the posture that the debt crisis was no more than a temporary liquidity problem which developing countries were faced with. Comfort was derived from the propositions that sovereign nations do not, like firms, go bankrupt, but on the contrary have strong incentives (connected with the retention of creditworthiness) never to default. Many of the indebted countries had considerable untapped natural resources, so it was concluded that eventually both principal and interest would be repaid. The perception that, on the contrary, heavily indebted countries faced a fundamental structural problem in servicing their debt, because the debt service burden itself undermines the possibility of economic growth, and thus of emerging from the debt crisis, was slow to penetrate official thinking.[12]

During this phase, the commercial banks followed various strategies of self-protection. One was to make use of the secondary market in sovereign debt, to allow small players to exit at a price, and larger players to re-arrange their exposure according to their assessment of country risks. (The debtors, too, used the heavy discounts in this market to make various kinds of debt buy-backs and debt-equity swaps – see French-Davis (1990) on Chile.) The value of secondary-market transactions rose from very little in 1984 to US $50 billion in 1989. The banks also protected themselves by increasing their capital, to reduce their exposure ratios, and by increasing their provisions against bad debts. The nine largest US commercial banks increased their capital from $29 bn (1982) to $55.8 billion (1988), thereby reducing their exposure to capital ratio for developing country loans from 288 to 108 per cent. By these means, the vulnerability of the US and UK banking system, which was substantial in 1982, was gradually decreased. The success of these self-protective measures by the banks in repairing the viability of the international banking system – which was seen as the primary objective of debt policy – seemed to validate the leave-it-alone, do-nothing philosophy of how to handle a world debt crisis.

Nevertheless, the pressures of the Anglo-American special relationship led to two major US initiatives intended to make progress in resolving the debt crisis, and their public endorsement by the UK. One was the Baker Plan, announced by Treasury Secretary James Baker in Seoul in September 1985. The other was the Brady Plan, announced by Treasury Secretary Nicholas Brady in March, 1989. The Baker Plan was aimed at fifteen highly indebted countries, mostly in Latin America, but also including the Philippines, Ivory Coast, Morocco, Nigeria and Yugoslavia. The intention was to encourage an increase in new commercial bank lending by proposing complementary increases in lending by the Bank and the Fund, to be accompanied by structural adjustment programmes. The Baker Plan achieved little progress, because it had no way of overcoming the banks' continuing unwillingness to supply 'new money' to countries still evidently in the grip of a debt crisis. The IFIs also failed to lend up to the Baker targets, fearing that the increase of their exposures when the banks were not increasing theirs meant that they were shouldering more of the risk, and thus bailing out the banks with public-sector money, and possibly putting their own credit in jeopardy. The UK continued to give formal support to the Baker Plan throughout 1985–9, even when its credibility had rather swiftly ebbed away.

The Brady Plan of 1989 broke new ground: (1) by recognizing that formal, negotiated debt reduction would be necessary to end the debt crisis; and (2) by providing that the IFIs could provide partial guarantees of the value of the paper which embodied the new, discounted debt. Both of these departures from past practice were made in a renewed attempt to persuade the banks to come forward with more 'new money'. Both were unwelcome to the British Chancellor Lawson. He distrusted all attempts to solve the debt crisis, which he regarded as 'grandiose' and likely to be counter-productive. His instinctive preference was for the case-by-case, step-by-step, pragmatically reactive approach (Lawson 1992: 530). Departure (1) implied that participating banks would, for the first time accept losses arising on their developing country loans, and not merely put aside provisions against losses. Departure (2) formalized the use of public-sector money to make that process less risky than it would otherwise be, and thus constituted a partial bail-out for the banks at the tax-payers' ultimate expense. Lawson disliked the latter feature of the Brady plan both because of its implications for public expenditure and because he believed that the banks alone should be left to cope with the consequences of debts which were 'negotiated freely' by them with the debtors (House of Commons 1990: 4–5).[13]

Why then did Britain's Chancellor publicly line up behind the Brady Plan, despite its breach of a principle which he strongly supported? Why had he supported the earlier Baker Plan, despite his dislike of 'grandiose solutions' in general? Part of the explanation may lie in the sterling crisis of January 1985. The fact that the pound fell almost to equal one dollar, and that the British government proved unwilling in the event to see that psychological barrier broken, finally disposed of the insularity component of the policy of insular monetarism. International cooperation to regulate the movement of exchange rates was put back on the policy agenda and quickly embodied in the Plaza Agreement of September 1985. Britain had turned out to need international help to overcome the strength of the US dollar. It is reasonable to suggest that the UK was willing to reciprocate with public support for other plans of international cooperation which were devised by James Baker, and his successor, to address the debt crisis, whatever private reservations were felt about their substance. Such willingness would be eased by the fact that these plans concentrated their attention on countries of major geopolitical importance to the United States.[14]

The major independent British move to ease the position of debtor countries came in April, 1987. It was a plan to relieve the pressure of official (not commercial) debts for poor debtor countries in sub-Saharan Africa. This came as a considerable surprise to public opinion, because the Chancellor who proposed it to the IMF in Washington was not well known either as a friend of sub-Saharan Africa or a sympathizer with those developing countries burdened by debt. He adhered to the view that the problem of excessive indebtedness was caused 'primarily by the mistaken policies' of the debtor countries themselves – the standard neo-liberal view (Griffith-Jones 1991: 108). A minor British initiative to help debtors had been unveiled at the autumn IMF meeting in 1984. It consisted of waiving the rule that re-scheduling debts automatically disqualified the country that re-scheduled from export credit cover (Keegan 1989: 139). This was helpful to debtors, but almost inevitable given the massive increase in debt re-scheduling through the Paris Club after 1982. The 1987 Lawson plan represented a recognition that official debt of SSA countries was unlikely ever to be repaid, plus a desire to steal a march on President Mitterrand who was meditating a similar plan.[15] The Lawson plan, and the later Mitterrand initiative, both became options of the 'Toronto terms', which effectively allow about one-third

TABLE 8.5 DEVELOPING COUNTRIES: EXTERNAL DEBT AND DEBT
SERVICE (US $, BILLIONS)

	External debt[a]		Debt service payments[a]	
	1983	*1990*	*1983*	*1990*
Total	889.0	1,306.4	120.6	161.8
Africa	126.9	226.4	17.3	25.4
Asia	207.5	361.7	26.6	47.4
Europe	84.8	136.0	11.5	16.6
Middle East	125.4	163.5	14.7	24.3
Western Hemisphere	344.5	418.7	50.5	48.1
Memo:				
15 Heavily indebted countries[b]	394.7	495.3	56.0	55.8

[a] Excludes debt owed to the IMF.
[b] Argentina, Bolivia, Brazil, Chile, Colombia, Cote d'Ivoire, Ecuador, Mexico, Morocco.
Source: IMF World Economic Outlook (1991)

debt service relief on Paris Club debt for certain poor developing countries (mainly African) who undertake to implement IMF stabilization programmes. By 1990, thirteen eligible countries had benefited from the Toronto terms (Mountfield 1990: 46). Just before Mrs Thatcher's fall from power, Lawson's successor as Chancellor, John Major, proposed *inter alia* that debt relief possibilities be raised to two-thirds. These 'Trinidad terms' have yet to be universally agreed by OECD countries.[16]

Despite substantial activity in debt reduction and conversion, both for commercial and for official debt, the absolute size of developing countries' external debt (not counting liabilities to the IMF) continued to rise, mainly as a result of the effective capitalization of interest that could not be paid. In 1983, the figure was US $880 billion. By 1990, it had risen to US $1306.4 bn. Debt service payments rose from US $120.6 billion in 1983 to US $161.8 bn in 1990. As table 8.5 shows, the situation of Latin America and the Caribbean – which in 1983 had the largest external debt and debt service payments – had improved somewhat relative to other regions by 1990. The indebtedness of Africa, Asia, Europe and the Middle East had increased rapidly between 1983 and 1990, although not enough to displace Latin America from its position as (still) the largest debtor region with the heaviest debt service payments. The composition of developing country debt had

TABLE 8.6   DEVELOPING COUNTRIES: EXTERNAL DEBT BY TYPE OF CREDITOR (US $, BILLIONS)

	1982	1983	1984	1985	1986	1987	1988	1989	1990
Official	249.4	279.9	303.7	353.5	409.2	488.7	496.7	526.3	575.7
Commercial Banks	433.7	461.5	471.5	487.1	507.4	545.0	532.2	515.5	517.9
Other private	156.1	147.5	154.8	163.9	179.7	182.2	194.8	192.3	212.7
Total	839.2	888.9	930.0	1,004.5	1,096.3	1,215.9	1,223.7	1,234.1	1,306.3

Source: IMF World Economic Outlook (1990, 1991)

TABLE 8.7   DEVELOPING COUNTRIES: COMPOSITION OF THE EXTERNAL DEBT BY TYPE OF CREDITOR (PERCENTAGE)

	1982	1983	1984	1985	1986	1987	1988	1989	1990
Official	29.7	31.5	32.7	35.2	37.3	40.2	40.6	42.6	44.1
Commercial banks	51.7	51.9	50.7	48.5	46.3	44.8	43.5	41.8	39.6
Other private	18.6	16.6	16.6	16.3	16.4	15.0	15.9	15.6	16.3
Total	100.0	100.0	100.0	100.0	100.0	100.0	100.0	100.0	100.0

Source: IMF World Economic Outlook (1990, 1991)

shifted somewhat away from commercial and towards official debt. The amounts and percentage shares are shown in table 8.6 and 8.7. This reflects the impact of the Baker and the Brady plans, which had more influence over the actions of the official sector than over those of the commercial banks.

It is more useful, in gauging the continuing impact of the debt crisis on developing countries, to look at external debt and debt service in relation to GDP and export earnings, than simply recording the absolute figures. Tables 8.8 and 8.9 show external debt and debt service in relation to GDP and to exports, both for developing countries as a whole and for the 'Baker 15' heavily indebted countries. These indicate that, since the debt crisis broke in 1982:

1   The ratios of total external debt to exports, and to GDP, worsened through the mid-1980s and then returned to their 1982 levels by 1990. These were, of course, considerably above those of 1979. Little difference is evident between all developing countries and the heavy indebted group in this regard.

TABLE 8.8 DEVELOPING COUNTRIES: RATIOS OF TOTAL EXTERNAL
DEBT TO EXPORTS AND GDP[a] (PERCENTAGE)

| | *Total Developing Countries* | | *15 Heavily Indebted Countries*[b] | |
	Debt/Exports	*Debt/GDP*	*Debt/Exports*	*Debt/GDP*
1979	90.9	24.2	183.7	31.0
1980	81.8	24.3	168.0	32.8
1981	95.0	27.7	202.6	37.6
1982	120.8	31.1	266.6	41.0
1983	135.6	33.0	288.9	46.0
1984	134.9	34.0	269.4	46.6
1985	152.0	35.9	284.3	45.5
1986	173.7	37.9	344.8	44.9
1987	162.1	37.6	339.3	44.4
1988	143.3	34.9	295.0	40.2
1989	129.3	32.3	264.1	38.9
1990	124.8	31.4	247.7	37.8

[a] Excludes debt owed to the IMF.
[b] Argentina, Bolivia, Brazil, Chile, Colombia, Cote d'Ivoire, Ecuador, Mexico,
Morocco, Nigeria, Peru, Philippines, Uruguay, Venezuela, Yugoslavia.
Source: IMF World Economic Outlook (1987–91)

TABLE 8.9 DEVELOPING COUNTRIES: RATIO OF DEBT SERVICE TO
EXPORTS OF GOODS AND SERVICES[a] (PERCENTAGE)

| | *Total Developing Countries* | | *15 Heavily Indebted Countries*[b] | |
	Total Service	*Interest*	*Total Service*	*Interest*
1979	14.3	6.1	35.0	14.7
1980	13.2	6.6	29.4	16.0
1981	16.1	8.7	40.9	22.6
1982	19.6	11.1	51.5	31.1
1983	18.4	11.0	41.0	29.2
1984	19.7	11.7	40.8	28.9
1985	21.3	11.9	40.0	28.1
1986	22.7	12.1	44.0	28.7
1987	20.5	9.4	38.0	21.1
1988	20.0	9.6	44.8	24.9
1989	16.8	8.2	32.2	18.5
1990	15.5	7.6	27.9	15.6

[a] Excludes debt service to the IMF.
[b] Argentina, Bolivia, Brazil, Chile, Colombia, Cote d'Ivoire, Ecuador, Mexico,
Morocco, Nigeria, Peru, Philippines, Uruguay, Venezuela, Yugoslavia.
Source: IMF World Economic Outlook (1987–91)

2   The ratios of debt service to exports tell a somewhat different story. For all developing countries, the ratio did fall after 1982, from 19.6 per cent to 15.5 per cent in 1990. Also, the ratio declined relatively more for the highly indebted countries, from 51.5 to 27.9 per cent (1982–90). This reflects both debt re-scheduling and the decline in total external debt that began after 1986.

The improvement in the debt service ratio, especially after 1987, is reflected in the changes in the size of current account imbalances in developing countries (see table 8.11). Although still in substantial deficit each year, the average absolute deficits of the late 1980s have been smaller than in the 1981–7 period for developing countries as a whole, and for the highly indebted countries. Nevertheless, it is not clear that the 1980s have laid the foundations for subsequent sustainable growth. Growth for the developing countries in the 1980s was markedly slower than for the whole period 1965–80. The heavily indebted countries would need to raise their current GDP by 45 per cent to reach the levels that would have prevailed if the average growth rate of 1965–80 had continued (Singer 1991: 3). There was no sign of any rising tempo of growth as the decade proceeded, either in developing countries as a whole, or among the highly indebted (see table 8.10).

By 1991, some chinks of light among the general gloom were visible, fortunately. A number of Latin American countries have benefited from negotiations completed under the Brady Plan: Mexico (February 1990), Costa Rica (May 1990), Venezuela (August 1990). The Philippines has also had a Brady deal. Early commentators noticed the small reductions in the debt service burden which Mexico experienced from its deal, and came to rather sombre conclusions (e.g. Williamson 1990). Later work has become more optimistic. Cline (1991: 44) concludes from an extensive study of Mexico's prospects: 'An important lesson of the Mexico agreement for future Brady Plans is that the largest effects are driven more by the restoration of investment confidence and the normalisation of domestic interest rates than by the direct savings on external obligations.'

Some evidence also exists that positive net transfers of resources resumed in Latin America and the Caribbean from the creditor countries in 1990 – although as yet only a few countries of the region have benefited (essentially Mexico, Chile, Columbia and Venezuela) (Griffith-Jones and Gottschalk 1991).

The position of sub-Saharan African economies remains dire, despite the reliefs offered under the G7 plans. These remain small relative both to debt service obligations and to the size of debt service payments actually being made. While obligations exceed US $20 billion per year, of which less than half is currently being paid, the additional relief

TABLE 8.10 DEVELOPING COUNTRIES: REAL GDP (ANNUAL CHANGES, PERCENTAGE)

	1979	1980	1981	1982	1983	1984	1985	1986	1987	1988	1989	1990
Total	4.3	3.4	1.8	2.1	2.1	4.3	4.2	4.1	3.8	4.4	3.1	1.3
Africa	3.3	3.6	1.8	2.0	-1.1	0.7	4.0	1.7	1.3	2.9	3.3	1.9
Asia	4.5	5.5	5.9	5.6	8.1	8.4	6.8	6.9	8.1	9.0	5.5	5.3
Europe	3.8	0.1	-0.1	1.2	2.4	4.9	2.7	4.4	2.6	1.6	-0.7	-4.7
Middle East	1.8	-2.5	-1.3	1.3	1.1	0.0	1.7	-0.7	0.1	4.7	3.2	-1.5
Western Hemisphere	6.1	6.0	-0.2	-1.1	-2.8	3.6	3.4	4.7	2.4	0.2	1.5	-1.0
Memo:												
HIC[a]	6.1	5.4	-0.3	-0.5	-3.0	2.3	3.7	4.6	2.1	0.7	1.9	-1.0

[a] Heavily indebted countries: Argentina, Bolivia, Brazil, Chile, Colombia, Cote d'Ivoire, Ecuador, Mexico, Morocco, Nigeria, Peru, Philippines, Uruguay, Venezuela, Yugoslavia.
Source: IMF World Economic Outlook (1987–91)

TABLE 8.11 DEVELOPING COUNTRIES: BALANCE OF PAYMENTS ON GOODS, SERVICES AND PRIVATE TRANSFERS (US $, BILLIONS)

	1979	1980	1981	1982	1983	1984	1985	1986	1987	1988	1989	1990
Total	6.4	25.2	−50.3	−84.4	−66.1	−37.0	−36.2	−57.6	−14.0	−32.3	−31.1	−29.1
Africa	−3.4	−5.8	−26.1	−25.1	−16.1	−11.2	−5.5	−15.5	−9.8	−17.4	−15.0	−11.8
Asia	−9.7	−17.2	−21.6	−18.8	−16.4	−6.9	−16.8	0.7	16.8	4.7	−4.7	−7.4
Europe	−13.6	−15.8	−4.1	−3.5	−2.6	−0.6	−0.8	−1.6	0.8	6.8	3.1	−3.7
Middle East	54.2	94.2	49.1	4.1	−21.0	−16.3	−9.6	−23.1	−10.4	−13.3	−4.6	7.3
Western Hemisphere	−21.1	−30.3	−42.6	−41.1	−10.0	−2.0	−3.5	−18.1	−11.4	−13.0	−9.9	−13.6
Memo: HIC[a]	−24.6	−29.5	−51.1	−50.8	−15.5	−1.4	−0.5	−18.1	−9.1	−11.1	−7.7	−13.6

[a] Heavily indebted countries: Argentina, Bolivia, Brazil, Chile, Colombia, Cote d'Ivoire, Ecuador, Mexico, Morocco, Nigeria, Peru, Philippines, Uruguay, Venezuela, Yugoslavia.
Source: IMF World Economic Outlook (1987–91)

TABLE 8.12   TOTAL NET RESOURCE FLOWS TO LDCS (US $, BILLIONS, AT 1988 PRICES AND EXCHANGE RATES)

	1981	1982	1983	1984	1985	1986	1987	1988	1989
Official development finance	67	66	64	73	75	70	66	66	70
ODA receipts	54	51	51	54	57	55	52	52	54
ODA receipts (DAC)	38	42	42	44	45	45	45	48	47
Total net resource flows	202	175	143	132	128	103	100	106	112

Source: OECD (1990: 123)

provided by the Toronto terms is in the region of US $0.1 billion. By itself, these terms do not reduce the stock of debt, although both the US and France promised in 1989 to forgive the debt owed to them by low-income countries with adjustment programmes. In these circumstances, it is obvious that 'substantial new commitments of foreign assistance will be needed' (Greene 1989: 872). The British commitment to implement the Trinidad terms, unilaterally if necessary, in late 1991, were welcome in this context. But it has yet to carry through against United States' opposition.

Aid Fatigue of the US and UK Governments

As the debt crisis turned off the flow of 'new money' from the commercial banks to the developing countries during the 1980s, nothing else took its place. The aid budgets of the industrialized economies did not expand to replace the commercial money, which by and large ceased once the debt crisis broke (except when coerced by the international financial institutions). As table 8.12 shows, once the effect of inflation and exchange-rate variations are removed from the figures, total flows of official development assistance ('aid') to developing countries are remarkably stable. Within the total of aid receipts, there is some substitution of DAC aid for non-DAC aid. This resulted from the impact of the falling oil price on OPEC donors and the disarray of the Soviet and East European economies in the latter half of the 1980s. But for total aid flows, the failure to expand in real terms is unmistakable. The period around 1979–80 seems to have been a transition point when aid donors decided that they could go thus far and no further (despite many unfulfilled pledges to raise the share of aid in GNP). This understanding seems to have been crucial in shifting the responsibility for adjustment from the shoulders of the industrialized nations onto the shoulders of the developing countries themselves. The prospect of evolving a new international economic order more favourable to developing countries vanished. Adjustment to whatever circumstances the international economy threw up now became the task of each individual developing country.

However, when we look more closely at this apparent collective aid fatigue of the 1980s, it is clear that it affected some countries much more than others. Most of the OECD countries actually increased their net disbursements of aid, in real terms, during the decade. This was so of Denmark, Finland, France, Germany, Italy, Japan, the Netherlands, Norway, Sweden and Switzerland. A minority did seem genuinely fatigued – unable to make any greater effort at resource transfer. Such countries were Australia, Austria, Belgium, Canada, Ireland. But only three countries reduced their aid effort over the decade: New Zealand (a minor donor), the United States and the United Kingdom. It was the behaviour of the US and the UK, in particular, which prevented DAC aid flows from rising to meet some of the financial needs which emerged in the wake of the debt crisis.

In 1986, one of Britain's aid ministers wrote to his successor that, while Mrs Thatcher had many qualities, 'over-enthusiasm for the aid budget' was not one of them (Byrd 1991: 66). Her lack of enthusiasm was most evident in the early 1980s, when between 1981–2 and 1986–7, the volume of British aid declined by 2.8 per cent a year in real terms. After this long decline, a small increase in the aid/GNP ratio was finally achieved by Christopher Patten, as minister responsible, in 1988. The figures in current prices, 1979 prices and as a percentage of GNP are given in table 8.13.

If the 1979 aid/GNP ratio is taken as the norm, a cumulative shortfall of aid resources equal to 1.43 per cent of UK GNP had occurred by 1988. Using the UN target of 0.7 of GNP as the norm would increase this shortfall to 3.33 per cent. Along with this loss of resources, the British aid programme was damaged in other ways. An explicit commitment to 'give greater weight to political, industrial and commercial considerations' in the allocation of aid had mixed results. On the one hand, it permitted the development of an intelligent strategy for post-apartheid Southern Africa, centred around Mozambique. On the other it permitted an expansion of low-quality export-related aid within a budget that was already shrinking in real terms (Toye 1991).

One other loss which the British aid programme suffered in the 1980s was in the skills required for an independent critical perspective on the

TABLE 8.13   UK OFFICIAL DEVELOPMENT ASSISTANCE, 1979–1988
(VARIOUS MEASURES)

	£ Millions	£ Millions (1979 prices)	% of GNP
1979	864	864	0.51
1980	842	704	0.35
1981	1062	798	0.42
1982	991	692	0.37
1983	1080	716	0.35
1984	1200	760	0.33
1985	1210	726	0.33
1986	1233	714	0.31
1987	1174	649	0.28
1988	1540	798	0.32

Source: Burnell (1991: 9–10)

activites of the international financial institutions. The deep cuts of the
early 1980s affected ODA staff and not merely the projects and programmes which they were administering. The capability of formulating
a different adjustment strategy from that proposed by the Fund and the
Bank, or of criticising what was proposed reasonably knowledgeably,
gradually decreased as the administration of aid was made leaner in
terms of middle and high-level personnel. Nor was what was lost in this
way made good in other departments of government. The Treasury's
international finance divisions also lack the skills and supporting staff
of a typical IMF mission (Mountfield 1990: 45). A naive attitude to
the efficacy of Fund and Bank conditionalities is a characteristic of
many of the public statements of British officials on the debt crisis. This
had its origin in the aid cuts as well as the more general pressure of the
Anglo-American special relationship and produced some over-rigid
attitudes about what is to be done as the debt crisis era is about to go
into double figures. Brady-type debt reduction programmes need to
be accompanied by sound adjustment programmes. But independent
input into the design of such programmes is vital. If the Fund/Bank
adjustment programmes prescribed for indebted countries are taken to
be unquestionably right, the persistence of the crisis is very easily as-
cribed to the debtors themselves, for having failed to do the right thing.
But in some cases, this intransigence will be justified, because of poor
programme design. A more discriminating approach could also be the
approach which leads to new opportunities for aid expansion.

Conclusion

Mrs Thatcher's first words on taking office were 'where there is discord, may we bring harmony . . . where there is despair, may we bring hope' (Young 1989: 136–7). For the developing countries of the world, these pious words must now have a somewhat hollow ring. After the Falklands episode, British and US foreign policy regressed to that of an earlier era of frequent military intervention, with scant respect for international law, against developing country regimes which were, often with good reason, disliked. The basis for sustaining this antagonistic posture was a re-invigorated 'special relationship' between the UK and the US. Built on shared political attitudes, this relationship was managed in a way which distracted attention from Britain's continuing structural dependence on the US, and thus the intrinsic sources of friction were kept tightly under control.

In the economic field, the effort at collusion was more difficult. Interpretations of requirements of the 'new monetarism' differed among the converts on either side of the Atlantic (not to mention the differences between those on the same side). The institutions for the execution of economic policy also differed. In addition, the Reagan camp tried hard to learn from the 'Thatcher experiment' in advance of their own advent to power. In the US, monetary policy was used against inflation more effectively than had been the case in Britain. But massive tax cutting created a large structural deficit for the US government. Nominal interest rates in both countries reached unprecedented levels, and when inflation decreased, real interest rates rose to, and remained at, roughly double their average level of the previous three decades (i.e. 4 per cent compared with 2 per cent, 1950–80).

This rise in real interest rates in the early 1980s as a result particularly of US policies put a major squeeze on those developing economies that had borrowed in the 1970s, at the behest of industrialized country governments and the international financial institutions. The new feature of variable interest rates had made them vulnerable to sudden changes in the international financial regime. The fragility of this re-cycling mechanism was finally revealed when falling oil prices forced Mexico to declare a debt moratorium in August, 1982. From this point onwards, commercial banks were very reluctant to continue lending on the normal voluntary basis. This precipitated a widespread crisis in the developing world, in which debt obligations spiralled by the power of compound interest, and a whole range of ingenious remedial measures were not able to prevent the debt overhang from growing.

The British government did occasionally hint in public that it would be nice if the US could control its budget deficit, to help alleviate the debtors' plight. But, when that hint fell on deaf ears in Washington, nothing else was to be done. The real priority was the deflection of any further threats to the international banking system, allowing individual banks time to take counter-measures against the consequences of future outright defaults. Once such threats – for example, the emergence of a well-organized debtors cartel – had receded, both governments had little interest in taking major actions to ease the plight of debtor countries.[17] The markets should be allowed to dictate the eventual outcome, it was strongly believed. The idea that governments should intervene to arrange a settling of accounts between creditors and debtors, to allow a fresh start on the international financial scene, was regarded as anathema (cf. Marcel and Palma 1988: 392–5).

Nevertheless, after 1985, more modest plans by the US government to ease the plight of countries with heavy commercial debts were announced and supported in public (but not in private) by the UK. Britain's formal support, despite reservations about the principles involved, resulted partly from its need for international economic co-operation after the sterling crisis of January 1985 and partly from unwillingness to interfere with the US pursuit of its own geopolitical interests. Britain's own debt initiatives have been more modest, to help African low-income countries with a burden of offical debt. These proposals have been helpful, and are to be welcomed, but their cost, and the relief they gave, was still small by the early 1990s.

The aid performance of both the US and the UK over the decade of the debt crisis has been one of steadily declining effort. The US volume of official development assistance fell in real terms between 1980–1 and 1988–9, and as a percentage of GNP from 0.27 to 0.18 per cent. The UK volume of aid also fell in real terms between the same years, and as a percentage of GNP from 0.39 to 0.32 (OECD 1990: 186–7). These performances were markedly worse than almost all other OECD aid donors. In Britain's case, the running down of the aid budget in the early 1980s had the additional unfortunate result that economic expertise on schemes of structural adjustment was impaired. This reinforced an existing tendency of naive and unquestioning support of the liberalization reforms so strongly promoted by the US.

By 1992, some hopeful signs had appeared, both of the initial successes of the Brady Plan, and increased vigour in implementing debt reduction schemes for the least developed countries. But many developing countries still have their debts treated much less favourably than terms which have been granted to Poland and Egypt, whose geopolitical significance requires no underlining. They are still having to extract themselves unaided from the aftermath of the 1970s re-cycling of petrodollars. They have not had their despair replaced by hope. Nevertheless, when they reflect on their situation in the global order, so harshly illuminated by the events of the 1980s debt crisis, they will surely agree with Mrs Thatcher's final words on losing power: 'It is a funny old world.'

Notes

1 The sentimentality and the riskiness of this approach were both neatly captured by a poster which showed Thatcher as Scarlett O'Hara to Reagan's Rhett Butler, over the legend: 'She promised to follow him to the end of the earth. He promised to arrange it.' More prosaically, 'Margaret was mesmerized by power, and she recognized in the American President a man whose writ far exceeded her own' (Lawson 1992: 528).

2 Critics of the 'new monetarism' compared these conversions unflatteringly with the periodic outbreaks of mass hysteria in the Middle Ages (Kaldor 1989: 178).

3 The mood of professional scepticism was captured in Britain by the 364 economists who criticized the 1981 budget in a letter to *The Times*.

4 Perhaps the reason was that, if they had been, a Thatcher government might not have been incoming after all. 'Unfortunately, in the heat of the election campaign, Margaret Thatcher felt electorally obliged' to honour Clegg's recommendations, according to Nigel Lawson (1992: 33).

5 It is to George Bush's credit that, when he first heard these supply-side doctrines in 1979, he described them as 'voodoo economics' (Congdon 1988: 27). He never repeated this remark, however, and served eight years as Vice-President in an administration which remained publicly committed to supply-side doctrines.

6 In a move that would have pleased the Mikado of Japan, Conable was subsequently appointed by Reagan in 1986 as President of the World Bank, with special responsibility for helping to alleviate the debt crisis.

7 In a rare (though veiled) public criticism of Reaganomics, Nigel Lawson had remarked in a speech in Zurich in January, 1981:

> The convenient theory so popular in some circles across the Atlantic – that cuts in tax rates produce increased tax revenue – is, alas, as a general proposition, simply too good to be true.
>
> (Keegan 1989: 86).

8 This characterization is somewhat misleading, in that the first Reagan administration abandoned Keynesian-style international macroeconomic management. Reaganomics was isolationist in just the same way that British monetarism was insular. At the G7 Summit at Williamsburg in May 1983, Reagan refused to raise taxes, despite being in a minority of one (Lawson 1992: 510–11). See also williamson in Milner 1987: 57.

9 It is true that in the 1980s, many developing countries ran larger current account deficits (as a per cent of GNP) than did the US (see Fry 1991: 3–4). What is relevant to the movement of interest rates is the *size* of the US economy, and its reliance on *commercial* rather than concessional finance.

10 In July 1982, just one month before the Mexican moratorium, the IMF published a document which concluded that 'over the medium term the rate of growth of international bank assets (on loans to LDCs) can be expected to remain high' (Griffith-Jones 1991: 102). On this point, see also Singer (1989: 37–8).

11 The Aid and Trade Provision of the UK aid programme was sometimes used as indirect bait when arms deals were to be clinched. Here is the story of the attempted Malaysian arms deal, which was referred to earlier.

> Aid to Malaysia declined from about £10m annually in the 1970s and early 1980s, but in 1986 the government offered Malaysia £50m in ATP. This spectacular reversal of policy was a cornerstone in a determined effort by the government, in which Mrs Thatcher appears to have taken a strong personal interest, to place relations with Malaysia on a new footing. In September 1988 Mrs Thatcher signed in Kuala Lumpur a 'memorandum of understanding' providing for arms sales to Malaysia of about £1.5 bn . . . No evidence has been produced of a *direct* link between the relatively modest ATP provision of 1986 and the very large arms deal of 1988 . . . Mrs Thatcher informed the Commons (23 June 1989) that her government had made it clear to the Malaysians on a number of occasions during 1988 that it remained 'most willing' to consider Malaysian requests for aid, although the provision of aid as an *integral* part of a negotiated agreement on the defence package was not possible.
>
> (Byrd 1991: 65–6, with emphases added)

Malaysia is not a debt-distressed country, of course. It decided to renegotiate the arms deal in May, 1990.

12 Keynes's efforts to persuade the establishment that post-First World War reparations would place Germany in this same impossible position present a strong historical parallel.

13 A significant disagreement had occurred in 1984 between Lawson and the Bank of England over whether Johnson Matthey Bankers should be rescued or allowed to fail. The Bank decided that to allow failure was too risky, given the fragility of the international banking system in the wake of the world debt crisis. Lawson, not having been fully informed of all the detail, was left publicly to defend the Bank's decision, which involved some partial loss of taxpayers' money. For more detail on JMB, see Keegan (1989: 152–5).

14 The only country among the Baker 15 of which this is not true is the Ivory Coast. The ten Latin American countries fall under the Monroe Doctrine; the US has bases in the Philippines and large commercial and military interests in Morocco; Nigeria is the economic giant of sub-Saharan Africa and Yugoslavia was pivotal in cold war politics.

15 The chemistry of the Lawson plan was the combination of a politician anxious to be seen taking high-profile international initiatives, with Treasury officials more imaginative and humane than is sometimes believed to be the case.

16 Interestingly, Mr Major as Prime Minister, decided that the UK would implement the Trinidad terms unilaterally, despite US opposition, in October 1991 (*Financial Times*, 18 October 1991).

17   With a frankness which comes with loss of office, Lawson has admitted
     after the event that 'the principal . . . objective of the Western world debt
     strategy, ably coordinated by the IMF, was to buy time . . . for it was
     perfectly clear that the vast bulk of these debts would never come good
     and be repaid – even though there was an understandable conspiracy of
     silence over admitting this unpalatable fact' (Lawson 1992: 520).

Postscript

Just as the revision of the text of the second edition was completed, the US electorate overwhelmingly swept away President Bush's hopes of a second term and installed his Democratic challenger, Bill Clinton in the White House. So ended twelve years of Republican tenure of the US Presidency, which have been so closely identified with the neo-conservative economic policies that have been discussed here. Is this the death knell for economic neo-conservativism in general, and for the development counter-revolution in particular? Have these policy attitudes and their underlying doctrines finally been relegated from current affairs to history?

It has been a recurring theme of this book that the strength of an economic idea at any time, and its influence on policy is determined not just by its intellectual coherence, but also – and usually very significantly, by the larger trends in world politics. If this is true, it must be expected that the Democratic Party's victory in the presidential polls of one of the most powerful countries in the world will produce an important change in the range of economic policies which will be considered practically useful and in the economic theories which find general favour. It would be surprising if, in the attempt to stimulate faster economic growth, a new President who campaigned on the need for change, did not change both the policies themselves and the prevailing policy discourse on economic management. The doctrine of minimal government intervention, in such matters as the fine-tuning of aggregate demand and the granting of selective subsidies, could also be expected to be re-appraised. The use of taxation for income distribution purposes is likely to return to the political agenda. Some widening of policy objectives beyond the search for low inflation is also likely.

Outside the US, such policies have already made some reappearances. Japan has already adopted a substantial new government spending package of infrastructure and transport projects in an explicitly Keynesian attempt to counter the deflationary effects of falling property prices, credit restriction and general industrial slowdown. The UK, after leaving the European Community's Exchange Rate Mechanism in September 1992, has placed increased policy emphasis on employment-creating capital investment as an instrument for reviving economic growth. In the face of a worldwide recession, the leaders of the industrial countries are finally allowing themselves to adopt, in varying degrees, the classical policies of reflation.

However, one should also note the many reasons why all the elements of the economic counter-revolution will not simply disappear, as if it had never been. The US is highly unlikely, whatever the content of the new political rhetoric, to move back to the extravagant welfare hand-outs of the Johnson era in the 1960s. The counter-revolution's focus on human resource development as central to economic growth will surely not be lost. Nor should its concern for the preservation and enhancement of personal incentives to undertake training, acquire employable skills and persist in job search. For these reasons, while the US government will almost certainly become more interventionist, the nature of its interventions will be more limited and better crafted from a micro-economic perspective than has historically been the case during Democrat administrations.

From the perspective of the developing countries, one of the most important questions about this transition is how the US fiscal deficit will be handled. Can it now be substantially reduced? Despite a campaign commitment to cut it by half, the room for manoeuvre is limited by, among other things, the extent of the recession. Such a reduction would require bold selective surgery on existing public expenditures to make room for new investment in education, training and infrastructure. It would also require substantial increases in revenue with a neutral distributional effect, given that the opportunities for effectively taxing the highest incomes is quite limited. To be confident that the US government's claim on world savings will dramatically fall is difficult. But without a smaller deficit in the US, it will be hard to lower the 1980s level of world real interest rates, and hard consequently to speed the easing of developing countries' debt burdens.

Other important imponderables remain on the present world scene. The 1989 liberal revolution in Eastern Europe and the former Soviet Union has dampened economic activity in capitalist economies with large military hardware sectors. A compensating surge in market-based civilian production in the formerly state socialist economies has not taken place, and massive programmes of external investment in those economies have not been forthcoming, on the reasonable ground that the conditions to make such investment fruitful are still absent. There was an important element of truth in the arguments of those Western neo-Marxists who claimed that capitalist prosperity was underpinned by armament production. It has taken the ending of the cold war to reveal this. Capitalist prosperity without the permanent arms economy has yet to be realized. To the extent that growth in developing countries is driven by world conditions, this is bad news for them.

Another major imponderable is the future growth of world trade. The Uruguay Round of GATT negotiations, launched in 1986, is still not concluded. As long as recession persists, industrial countries remain tempted to cling to, or even intensify, trade protection to achieve short-term national gains, rather than to commit themselves to trade liberalisation in the expectation of mutual long-term gains. Yet it is from trade, much more than from aid, that the developing countries will benefit in stimulating their own economic growth. The development counter-revolution, for all its excesses and hyperbole has produced a near-consensus on one key point. The comprehensive and crude controls on trade and foreign exchange adopted by most developing countries by the 1970s were economically damaging and blocked off existing opportunities to trade that would have been advantageous. It would be tragic if, once this has been achieved, trade opportunities are now increasingly closed off by the developed countries' defensive actions.

The international financial institutions have in recent years already moved a long way from the harsh neo-liberal certainties which they preached in the mid-1980s. The notion of development policies which are 'market-friendly', in that they understand and respect the functions which markets perform, has replaced the strident insistence that getting prices right is the alpha and omega of development. Structural adjustment has had the human dimension increasingly integrated into other strands of policy reform. The reduction of poverty has been moved back as the central objective which international assistance is intended to serve. As has been noted at the end of chapter 7, the World Bank has increasingly highlighted the policy deficiencies of developed countries' economic management and called for a retreat from monetarism and minimal government. All of this constitutes a more enlightened approach to development policy.

Various attempts have already been made to construct a new intellectual consensus around these shifts in policy emphasis within the international financial institutions. Many policy-makers seem to be happy only when they can work within some codification of agreed truth, regardless of its content. But any such attempt is necessarily strained and artificial, given the diversity and open-endedness of on-going research and enquiry on development issues. This book has argued that the negative features of the development counter-revolution arose precisely from a misconceived and politically driven attempt to foreclose debate and to anathematize opposing intellectual approaches. Now that the negative features of that codification have come to be seen with increasing clarity, the last thing that is needed is a new catechism, a counter-counter-revolution, which tries to provide a new alternative simplification, appropriate to the political demise of neo-conservatism. To outlaw even what was positive, and should be enduring from the counter-revolution which we have tried here to describe and evaluate, would not only be a great mistake in itself. It would indicate that the fundamental basis of our critique of that curious episode has been well and truly misunderstood.

References

Ahluwalia, I. J. (1983) *Industrial Stagnation in India since the mid-Sixties*. New Delhi: Indian Council of Research in International Economic Relations.

Balassa, B. (1971) 'Trade Policies in Developing Countries'. *American Economic Review*, 61, Papers and Proceedings, May.

Balassa, B. and Associates (1982) *Development Strategies in Semi-Industrial Countries*. Baltimore: Johns Hopkins University Press.

Bale, M. D. and Lutz, E. (1979) *Price Distortions in Agriculture and their Effects: An International Comparison*. Washington, DC: World Bank, Staff Working Paper, No. 359, October.

Baran, P. A. (1957) 1973, *The Political Economy of Growth*. Harmondsworth: Penguin.

Bardhan, P. K. (1984) *The Political Economy of Development in India*. Oxford: Basil Blackwell.

Barry, B. M. (1970) *Sociologists, Economists and Democracy*. London: Collier-Macmillan.

Bates, R. H. (1981) *Markets and States in Tropical Africa*. Berkeley and Los Angeles: University of California Press.

Bates, R. H. (1989) 'Some Skeptical Notes on the "New Political Economy" of Development'. Durham, North Carolina: Duke University (mimeo).

Bauer, P. T. (1947) 'Malayan Rubber Policies'. *Economica* (new series), 14, May.

Bauer, P. T. (1959) *United States Aid and Indian Economic Development*. Washington, DC: American Enterprise Association.

Bauer, P. T. (1972) *Dissent on Development*. London: Weidenfeld & Nicolson.

Bauer, P. T. (1981) *Equality, the Third World and Economic Delusion*. London: Methuen.

Bauer, P. T. (1984) *Reality and Rhetoric: Studies in the Economics of Development*. London: Weidenfeld & Nicolson.

Berlin, I. (1979) *Against the Current: Essays in the History of Ideas*. London: Hogarth Press.

Bhagwati, J. N. (1971) 'The Generalized Theory of Distortions and Welfare'. In J. N. Bhagwati, R. W. Jones, R. A. Mundell and J. Vanek (eds) *Trade,*

Balance of Payments and Growth: Papers in International Economics in Honour of Charles P. Kindleberger. Amsterdam: North Holland.

Bhagwati, J. N. (1982) 'Directly Unproductive, Profit Seeking (DUP) Activities'. *Journal of Political Economy*, October.

Bhagwati, J. N. and Desai, P. (1970) *India: Planning for Industrialization. Industrialization and Trade Policies since 1951.* London: Oxford University Press, for the OECD Development Centre, Paris.

Bhagwati, J. N. and Srinivasan, T. N. (1975) *Foreign Trade Regimes and Economic Development: India.* New York and London: Columbia University Press (published for the US NBER).

Brandt Report (1980) *North–South: A Programme for Survival. The Report of the Independent Commission on International Development Issues under the Chairmanship of Willy Brandt.* London and Sydney: Pan Books.

Brewer, A. (1980) *Marxist Theories of Imperialism: a Critical Survey.* London: Routledge & Kegan Paul.

Brookfield, H. (1988) 'Sustainable Development and the Environment'. *Journal of Development Studies*, 25 (1), October.

Buchanan, J. M., Tollison, R. D. and Tullock, G. (eds) (1981) *Toward a Theory of the Rent-seeking Society.* College Station: Texas A. & M. University Press.

Burnell, P. (1986) *Economic Nationalism in the Third World.* Brighton: Wheatsheaf Books.

Burmell, P. (1991) 'Introduction to Britain's Overseas Aid: between Idealism and Self-interest'. In A. Bose and P. Burnell (eds) *Britain's Overseas Aid since 1979.* Manchester: Manchester University Press.

Bury, J. B. (1955) *The Idea of Progress: an Enquiry into its Growth and Origin.* New York: Dover Publications.

Byrd, R. (1991) 'Foreign Policy and Overseas Aid'. In A. Bose and P. Burnell (eds) 1991, *Britain's Overseas Aid since 1979.* Manchester: Manchester University Press.

Byres, T. J. (1979) 'Of Neo-Populist Pipe-Dreams: Daedalus in the Third World and the Myth of Urban Bias'. *Journal of Peasant Studies*, 6 (2).

Cardoso, F. H. (1984) *Les Idées à leur Place: le Concept de Développement en Amérique Latine* (translated by Danielle Ardaillon and Cecile Tricoire). Paris: Editions A. M. Metaillie.

Cardoso, F. H. and Faletto, E. (1979) *Dependency and Development in Latin America* (translated by Marjory Mattingly Urquidi). Berkeley and Los Angeles: University of California Press.

Cassen, R. H. and Associates (1986) *Does Aid Work?.* Oxford: Oxford University Press.

Chamberlain, M. E. (1985) *Decolonization: the Fall of the European Empires.* Oxford: Basil Blackwell.

Chambers, R. (1983) *Rural Development: Putting the Last First.* London, New York and Lagos: Longman.

Chandavarkar, A. (1989) *Keynes and India: a Study in Economics and Biography.* Basingstoke: Macmillan.

Chang, H.-J. (1991) 'The Political Economy of Industrial Policy: Reflections on the Role of the State Intervention'. University of Cambridge: unpublished Ph.D. dissertation.

Chatterji, R. (1986) 'The Behaviour of Industrial Prices in India, 1947–77'. University of Cambridge: unpublished Ph.D. dissertation.

Clarkson, S. (1979) *The Soviet Theory of Development: India and the Third World in Marxist-Leninist Scholarship*. Basingstoke: Macmillan.

Cline, W. R. (1991) 'Mexico: Economic Reform and Development Strategy', *EXIM Review*, Special Issue. Tokyo: Export–Import Bank of Japan.

Colclough, C. (1982) 'Lessons from the Development Debate'. *International Affairs*, 58 (3), summer.

Collander, D. (1984) *Neoclassical Political Economy*. Cambridge, Mass.: Ballinger.

Congdon, T. (1988) *The Debt Threat*. Oxford: Basil Blackwell.

Cornia, A., Jolly, R. and Stewart, F. (1987) *Adjustment with a Human Face*, 2 vols. Oxford: Clarendon.

Cowling, M. (1990, 1963) *Mill and Liberalism*, 2nd edn. Cambridge: Cambridge University Press.

Crow, B. and Thomas, A. (1983) *Third World Atlas*. Milton Keynes and Philadelphia: Open University Press.

CW (1971–89) *The Collected Writings of John Maynard Keynes*, 30 vol. Basingstoke: Macmillan.

Deane, P. (1983) 'The Scope and Method of Economic Science'. *Economic Journal*, 93 (369), March.

Dearlove, J. (1989) 'Neoclassical Politics: Public Choice and Political Understanding'. *Review of Political Economy* 1 (2), 208–37.

De Condorcet, A. N. (1955) *Sketch for a Historical Picture of the Progress of the Human Mind*. London: Weidenfeld & Nicolson.

De Rosa, D. and Greene, J. (1991) 'Will Contemporaneous Devaluation Hurt Exports from Sub-Saharan Africa?'. *Finances and Development*, 28 (1), March.

Desai, M. (1982) 'Homilies of a Victorian Saga: a Review Article on Peter Bauer'. *Third World Quarterly*, 4 (2), April.

Desai, M. (1985) 'Men and Things'. Inaugural lecture, London School of Economics and Political Science, 7 March.

Downs, A. (1960) 'Why the Government Budget is Too Small in a Democracy'. *World Politics*, 12 (4), July, 541–63.

Dyker, D. A. (1992) *Restructuring the Soviet Economy*. London: Routledge.

Elkan, W. (1984) Review of Lal, D. (1983) *The Poverty of 'Development Economics'*. London: Institute of Economic Affairs. In *Economic Journal*, 94 (376), December.

Emmet, D. (1960) 'How Far Can Structural Studies Take Account of Individuals'. *Journal of the Royal Anthropological Institute*, 90.

Evans, D. (1985) 'Back to Benoit'. *IDS Bulletin*, 16 (4), October.

Evans, D. and Alizadeh, P. (1984) 'Trade Industrialization and the Visible Hand'. *Journal of Development Studies*, 21 (1), October.

Fanon, F. (1967) *The Wretched of the Earth*. Harmondsworth: Penguin.

Findlay, R. (1989) 'Is the New Political Economy Relevant to Developing Countries?'. *PPR Working Papers* (WPS 292). Washington DC: The World Bank.

Fisher, F. M. (1969) 'The Existence of Aggregate Production Functions'. *Econometrica*, 37 (4), October.

Forbes, D. (1966) *Adam Ferguson: an Essay on the History of Civil Society, 1767.* Edinburgh: Edinburgh University Press.

Frank, A. G. (1958) 'General Productivity in Soviet Agriculture and Industry: the Ukraine 1928–35'. *Journal of Political Economy,* 66, December.

Frank, A. G. (1972) *Lumpenbourgeoisie: Lumpendevelopment. Dependence, Class and Politics in Latin America* (translated from the Spanish by Marion Davis Berdecio). New York and London: Monthly Review Press.

Frankel, F. (1978) *India's Political Economy, 1947–1977: the Gradual Revolution.* Princeton, NJ: Princeton University Press.

Fransman, M. (1984) 'Explaining the Success of the Asian NICs: Incentives and Technology'. *IDS Bulletin,* 15 (2), April.

French-Davis, R. (1990) 'Debt–equity swaps in Chile'. *Cambridge Journal of Economics,* 14 (1).

Friedrich, C. J. (1949) *The Philosophy of Kant – Immanual Kant's Moral and Political Writings.* New York: The Modern Library.

Fry, M. J. (1991) 'Debts and Deficits in 26 Developing Countries: Financial and Fiscal Effects of Foreign Debt Accumulation', *International Finance Group Working Papers.* Birmingham: University of Birmingham.

Fukuyama, F. (1992) *The End of History and the Last Man.* London: Hamish Hamilton.

Gellner, E. (1983) *Nations and Nationalism.* Oxford: Basil Blackwell.

Giddens, A. (1984) *The Constitution of Society.* Oxford: Polity Press.

Greene, J. (1989) 'The External Debt Problem of Sub-Saharan Africa'. *IMF Staff Papers,* 36 (4).

Griffin, K. and Gurley, J. (1985) 'Radical Analyses of Imperialism, the Third World, and the Transition to Socialism: a Survey Article'. *Journal of Economic Literature,* 23 (3), September.

Griffith-Jones, S. (1991) 'International Financial Markets: a Case of Market Failure'. In C. Colclough and J. Manor (eds), *States or Markets? Neo-Liberalism and the Development Policy Debate.* Oxford: Clarendon Press.

Griffith-Jones, S. and Gottschalk, R. (1991) 'Is There Still a Latin American Debt Crisis?' mimeo. Brighton: Institute of Development Studies.

Griliches, Z. and Jorgenson, D. W. (1967) 'The Explanation of Productivity Change'. *Review of Economic Studies,* 34.

Grillo, R. and Rew, A. (eds) (1985) *Social Anthropology and Development Policy.* London and New York: Tavistock Publications, ASA Monographs 23.

Grindle, M. (1989) 'The New Political Economy: Positive Economics and Negative Politics'. Cambridge, Mass (mimeo).

Hahn, F. H. (1981) 'General Equilibrium Theory'. In D. Bell and I. Kristol (eds), *The Crisis in Economic Theory.* New York: Basic Books.

Hahn, F. H. and Matthews, R. C. O. (1965) 'The Theory of Economic Growth: a Survey'. In *Surveys of Economic Theory, Volume II: Growth and Development.* London: Macmillan.

Harcourt, G. C. (1972) *Some Cambridge Controversies in the Theory of Capital.* Cambridge: Cambridge University Press.

Harris, J. and Todaro, M. P. (1970) 'Migration, Unemployment and Development: a Two-Sector Analysis'. *American Economic Review,* March.

Hayek, F. A. (1962, 1944) *The Road to Serfdom.* London. Routledge & Kegan Paul.

Hegel, G. W. F. (1953, 1837) *Reason in History.* Indianapolis: Bobbs-Merrill, Library of the Liberal Arts.

Hexter, J. H. (1979) *On Historians: Reappraisals of some of the Masters of Modern History.* Cambridge, Mass.: Harvard University Press.

Hindess, B. (1988) *Choice, Rationality and Social Theory.* London: Unwin Hyman.

Hirsch, F. (1977) *Social Limits to Growth.* London: Routledge & Kegan Paul.

Hirschman, A. O. (1971) *A Bias for Hope: Essays on Development and Latin America.* New Haven and London: Yale University Press.

Hirschman, A. O. (1977) *The Passions and the Interests: Political Arguments for Capitalism before its Triumph.* Princeton, NJ: Princeton University Press.

Hirschman, A. O. (1981) *Essays in Trespassing: Economics to Politics and Beyond.* Cambridge: Cambridge University Press.

Hirschman, A. O. (1982a) *Shifting Involvements: Private Interest and Public Action,* Oxford, Martin Robertson.

Hirschman, A. O. (1982b) 'Rival Interpretations of Market Society: Civilizing, Destructive or Feeble?'. *Journal of Economic Literature,* 20, December

Hirschman, A. O. (1991) *The Rhetoric of Reaction. Perversity, Futility, Jeopardy.* Cambridge, Mass.: Belknap Press.

Hodgson, G. M. (1988) *Economics and Institutions: a Manifesto for a Modern Institutional Economics.* Oxford: Polity Press.

House of Commons (1983) *International Monetary Arrangements: International Lending by Banks,* 4th Report from the Treasury and Civil Service Committee, Session, 1982–83.

House of Commons (1990) *International Debt Strategy,* 3rd Report from the Treasury and Civil Service Committee, Session 1989–90.

International Monetary Fund (IMF) (1987) *World Economic Outlook.* Washington DC.

International Monetary Fund (1991) *World Economic Outlook.* Washington DC.

Jha, P. S. (1980) *India: a Political Economy of Stagnation.* Bombay: Oxford University Press.

Johnson, C. (1991) *The Economy under Mrs Thatcher 1979–1990.* London: Penguin.

Johnson, H. G. (1971a) 'The Keynesian Revolution and the Monetarist Counter-Revolution'. *American Economic Review,* 61, Papers and Proceedings, May.

Johnson, H. G. (1971b) 'A Word to the Third World: a Western Economist's Frank Advice'. *Encounter,* 37, October.

Johnson, E. S. and Johnson, H. G. (1978) *The Shadow of Keynes: Understanding Keynes, Cambridge and Keynesian Economics.* Oxford: Basil Blackwell.

Joshi, V. and Little, I. M. D. (1986) *Indian Macro-Economic Policies.* Oxford (mimeo).

Kaldor, N. (1978) *Further Essays on Applied Economics,* London: Duckworth.

Kaldor, N. (1989) *Further Essays on Economic Theory and Policy.* London, Duckworth.

Kalecki, M. (1972) *Selected Essays on the Economic Growth of the Socialist and the Mixed Economy.* Cambridge: Cambridge University Press.

Kamarck, A. M. (1976) *The Tropics and Economic Development: a Provocative Inquiry in to the Poverty of Nations.* Baltimore and London: Johns Hopkins University Press, for the World Bank.

Kanbur, S. M. R. (1983) *How to Analyse Commodity Price Stabilization? A Review Article.* Coventry: Development Economics Research Centre, University of Warwick, Discussion Paper 35.

Kay, C. (1989) *Latin American Theories of Development and Underdevelopment*. London: Routledge.

Kautsky, D. (1971) *The Class Struggle (Erfurt Program)*. New York: W. W. Norton.

Keegan, W. (1984) *Mrs Thatcher's Economic Experiment*. Harmondsworth: Penguin.

Keegan, W. (1989) *Mr Lawson's Gamble*. London, Hodder & Stoughton.

Keynes, J. M. For all references to Keynes, please see CW (1971–89).

Kiernan, V. G. (1982) *European Empires from Conquest to Collapse, 1815–1860*. London: Fontana.

Kilby, P. (1983) 'An Entrepreneurial Problem'. *American Economic Review*, 73 (2), May

Killick, A. (ed.) (1984) *The Quest for Economic Stabilization: the IMF and the Third World*. London: Gower, in association with the Overseas Development Institute.

Killick, A. (1986) 'Twenty Five Years in Development: the Rise and Impending Decline of Market Solutions'. *Development Policy Review*, 4 (2), June.

Kolakowski, L. (1978) *Main Currents of Marxism*, 3 vols. Oxford: Oxford University Press.

Krueger, A. O. (1974) 'The Political Economy of the Rent-Seeking Society'. *American Economic Review*, 64 (3), June.

Kurian, K. M. (1975) *India – State and Society: a Marxian Approach*. Bombay: Longman.

Lal, D. (1983) *The Poverty of 'Development Economics'*. London: Institute of Economic Affairs, Hobart Paperback 16.

Lal, D. (1992) *Development Economics*, International Library of Critical Writings in Economics 18. Aldershot: Edward Elgar Publishing Ltd.

Lall, S. (1981) *Developing Countries in the International Economy*. Basingstoke: Macmillan.

Lawson, N. (1992) *The View from No. 11: Memoirs of a Tory Radical*. London: Bantam Press.

Lawson, T. (1985) 'Uncertainty and Economic Analysis'. *Economic Journal*, 95 (380), December.

Leff, N. H. (1979) 'Entrepreneurship and Development: the Problem Revisited'. *Journal of Economic Literature*, 17 (1), March.

Leff, N. H. (1985a) 'Optimal Investment Choice for Developing Countries: Rational Theory and Rational Decision-Making'. *Journal of Development Economics*, 18, 355–60.

Leff, N. H. (1985b) 'The Use of Policy Science Tools in Public Sector Decision-making: Social Benefit–Cost Analysis in the World Bank'. *Kyklos*, 38 (1).

Leijonhufvud, A. (1968) *On Keynesian Economics and the Economics of Keynes. A Study in Monetary Theory*. New York, Oxford University Press.

Lever, H. and Huhne, C. (1985) *Debt and Danger: the World Financial Crisis*. Harmondsworth: Penguin.

Levi, M. (1988) *Of Rule and Revenue*. Berkeley: University of California Press.

Lewis, S. R. (1968) 'Effects of Trade Policy on Domestic Relative Prices: Pakistan, 1951–64'. *American Economic Review*, 58 (1), March.

Lewis, W. A. (1954) 'Economic Development with Unlimited Supplies of Labour'. *The Manchester School*, 22 (2), May.

Leys, C. (1989) *Politics in Britain. From Labourism to Thatcherism* (revised edn). London: Verso.

Lipton, M. (1977) *Why the Poor Stay Poor.* London: Maurice Temple Smith.

Lipton, M. (1981) 'Bauer's Fulminations Against Aid'. *Financial Times*, 1 August.

Lipton, M. (1984) 'Urban Bias Revisited'. *Journal of Development Studies*, 20 (3), April.

Lipton, M. and Toye, J. (1990) *Does Aid Work in India? A Country Study of the Impact of Official Development Assistance.* London: Routledge.

Little, I. M. D. (1978) 'Distributive Justice and the New International Order'. In P. Oppenheimer (ed.), *Issues in International Economics*, London: Oriel Press.

Little, I. M. D. (1979) 'An Economic renaissance'. In W. Galenson (ed.), *Economic Growth and Structural Change in Taiwan.* Ithaca and London: Cornell University Press.

Little, I. M. D. (1982) *Economic Development: Theory, Policies and International Relations.* New York: Basic Books.

Little, I. M. D. and Mirrless, J. A. (1974) *Project Appraisal and Planning for Developing Countries.* London: Heinemann Educational.

Little, I. M. D. Scitovsky, T. and Scott, M. F. G. (1970) *Industry and Trade in Some Developing Countries.* Oxford: Oxford University Press, for OECD Development Centre, Paris.

Lundahl, M. (1991) Review of Toye (1987). *Journal of Development Studies*, 27 (4), July.

MacDonagh, O. (1977) *Early Victorian Government 1930–1970.* London: Weidenfeld & Nicolson.

McGranahan, D., Pizarro, E. and Richard, C. (1985) *Measurement and Analysis of Socio-Economic Development.* Geneva: UNRISD.

McLellan, D. (1975) *Marx.* Glasgow: Fontana/Collins.

Macpherson, C. B. (1985) *The Rise and Fall of Economic Justice and Other Papers.* Oxford and New York: Oxford University Press.

Mair, L. (1965) 'How Small-scale Societies Change'. In J. Gould (ed.), (1965), *Penguin Survey of the Social Sciences 1965.* Harmondsworth: Penguin.

Malinowski, B. (1926) *Crime and Custom in Savage Society.* London: Routlege Kegan Paul.

Marcel, M. and Palma, J. G. (1988) 'Third World Debt and its Effects on the British Economy: a Southern View of Economic Mismanagement in the North'. *Cambridge Journal of Economics*, 12 (3).

Marx, K. (1964) *Pre-Capitalist Economic Formations*, (edited by E. J. Hobsbawm). London: Lawrence & Wishart.

Marx, K. (1973a) *Grundrisse.* Harmondsworth: Penguin.

Marx. K. (1973b) *The Revolutions of 1848 (Political Writings, Vol. 1).* Harmondsworth: Penguin.

Marx, K. (1973c) *Surveys from Exile (Political Writings, Vol. 2).* Harmondsworth: Penguin.

Meier, G. M. (1989) 'Do Development Economists Matter?'. *IDS Bulletin*, 20 (3), July.

Meier, G. M. (1991) *Politics and Policymaking in Developing Countries.* San Francisco, California: ICS Press.

Meier, G. M. and Seers, D. (eds) (1984) *Pioneers in Development*. New York and Oxford: Oxford University Press, for the World Bank.

Mellor, J. W. (1976) *The New Economics of Growth: a Strategy for India and the Developing World*. Oxford: Oxford University Press.

Millward, R. (1985) 'Nationalization'. In A. Kuper and J. Kuper (eds) *The Social Science Encyclopaedia*. London and Boston: Routledge & Kegan Paul.

Milner, C. (ed.) (1987) *Political Economy and International Money. Selected Essays of John Williamson*. Hemel Hempstead: Harvester Wheatsheaf.

Moore, M. P. (1984) 'Political Economy and the Rural–Urban Divide'. *Journal of Development Studies*, 20 (3), April.

Moore, M. P. (1991) 'Rent-seeding and Market Surrogates: the Case of Irrigation Policy'. In C. Colclough and J. Manor (eds), *States or Markets?*. Oxford: Oxford University Press.

Morawetz, D. (1977) *Twenty-five Years of Economic Development 1950 to 1975*. Baltimore and London: Johns Hopkins University Press.

Mosley, P. (1984) Review of Mikesell, R. F. and Associates (1983) *The Economics of Foreign Aid and Self-Sustaining Development*. Boulder, Colo.: Westview Press. In *Journal of Development Studies*, 21 (1), October.

Mosley, P., Harrigan, J. and Toye, J. (1991) *Aid and Power: the World Bank and Policy-based Lending*, 2 vols London: Routledge.

Mountfield, P. (1990) 'The Paris Club and African Debt'. *IDS Bulletin*, 21 (2).

Mulji, S. (1990) 'Vision and Reality in Public Sector Management: the Indian Experience'. In M. Scott and D. Lal (eds), *Public Policy and Economic Development. Essays in Honour of Ian Little*. Oxford: Clarendon Press.

Munasinghe, M. (1985) *Bioenergy Management Policy and Integrated National Energy Planning*. Brussels: Centre of European Studies (mimeo).

Muscatelli, V. A. and Vines, D. (1991) 'Third World Debt and Macroeconomic Interactions between North and South'. *Journal of Development Studies*, 27 (3).

Myrdal, G. (1968) *Asian Drama: an Enquiry into the Poverty of Nations*, (3 vols). London: Pelican.

Myrdal, G. (1970) 'The "Soft State" in Underdeveloped Countries'. In P. Streeten (ed.), *Unfashionable Economics: Essays in Honour of Lord Balogh*. London: Weidenfeld & Nicolson.

Nabli, M. K. and Nugent, J. B. (1989) 'The New Institutional Economics and its Applicability to Development'. *World Development*, 17 (9).

Nelson, R. R. (1964) 'Aggregate Production Functions and Medium-range Growth Projections'. *American Economic Review*, 54 (5), September.

Newbery, D. and Stigltz, J. (1981) *The Theory of Commodity Price Stabilisation: a Study in the Economics of Risk*. Oxford and New York: Oxford University Press.

Nordhaus, W. D. (1973) 'World Dynamics: Measurement without Facts'. *Economic Journal*, 83, December.

Olson, M. (1971) *The Logic of Collective Action. Public Goods and the Theory of Groups* (revised edn). New York: Schocken Books.

Olson, M. (1982) *The Rise and Decline of Nations: Economic Growth, Stagflation and Social Rigidities*. London and New Haven: Yale University Press.

Organisation for Economic Cooperation and Development (OECD) (1990) *Development Cooperation. Efforts and Policies of the Members of the Development Assistance Committee*. Paris.

Palma, G. (1978) 'Dependency: a Formal Theory of Underdevelopment or a

Methodology for the Analysis of Concrete Situations of Underdevelopment?'. *World Development*, 6 (7–8).

Patinkin, D. (1982) *Anticipations of the General Theory? And Other Essays on Keynes.* Oxford: Basil Blackwell.

Perez-Lopez, J. F. (1992) 'The Cuban Economy: Rectification in a Changing World'. *Cambridge Journal of Economics*, 16 (1), March.

Please, S. (1984) *The Hobbled Giant: Essays on the World Bank.* Boulder, Colo. and London: Westview Press.

Pollard, S. (1971) *The Idea of Progress: History and Society.* Harmondsworth: Penguin.

Ponting, C. (1989) *Breach of Promise.* London: Hamish Hamilton.

Prawer, S. S. (1978) *Karl Marx and World Literature.* Oxford: Oxford Paperbacks.

Rawls, J. (1972) *A Theory of Justice.* London and New York: Oxford University Press.

Robinson, J. (1975) 'What has Become of the Keynesian Revolution?'. In Keynes, M. (ed.), *Essays on John Maynard Keynes.* Cambridge: Cambridge University Press.

Rosen, G. (1985) *Western Economists and Eastern Societies: Agents of Change in South Asia, 1950–1970.* Baltimore: Johns Hopkins University Press.

Rosenthal, D. B. (1970) *The Limited Elite: Politics and Government in Two Indian Cities.* Chicago and London: University of Chicago Press.

Roxborough, I. (1984) 'Unity and Diversity in Latin American History'. *Journal of Latin American Studies*, 16 (1).

Roy, S. (1984) *Pricing, Planning and Politics: a Study of Economic Distortions in India.* London: Institute of Economic Affairs.

Rubin, B. R. (1982) 'Private Power and Public Investment in India: a Study in the Political Economy of Development'. University of Chicago: unpublished Ph.D. dissertation.

Runciman, W. G. (1989) *Confessions of a Reluctant Theorist. Selected Essays.* New York: Harvester Wheatsheaf.

Salazar-Xirinachs, J. M. (1985) *Researching the Case for State Intervention: a Theoretical Critique of Free Market Views on Economic Incentives and Development Strategy.* School of Economics, University of Costa Rica, February, (mimeo).

Sandel, M. (ed.) (1984) *Liberalism and its Critics.* Oxford: Basil Blackwell.

Schultz, T. W. (1964) *Transforming Traditional Agriculture.* New Haven: Yale University Press.

Seers, D. (1962) 'A Theory of Inflation and Growth in Underdeveloped Economies Based on Experiences of Latin America'. *Oxford Economic Papers* 14 (2), June.

Seers, D. (1963) 'The Limitations of the Special Case'. *Bulletin of the Oxford Institute of Economics and Statistics*, 25 (2).

Seers, D. (1979a) 'Introduction: the Congruence of Marxism and other Neo-classical Doctrines'. In K. Q. Hill (ed.), *Towards a New Strategy for Development: a Rothko Chapel Colloquium.* New York and Oxford: Pergamon.

Seers, D. (1979b) 'The Birth, Life and Death of Development Economics (Revisiting a Manchester Conference)'. *Development and Change*, 10 (4), October.

Seers, D. (1983) *The Political Economy of Nationalism.* Oxford: Oxford: Oxford University Press.

Sen, A. K. (1975) *Employment, Technology and Development*. Oxford: Clarendon Press.

Sen, A. K. (1982) 'Just Deserts', *New York Review of Books*, 4 March.

Sen, A. K. (1983) 'Development: Which Way Now?', *Economic Journal*, 93 (372), December.

Sen, A. K. (1984) *Resources, Values and Development*. Oxford: Basil Blackwell.

Senses, F. (1984) 'Development Economics at a Crossroad'. *METU Studies in Development*, 11 (1–2).

Singer, H. W. (1975) *The Strategy of International Development: Essays in the Economics of Backwardness* (edited by Sir Alec Cairncross and Molinder Puri). Basingstoke: Macmillan.

Singer, H. W. (1985) 'What Keynes and Keynesianism Can Teach Us About Less Developed Countries'. Paper presented to the 7th Keynes Seminar on 'Keynes and Economic Development' at University of Kent, Canterbury, 15 November 1985.

Singer, H. W. (1989) 'Lessons of Post-War Development Experience: 1945–1988', *IDS Discussion Paper 260*. Brighton: Institute of Development Studies.

Singer, H. W. (1991) 'Beyond the Debt Crisis'. *Journal für Entwicklungspolitk*, 3, 53–7.

Singh, A. (1986) 'The Interrupted Industrial Revolution of the Third World: Prospects and Policies for Resumption'. *Industry and Development* (12).

Skidelsky, R. (1992) 'Keynes Here, How Can I Help You?'. *Financial Times*, 4–5 April.

Smith, S. (1982) 'Stories about the World Economy: the Quest for the Grail'. *Third World Quarterly*, 4 (3), July.

Smith, S. B. (1989) *Hegel's Critique of Liberalism*. Chicago: University of Chicago Press.

Solow, R. M. (1957) 'Technical Change and the Production Function'. *Review of Economics and Statistics*, 39, August.

Solow, R. W. (1970) *Growth Theory: an Exposition*. Oxford: Clarendon Press.

Srinivasan, T. N. and Narayana, N. S. S. (1977) 'Economic Performance since the Third Plan and Its Implications for Policy'. *Economic and Political Weekly*, annual number, February.

Srinivasan, T. N. (1985) 'Neoclassical Political Economy, the State and Economic Development'. *Asian Development Review*, 3 (2).

Staniland, M. (1985) *What is Political Economy? A Study of Social Theory and Underdevelopment*. New Haven and London: Yale University Press.

Steinberg, D. I. (1984) *On Foreign Aid and the Development of the Republic of Korea: the Effectiveness of Concessional Assistance*, Washington: Agency for International Development, June, (mimeo).

Stevens, C. and Kennan, J. (eds) (1992) *Reform in Eastern Europe and the Developing Country Dimension*. London: Overseas Development Institute.

Stewart, F. (1971) 'Appropriate Intermediate or Inferior Economics'. *Journal of Development Studies*, 7 (3), April.

Stewart, F. (1985) 'The Fragile Foundations of the Neoclassical Approach to Development'. *Journal of Development Studies*, 21 (2), January.

Stewart, F. (1992) 'The Many Faces of Adjustment'. In P. Mosley (ed.) *Development Finance and Policy Reform*. Basingstoke: Macmillan.

Stockman, D. A. (1985) *The Triumph of Politics: the Crisis in American Government and How it Affects the World.* London: Bodley Head.

Sutherland, G. (ed.) (1972) *Studies in the Growth of Nineteenth Century Government.* London: Routledge & Kegan Paul.

Taylor, L. (1979) *Macro Models for Developing Countries.* New York: McGraw-Hill.

Taylor, L. (1988) *Varieties of Stabilisation Experience.* Oxford: Clarendon Press.

Thirlwall, A. P. (ed.) (1978) *Keynes and Laissez-Faire: the Third Keynes Seminar held at the University of Kent at Canterbury 1976.* Basingstoke: Macmillan.

Thirlwall, A. P. (1984) 'In Praise of Development Economics'. *METU Studies in Development,* 11 (1–2).

Thirlwall, A. P. (1985) Paper presented to the 7th Keynes Seminar on 'Keynes and Economic Development' held at the University of Kent, Canterbury, 15 November 1985.

Thirlwall, A. P. (ed.) (1987) *Keynes and Economic Development.* Basingstoke: Macmillan.

Tinbergen, J. (1984) 'Lessons and Prospects'. *METU Studies in Development,* 11 (1–2).

Toye, J. F. J. (1976), 'Economic Theories of Politics and Public Finance'. *British Journal of Political Science,* 6.

Toye, J. F. J. (1981) *Public Expenditure and Indian Development Policy 1960 to 1970.* Cambridge: Cambridge University Press.

Toye, J. F. J. (1983a) 'Interdependence: from Kant to Brandt'. In *Third World Studies, Block 4. The International Setting.* Milton Keynes: Open University Press.

Toye, J. F. J. (1983b) 'The Disparaging of Development Economics'. *Journal of Development Studies,* 20 (1), 87–107.

Toye, J. F. J. (1984) 'The Recession, the Third World and the Base Metals Industries'. *World Development,* 12 (9).

Toye, J. F. J. (1985) '*Dirigisme* and Development Economics'. *Cambridge Journal of Economics,* 9 (1), March.

Toye J. F. J. (1987) *Dilemmas of Development. Reflections on the Counter-Revolution in Development Theory and Policy.* Oxford: Basil Blackwell.

Toye J. F. J. (1990) 'The Year of Liberal Revolution. A Survey of 1989'. *World Economic and Business Review.* Oxford: Blackwell Reference.

Toye J. F. J. (1991) 'The Aid and Trade Provision of the British Aid Programme'. In A. Bose and P. Burnell (eds), *Britains' Overseas Aid Since 1979.* Manchester: Manchester University Press.

Toye, J. F. J. (1993) 'Keynes, Russia and the State in Developing Countries'. In Thirlwall, A. P. (ed.), *Keynes and the Role of the State.* London: Macmillan.

Toye, J. F. J. and Clark, G. (1986) 'The Aid and Trade Provision: Origins, Dimensions and Possible Reforms'. *Development Policy Review,* 4 (4), December.

Tucker, D. F. B. (1980) *Marxism an Individualism.* Oxford: Basil Blackwell.

UNDP (1992) *Human Development Report 1992.* New York: Oxford University Press.

UN Department of Economic Affairs (1951) *Measures for the Economic Development of Under-Developed Countries.* New York.

Van Arkadie, B. and Frank, C. R. (1969) *Economic Accounting and Development*

Planning (revised American edn). New York, London and Toronto: Oxford University Press.

Visvesvaraya, M. (1934) *Planned Economy for India*. Bangalore: Bangalore Press.

Wade, R. (1984) Review of Toye, J. F. J. (1981) *Public Expenditure and Indian Development Policy 1960 to 1970*. Cambridge: Cambridge University Press. In *Economic Development and Cultural Change*, 32 (2), January.

Wade, R. (1988) *Village Republics. Economic Conditions for Collective Action in South India*. Cambridge: Cambridge University Press.

Wade, R. (1990) *Governing the Market. Economic Theory and the Role of Government in East Asian Industrialisation*. Princeton, NJ: Princeton University Press.

Wallich, C. (1982) *State Finances in India, Volume 2. Studies in State Finances*. Washington DC: World Bank, Staff Working Paper 523, June.

Walters, A. A. (1969) *Money in Boom and Slump*. London: Institute of Economic Affairs, Hobart Paper 44.

Warren, B. (1980) *Imperialism: Pioneer of Capitalism* (ed. by John Sender). London: NLB and Verso.

White, G. (1984) 'Development States and Socialist Industrialization in the Third World'. *Journal of Development Studies*, 21 (1), October.

Wilber, C. K. (1970) *The Soviet Model and Underdeveloped Countries*. London: North Carolina Press.

Willetts, P. (1978) *The Non-Aligned Movement: the Origins of the Third World Alliance*. London: Frances Pinter.

Williams, B. (1985) *Ethics and the Limits of Philosophy*, London: Fontana/Collins.

Williams, G. (1987, 1981) *Third World Political Organisations*, 2nd ed. London: Macmillan.

Williamson, J. (1985) Paper presented to 7th Keynes Seminar on 'Keynes and Economic Development' at University of Kent, Canterbury, 15 November 1985.

Williamson, J. (1990) 'The Debt Crisis at the Turn of the Decade'. *IDS Bulletin*, 21 (2).

World Bank (1983) *World Development Report 1983*. New York: Oxford University Press, for the World Bank.

World Bank (1984) *World Development Report 1984*. New York: Oxford University Press, for the World Bank.

World Bank (1985a) *Research News*, 6 (1), summer.

World Bank (1985b) *World Development Report 1985*. Washington, DC.

World Bank (1986) *Research News*, 6 (3), winter.

World Bank (1990) *Pretty World Development Report* 1990. Washington, DC: World Bank.

World Bank (1991) *The Challenge of Development. World Development Report 1991*. Washington, DC.

World Bank (1992) *The World Bank Annual Report 1992*. Washington, DC.

Wylie, R. F. (1983) Review of Bauer, P. T. (1981) *Equality, the Third World and Economic Delusion*. London: Methuen. In *Journal of Developing Areas*, 18 (1), October.

Young, H. (1989) *One of Us*. London: Pan Books for Macmillan.

Index